World Trade Organisation
Regional Trading Arrangements and India

WORLD TRADE ORGANISATION REGIONAL TRADING ARRANGEMENTS AND INDIA

Edited by

M.G. Basava Raja

Reader, Division of Economics
Mysore University
Sir M. Visvesvaraya P.G. Centre
Mandya—571 402
Karnataka

SERIALS PUBLICATIONS
New Delhi

First Published–2003

ISBN: 81-86771-15-8

Published by

Head Office : **SERIALS PUBLICATIONS**
4, B.S.S. Hall, Khyber Pass Market
Civil Lines, Delhi–110054 (India)
Fax: 91-11-23272135
E-mail: serials@satyam.net.in

Branch Office : 4830/24, Prahlad Street, Ansari Road
Darya Ganj, New Delhi-110002 (India)
Phone: 23245225

Typeset By : *Shankar Bose*

Printed at :

PRINTED IN INDIA

PREFACE

The World Trade Organisation-the successor to GATT-is one of the youngest of the international organisations. While the WTO is still young, the multilateral trading system that was originally set up under GATT is more than 54 years old. When we go through the economic history of GATT/WTO; we will come to know the fact that the multilateral trading system was not developed along a smooth path since the early 1980s; on the contrary, the trade policy has experienced a long periods of only minimal progress, occasional full stops and sudden leap forward.

The period after World War II has seen a growing interest in integrating national economies at regional level in the form of regional trading arrangements. RTAs are a part and parcel of the present international economic order, and they are pursued for a variety of reasons. RTAs, called a 'Spaghetti Bowl' due to their over lapping nature, are accepted as the 'Second Best' of free trade/multilateralism. At present, WTO has 144 member contouries and the number of RTAs is 198. True, the number of RTAs is higher than the number of members of WTO; those of consequence are few and concern the major economies of the world such as the NAFTA in the north, and the ASEAN, and MERCOSUR in the south. The SAARC- though it includes the fourth largest economy of the world and six other countries-has yet to really become a well developed RTA-based group. The emerging APEC may broaden the base. Indeed, negotiating with a small number of countries is considered easier and more expedient than negotiating with 144 countries . From 1947-2003, the GATT/WTO had been informed of more than 144 RTAs although some no longer exist or they remain insubstantial. Look at the question. RTAs and the multilateral trading system: Are they complements or substitutes?. The debate will probably never end. Economists have different views of the pros and cons of the WTO's multilateral trading system and promotion of freer trade among the member states of RTAs. Some developing countries express alarm at the growing strength of RTAs organised by advanced countries and feel that they could create a "Big Powers Bloc"; But WTO is confident that proliferating RTAs will not turn into big powers' isolationist blocs undermining progress of worldwide free trade. The deep and wide ranging tariff cuts agreed upon in the Uruguay Round of Trade Negotiations by some 125 countries have meant that there is little scope for greater reductions in purely regional accords. So regional and multilateral integration initiatives are complementary rather than alternatives in the pursuit of open trade.

This book is a product of a two-day national seminar organised by the Division of Economics, Mysore University, Sir M. Visvesvaraya P. G. Centre, Mandya, during 17th and 18th of April 2002 on the theme entitled "The World Trade Organisation, Regional Trading Arrangements and India ". This seminar was inaugurated by Dr. Netaji Ganesan, Executive Director, Karnataka Stated Financial Corporation, Bangalore, under the chairmanship of A. K. Chattopadhyay, General Manager, Bharathiya Reserve Bank Note Mudran Unit, Mysore. On that occasion, Dr. B. S. Sreekantaradhya, SBM Professor of Economics of Mysore University and Member, Revenue Reforms Commission of Government of Karnataka delivered the keynote address. Dr. C.K. Renukarya, Professor of Economics of Mysore University was the chief guest. Prof. Nageswara Rao of S.K. University

Anantapur released the seminar volume. The valedictory address of the seminar was delivered by Prof. Francis Cherunilam of Cochin University, under the chairmanship of Prof. C.N. Srinath, Director, Sir. M. Visvesvaraya P. G. Centre, Prof. S. Indumati Madaiah, Chairperson, Department of Studies in Economics and Co-operation, University of Mysore was the chief guest. Dr. H.R. Krishnaiah Gowda, of Co-operation Department, Government of Karnataka provided an overview of the seminar.

The papers brought out here contributed by different scholars/administrators/policy makers were presented in three technical sessions. Dr. G. T. Marulasiddappa former Registrar of Kuvempu University, Prof. K. Nageswara Rao of S.K. University, and Prof. H.G. Devraj of P.G. Centre, Davanagere, presided over Technical sessions I, II and III respectively, Dr. D.S. Leelavathi, Dr. B.K. Tulasimala, Dr. M. Indira, Dr. B.P. Veerabhadrappa, Prof. K.M. Veeraiah, S.M. Basavaraju acted as rapporteurs, Prof. O.D. Heggade, Dr. G.V. Swamy, Dr. S. Rajendran, K.C. Basavaraju, K.M. Jayaramaiah participated as discussants. Ms. Vanamala, Dr. B.P. Veerabhadrappa and Dr. Jayakumar Shetty compered the technical sessions programmes.

The contributors to this volume and the persons participated in the seminar consist of scholars/administrators/ Policy makers. 31 papers brought out here on a very vast subject like the one to which this volume is devoted cannot do full justice to all of its aspects and may raise more questions/comments than can be answered in this context. If the authors of the papers succeed in stimulating further and more comprehensive studies on this highly dynamic subject, they will have achieved their aim of contributing to a creative discourse. This book is a significant resource that will be indispensable to students/professionals and all people seeking to increase their understanding of this highly topical subject. Prof. S.N. Hegde, erudite Vice-Chancellor, University of

Mysore, Mysore, IGP Mr. K.S.N. Chikkerur, our past Registrar, and Mr. N.D. Tiwari, I.F.S. our present Registrar, Prof. C.N. Srinath past Director of the P.G. Centre, provided administrative and moral support all along. Prof. O.D. Heggade, the present Director of the P.G. Centre and Co-ordinator of the Division of Economics, G.S. Premkumar, K. Sivachithappa, Manohar, Ashok Hulibandi, and all the teaching and non-teaching staff of the P.G. Centre helped me in different ways in organising this national seminar.

The seminar would not have been possible without the financial help extended by Shri V. Umesh, IAS, Managing Director of Karnataka State Financial Corporation, Bangalore, Dr. H.R. Krishnaiah Gowda, Deputy Registrar of Co-operative Societies, Mandya, Shri R. Guru, Proprietor Cycle Brand Agarbathies and Chairman, MATF, Mysore, A.K. Chattopadhyay, General Manager, Bharathiya Reserve Bank Note Mudran Unit of Mysore, K.P. Basava Raju, Deputy Commissioner of Commercial Taxes, Dr. Bhavanishankar, Plant Controller, Bacardi Martini, Nanjanagud for which we are ever grateful to them.

We have no words to express our sincere thanks to Shri S.K. Jha, Director, Serials Publications, Delhi for publishing this book.

M.G. Basavaraja

LIST OF CONTRIBUTORS

Arabi, U, Department of Economics, Mangalore University-574199, Karnataka.

Balakrishnan, K., Associate Professor, S.D.M. Institute for Management Development, Mysore-570005.

Basava Raja, M.G., Reader, Division of Economics, Mysore University, Sir M. Visvesvaraya P.G. Centre, Mandya-571402.

Chattopadhyay, A.K., General Manager, Bharathiya Reserve Bank, Note Mudran Unit, Note Mudran Nagar, Mysore-570003.

Cherunilam, Francis, Professor, School of Management Studies, Cochin University of Science and Technology, Cochin-682022.

Devaraj, H.G., Professor of Economics, Kuvempu University, P.G. Centre, Davanagere-577002.

Heggade, O.D., Professor, Co-ordinator, Division of Economics, Director of Sir M. Visvesvaraya P.G. Centre, Mandya-571402.

Jayakumar Shetty, A., Dept. of Economics, S.D.M. College, Ujire-574240.

Jagadhish, R.L. Lecturer, Department of Polymer Science, P.G. Centre, Mandya-571402.

Kallur, M.S., Professor and Head, Department of Economics, Gulbarga University, Gulbarga, Karnataka.

Krishnaiah Gowda, H.R., Deputy Registrar of Co-operative Societies, Mandya, Karnataka.

Krishnakumar, Suchithra, Head, P.G. Department of Economics, Vivekananda College, Bangalore.

Leelavathi, D.S., Reader, Department of Studies in Economics, Manasagangotri, Mysore University, Mysore 570006.

Mahadevaiah, Lecturer, Department of Sugar Technology, P.G., Centre, Mandhya.

Mallikarjunappa, T., Reader, Department of Business Administration, Mangalore University-574199, Karnataka.

Meenakshi, R., Reader, Department of P.G. Studies in Economics, Sri Sarada College, Salem-636016, Tamil Nadu.

Mohanty, D.K., Bharathiya Reserve Bank, Note Mudran Unit, Note Mudran Nagar, Mysore-570003.

Nageswara Rao, K., Professor, Department of Economics, Sri Krishnadevaraya University, Anantapur-515003, Andhra Pradesh.

Nambiar, A.C.K., Professor, Department of Economics, University of Calicut, Thrissur-680618, Kerala State.

Padoshi, A.R., Department of Economics, Goa University,. Goa.

Patil, G.R., Professor, Department of Studies in Economics, Karnataka University, Dharwad.

Raghavendra, T.S., Professor, Department of Economics, Shri Lal Bahadur Shastri College, Sagar-577401, Karnataka.

Ramachandran, Lija, Research Scholar, Institute for Socio-Economic Change, Nagarabhavi, Bangalore-72, Karnataka.

Rego, P.A., Department of Economics, Mangalore University, Mangalagangotri-574199, Karnataka.

Renukarya, C.K., Visiting Professor, P.G. Department of Economics, JSS Women's College, Saraswathipuram, Mysore-570006.

Sabanna, Talwar, Department of Studies in Economics, Karnataka University, KRC PG Centre, Belgaum, Karnataka State.

Shripathi, K.P., Department of Economics, Mangalore University, Mangalagangotri-574199, Karnataka.

K. Sivachithappa, Lecturer, Division of Economics, P.G. Centre, Mandya-571402.

Sreekantaradhya, B.S., Member, Revenue Reforms Commission, Govt. of Karnataka and Professor of Economics, SBM Chair, Mysore University, Mysore-570006.

Suryanarayana, N.P., Visiting Professor, Department of Polymer Science Mysore University, Sir M. Visvesvaraya, P.G. Centre, Mandya, Karnataka State.

Swamy, Gajavelli, Associate professor, SDM Institute for Management Development, Mysore-570005.

Veerabhadrappa, B.P., Dept of Economics, Kuvempu University, P.G. Centre, Davanagere-577002.

Veeraiah, K.M., Professor, Department of Economics, J.S.S. College, Ooty Road, Mysore.

Yogeesh, S.N., Department of Studies in Economics, Kuvempu University, Jnana Sahyadri-577451, Shimoga Disrict, Karnataka.

CONTENTS

Part—II

WTO AND INDIAN AGRICULTURE

Part—III

WTO AND INDIAN LABOUR SERVICE SECTOR INDUSTRY

Part—I
WTO and its Trade Policy

1

Key Note Address
WTO and India: The Road Ahead

B.S. Sreekantaradhya

World Trade Organisation, which is a successor to General Agreement on Trade and Tariffs, came into being in 1995 after the conclusion of the Uruguay Round of Trade Negotiations. It has the responsibility of supervising the implementation of the final Uruguay round agreement and of settlement of disputes arising among the members in implementing the agreement, besides providing a forum for arranging new negotiations for fulfilling the objective of promoting world trade in goods and services. Throughout the negotiations of the Uruguay Round as well as following the conclusion of the final agreement, there was unprecedented controversy and though much of it has been resolved by now by simply accepting and implementing the various provisions of the agreement, new issues are coming up for discussion and that way there seems to be no end to the controversies surrounding WTO. New issues are coming up before the ministerial meetings, which need close scrutiny. This note takes a look at the new issues to be addressed at the ongoing and future negotiations.

Tariff Reduction on Manufacturers

Multilateral trade negotiations of several rounds have resulted in considerable reduction of tariffs on manufacturers, especially in the developed countries. This should be of great help to the developing countries, since their share of exports of manufacturers in total exports has greatly increased in recent years. But as a matter of fact, tariffs levied by developed countries on imports from developing countries are still high. This is because of the fact that the export basket of developing countries including India consists to a great extent of products like textiles and sugar, which attract relatively high tariffs. In any case, 40 per cent of India's exports enter the world market duty-free and 60 per cent at 4.5 per cent.

With regard to the tariffs on manufactures, one important question that needs to be addressed is whether in the next round of negotiation, further reduction in tariffs should be considered. Since the tariff level in the developed countries is already low except in respect of some items like textiles and sugar, perhaps there is not much scope for reducing the tariffs of developed countries. Therefore, if at all there should be any reduction in tariffs for manufactures, it will be in the case of developing countries. Tariff reduction in developing countries is an issue, which needs careful consideration. Since the volume of trade among developing countries has considerably increased, reduction of tariffs of developing countries would promote trade among themselves. However, the market access to developed countries in developing countries will also increase and this will hurt the industries of developing countries.

While India's market access has improved because of lowering of tariffs by developed countries, concerns have been expressed about reduction in tariffs given effect to by India as per the commitment in the Uruguay Round of negotiations. India agreed to reduce the basic duty rate by 30 per cent on items having duty rate above 25 per cent. India's rates were very high going up to 300 per cent in some cases. Starting from the early 1990s, tariffs have been reduced drastically with the objective of bringing down the peak rate to 20 per cent in the near future. Fears of dumping by other countries putting Indian industries into disadvantage are no doubt genuine. But there are safeguards in the form of anti-dumping measures, which can be implemented in case of adverse impact on Indian industry. Besides tariff reduction, quantitative restrictions have been removed. This has created an impression that Indian imports will increase and destroy the Indian industry in general and the small scale industries in particular. The generally accepted view is that India should liberalize imports and import more in order to export more. Before agreeing for any further reduction in tariffs, it is necessary to make a careful study of the impact of the import liberalisation that has taken place so far on the Indian industry. What is the extent of increase in imports after liberalisation? What industries are affected and to what extent? A case by case study of Indian industries is necessary to have a clear idea of the actual impact on Indian industry. Having reduced the tariffs as per the earlier rounds of negotiations, what stand India should take with regard to further reduction in the next round of negotiations needs to be carefully examined.

Tariffs on Agriculture

While the tariffs on manufacturers are quite low, the tariffs on agricultural products are still high. The rates on an average are 15.6 per cent in developed countries and 20.1 per cent in developing countries. In the next round of negotiations, it would be necessary to examine whether reduction in tariffs on agricultural products is necessary and whether the reduction would benefit the developing countries. The questions of reducing domestic support and export subsidies are also important. In the Uruguay Round, India did not suffer in respect of domestic subsidies because India's Aggregate Measure of Support was less than the limit fixed by WTO and consequently there was no need to cut subsidies. Public distribution system also remained unaffected. But the expansion of agricultural exports has not been satisfactory. The reasons for this are stringent sanitary and phytosanitary conditions, product standardisation and quality assurance. India and other developing countries should press for standardisation of these requirements in the next round of negotiations.

Liberalisation of Services

While merchandise trade is restricted through tariffs and quantitative restrictions, trade in services is restricted through regulations on entry or operations. These regulations have to be removed or greatly minimised if the trade in services is to be promoted. Limited liberalisation of services took place under the Uruguay Round of Negotiations as per the provisions of General Agreement on Trade in Services (GATS). There are new proposals, for further liberalisation in respect of services like banking, insurance, telecom, maritime transport etc. More services like health, education, technological services etc. have to be brought under negotiations.

It would be interesting to look into banking and education in particular because of the great importance of these services for the national economy. Major demands in respect of financial services are that India should allow greater market share to foreign banks and subsidiaries and joint ventures of foreign banks should be allowed and that discrimination against foreign banks in terms of taxation and placement of surplus funds by public sector units be removed. Financial Services Agreement, 1997 under GATS deals with these issues. The presence of foreign banks undoubtedly confers certain benefits like better quality services, providing stimulus to competition leading to improvement in efficiency and improvement in prudential regulation. But very large presence of foreign banks will also create certain problems. Lending policy of foreign banks being pro-rich, there will be less finance for the disadvantaged groups and also less credit-worthy borrowers will be left to the local banks and further, there is also the fear of foreign banks becoming dominant and local banks getting marginalised. More than everything else, several instances of financial crises triggered by foreign banks in different parts of the world in recent years, have made it amply clear that financial liberalisation needs a very cautious approach.

Regarding the issue of branches vs subsidiaries, until recently India's policy was to allow only branches of foreign banks. But the Finance Minister announced in his Budget for 2002-03 that foreign banks may continue as branches of their parent banks or set up their subsidiaries and thus setting up of subsidiaries is no longer an issue. There are other issues on which India should take a definite stand. How many branches of foreign banks be permitted to be set up per year; whether the present restriction on foreign share of banking assets at 15 per cent of the total banking assets in India should be retained or enhanced to 20 or 30 per cent, whether the restrictions on national treatment be removed and whether the investment limits of foreign banks in finance companies can be raised from 30 per cent to 49 per cent are some of the important issues to be addressed. It is in respect of the movement of natural persons that India has advantage. India has a vast pool of technical people who can provide financial services in other countries and therefore India should strive hard to get the restrictions on the movement of natural persons removed or substantially reduced.

Educational service is another area in which liberalisation is proposed under GATS. Education has come to be treated as tradable service and the member countries may open up any of the five categories of education listed by WTO namely primary, secondary, university, adult and others. Further, trade in educational services is classified into four modes namely cross-border supply, consumption abroad, commercial presence and movement of natural persons. Negotiations have to take place for liberalisation in all these areas. Some countries have already made their proposals and commitments. India has to make its own proposals and commitments and great care is necessary in this regard. While the entry of foreign educational institutions may be helpful from the point of view of improving educational standards, there is the fear of our own educational institutions getting marginalised. We should accept what is good in the other systems and at the same time preserve what is good in our system. While a large number of Indian students are going abroad for studies, the number of foreign students coming to India for studies is very small. It is necessary to introduce appropriate measures to attract more foreign students. Some of these concerns have to be kept in mind while participating in the negotiations for liberalisation of educational services.

Social Clause

Developing countries have been insisting on the adoption of labour standards by the developing countries. Labourers of developed countries want inclusion of labour standards in the trade negotiations not for protecting the interests of labour in developing countries, but because of the desire to protect their own interest i.e. to avoid import of products of cheap labour. Putting restrictions on the import of products of child labour is also for similar reasons. Labour standards like wages, employment protection and protection of women and children are no doubt important. But they are not trade issues. They are matters of concern for International Labour Organisation (ILO). But ILO has no teeth and if these issues are related to trade, their implementation would be easy and that is the reason why the developed countries wish to include the social clause in the trade negotiations. Should developing countries resist inclusion of social clause altogether or concentrate on what aspects of social clause should be included is an important issue on which India and other countries should take a definite stand.

Environmental Concerns

Environmental issues, which the developed countries want to include in the negotiations, are also a matter of concern to India and other developing countries. Doha declaration provides for the negotiation on trade and environment in the Post-Doha work programme of the WTO. U.S.A. has been using environmental concerns as a disguised form of protection. The shrimp-turtle case is the best example of this. U.S.A. placed restrictions on import of shrimp harvested with shrimp trawl nets not equipped with turtle excluder devices. India, Malaysia, Thailand and Pakistan filed a case, but WTO's Dispute Settlement Mechanism upheld the U.S. position. Environmental concerns are no doubt important. But using them as protectionist devices is not acceptable. This is an issue on which developing countries should take a united stand.

Review of TRIPS and TRIMS

Agreement on Trade Related Intellectual Property Rights and the Agreement on Trade Related Investment Measures have been extensively debated and the developed-country bias in these agreements has been very well recognised. It is now time to review these agreements in the interest of the developing countries.

Developing countries have committed to make their IPR regimes TRIPS compliant. In India, amendments have been made to the Patents Act of 1970. But this does not cover the product patenting to be introduced by January 1, 2005. Separate legislation in this regard will be necessary. What will happen to the prices of pharmaceuticals in particular after the introduction of product patenting is to be seen. Developing countries want the deadline for introducing product patenting to be postponed since public health interest will suffer because of the possible increase in the prices of drugs for Malaria, T.B. and HIV/AIDS. At the Doha Ministerial Conference, least developed countries were given time till 2016 to switch over to product patenting. But this concession should have been given to the other developing countries as well. Least developed countries will not benefit much from this concession since they do not have the capacity to produce the most essential drugs. India has the capacity to produce the drugs for Malaria, T.B. and HIV/AIDS and it can export them to least developed countries at a very low price. From that point of view, in addition to India's public health concerns, extension of time for India to go in for product patenting would have been useful. TRIPS agreement, by denying access to cheap medical treatment, comes in the way of the right to health and thus violates the human rights. Therefore, a review of TRIPS is essential to remove all those provisions, which are inimical to the basic rights of the people of developing countries including India.

Regarding the Trade Related Investment Measures (TRIMS) also a review is necessary, particularly to remove the asymmetry that exists between the host country and the foreign investors. While the TRIMS agreement requires national treatment and removal of restrictions on exports or imports by the host countries, restrictions that are imposed by the multinationals on their affiliates with regard to exports and imports are not sought to be removed. In any case, WTO is not the appropriate body to deal with investment issues. Multilateral Agreement on Investments (MAI) proposed by the OECD, which aimed at subjecting the host countries to a code of conduct failed to come into being. But now there is a move on the part of the advanced countries to bring into force something similar to MAI. India and other developing countries should resist such a move. Any attempt to widen the scope of investment under the WTO beyond TRIMS should be opposed.

Developed-country bias has been the major problem with regard to all the WTO issues. Developed countries have obviously better bargaining capacity and they have always been striving to ensure that all the decisions are favourable to them. Unless the developing countries get united on all major issues, the problem of asymmetry between the developed and developing countries cannot be solved. India's assertion at the Doha Ministerial conference has yielded some good results. It has been decided that negotiations on issues like investment, competition, trade facilitation and Government procurement will start only after explicit consensus by all members. India should take the leadership and work with other developing and like-minded countries and as rightly pointed out by the Commerce and Industries Minister, Mr. Murasoli Maran, soon after his return from the Doha Ministerial Conference, there is need for forging a `development coalition' to champion the cause of India and other developing countries.

2

Presidential Address: WTO—A Few Thoughts

A. K. Chattopadhyay

First of all let me congratulate the Division of Studies in Economics, University of Mysore for having chosen for the seminar a topic, which is not only contemporaneous but also relevant, controversial and hence interesting. In fact, any reference to WTO evokes a mixed reaction,—a sense of outrage combined with a resigned acceptance of its inexorability and inevitability. The Macbethian dilemma of 'to be or not to be' is all the more pronounced in a developing country like India,—which is trying to cope with its backwardness overshadowed by the impact of globalisation in trade and commerce as a member of the WTO.

There is no denying the fact that in a unipolar world of today, our country cannot afford to remain isolated, and allow itself to miss the opportunity of international trade liberalisation and removal of protectionist practices of advanced countries. But at the sametime, we cannot keep our eyes closed to the negative impact of it all on our tottering small and medium scale industries, the large unorganized labour force, our traditional agricultural and ayurvedic products,—examples of which are many and wellknown.

The apprehension of MNC's gobbling up our industries, flooding of our markets with cheap articles from China and elsewhere, life saving drugs going out of reach of common people, misuse of IPR and patenting procedure, increase in unemployment due to takeovers and mergers, etc.,—cannot be wished away. In areas of labour laws, it cannot be over emphasized that aberrations and restrictive practices borne out of existing archaic laws, have been seriously affecting industrial climate and investment, and these laws have to be reviewed and reformed in order for the industries/PSU's to survive and prosper in a competitive market, for the investment climate to look up and generate employment. However, in absence of social security in India, a holistic view needs to be taken in the direction of multi--skilling, unemployment security, liberal outsourcing etc., in correcting the present shortcomings and to fall in line with WTO regulation. Perhaps we may take a cue from China,—which has opened up its economy to invite FDI, simultaneously with maintaining its own totalitarian policies. As a democracy, the methodology will not be the same for us. But it must be kept in mind that both may be clubbed in the same bracket in so far as the stage of economic development, living standards etc., are concerned.

Finally, we have to have our own remedy for our ills, and for using the WTO objectives/guidelines to our advantage. It is an emotive issue and has socio-political implications. We have to work from within to fight out its negative features to suit our stage of development and state of economy. The scholars and experts gathered here will surely throw more light in this direction and come up with prescription.

3

The WTO and India's Trade Policy Regime–with Some Reference to LDCs

G.R. Patil

Although the WTO was the outcome of Uruguay Round, it had been in existence in the form of GATT ever since the close of the Second World War. GATT was established with the intention of introducing rule of law in international trade relations. It prohibited discriminatory tariffs. Under GATT agreement each country had to apply the same rate to the imports from all member countries. It contained the rules for the regulation of tariffs, non-tariff barriers and other trade measures. It insisted on equality of treatment between domestically produced goods and foreign goods after importation. It prohibited quotas because of their trade distorting effects. It laid down the principles of valuation for customs purposes, the procedure for imposition of antidumping and countervailing duties, the treatment of subsidies and conditions for introduction of restrictions to maintain balance of payments to further a country's economic development.

(i) Uruguay Round

The principal objective of Uruguay Round was to strengthen the multilateral trading system to face the needs of the future. GATT was successful in reducing the tariff levels in the developed countries from the average of 40% in 1948 to less than 4% in 1995. It was feared that with the reduction in tariffs to insignificant levels, countries might be tempted to misuse non-tariff measures for purposes of protection. New sectors of trade such as service sector were developing at a much faster pace. Because of these reasons the GATT approached the strengthening of the system in the Uruguay Round from four directions. First, Uruguay Round was aimed at improving the overall effectiveness of the GATT as an institution. A new safeguard agreement was developed to govern the introduction of protective actions. A comprehensive dispute settlement machinery was installed. A new institution was created in succession to GATT, the WTO, with a wider ambit covering international trade in both goods and services. Second, GATT rules pertaining to anti-dumping actions, subsidies, countervailing measures and customs valuation methods were strengthened. Third, the trade in agricultural goods and textiles was brought under the preview of WTO rules, because these two sectors were heavily protected in most of the developed countries. It was accepted that the multilateral trading system would not be healthy if the trade in the two sectors were not subjected to the GATT disciplines. Fourth, new rules were formulated to govern the trade in services which had assumed significant proportions and for which there were existing no rules in the GATT The conclusion of Uruguay Round of negotiations took ten years and WTO was established in 1995. It has helped the global community of trading nations to move towards freer trade and open market.

(ii) India's Trade Policy Regime

India is a founder member of both GATT and WTO but had not made significant contributions for the development of the GATT system. India's exports had benefited from progressive reductions of tariff levels in the developed countries. But it had not reduced its tariffs nor did it offer to bind them against future increases. On the contrary, its tariffs had reached an astronomical heights before the start of Uruguay Round with the levels as high as 300% for some goods. Such abnormal level shielded domestic producers from competition by the more efficient producers elsewhere. The government did not even receive the full benefit of the high customs revenue because smugglers, taking advantage of the high tariffs and import controls, began large-scale illicit trade. A well-organised clandestine traffic was developed between West Coast of India and the centres of contraband trade in the Gulf.

India had faced a severe foreign exchange crisis at the close of the Second Plan. India had to initiate import restriction to meet foreign exchange crisis. Some imports were banned, some could be imported in limited quantities and some goods were permitted against equivalent exports. Some were canalised for imports through state trading agencies. Consumer goods were more or less completely prohibited for imports. While imports of industrial raw materials and intermediate goods were allowed depending upon the availability of foreign exchange. The domestic market was insulated from competition of local and foreign origins by an extensive system of centralised planning and import controls. The domestic producers were protected from competition and became more and more inefficient, but they were helped by state aid. The production base was fragmented. Important segments of production were reserved for small-scale sector, which were given subsidies to remain small and inefficient. The public sector inefficiency was hidden by massive doses of capital fusion from the public exchequer. The public sector units were overstaffed and little shareholder pressure to improve the performances. Organised labour was pampered and assured rising wages without any linkages with productivity. There was not a sector, whether it was agriculture, export, industry or services that was denied subsidies. The interest of the ordinary consumer was ignored in favour of those of a selected few. The protection of the domestic market and unrestrained flow of subsidies has created vested interests in India. These vested interests are resisting introduction of market forces and competition. The manufacturing sector wants to deny consumers the choice to buy better and cheaper goods from outside in preference to its high priced shoddy goods. The small-scale sector wishes to produce spurious and non-standard goods in unhygienic conditions. Agriculture would fight hard to maintain free supply of electricity, subsidised fertilisers and other inputs. The vested interests have created nexus between politicians, bureaucrats and producers. The politicians were happy to exploit the system for their vote bank politics. The bureaucrats were happy with the license permit quota raj for their own selfish ends. The industry and Trade was happy with the continuation of the congenial conditions that assured a regular flow of profits. The political Parties of socialist pretensions that had remained prisoners of the discarded ideology aided them. This unholy alliance of the vested interests and political parties of different hues, in order to preserve the status quo, claims that India's acceptance of the Uruguay Round results in threatening the sovereignty of the nation and the supremacy of its parliament.

WTO embodies rule of law in trade relations and its constituent agreements and decisions represent a distinct movement towards liberalisation of World Trade. Withdrawal from WTO implies that India has lost faith in the rule of law and it is opposed to trade liberalisation. Withdrawal from WTO membership is not a very simple affair. There are serious consequences. WTO members extend to each other, without discrimination, the most favoured nation tariffs that currently average around 4% in the developed countries. Without WTO membership, these countries will be under no obligation to apply the low import duties to imports from India. Without the protection of WTO agreements India's exports could be subjected to quotas, anti-dumping actions or countervailing measures in a totally arbitrary manner. The dispute settlement machinery would be outside India's reach. In the absence of this facility. India would be reduced to bilateral appeals to its trading partner for whatever they are worth. India had insulated itself with import substitution policies. It had resorted state interventions in production and trade with all its attendant inefficiencies. Therefore, India lagged behind the other Asian Countries, South Korea, Thailand, Taiwan and Indonesia achieved higher rates of economic growth. India can no longer afford to resist market opening if it had to grow faster and forge ahead. It will have to remove inefficiencies and will have to welcome competition. India having become leading player in I.T, having entered the field of space technology, having become a nuclear power, and having claimed a permanent seat in the Security Council, surely it can not turn around and declare that it can not face import competition and economic liberalisation.

(iii) Unfounded Fears

The quota libealisation has been going on progressively during past four years. There is no flood of imports of the liberalised goods. When quotas on nearly 1400 products were removed, non-oil imports increased marginally by 2.5%. The quotas had always been a strong incentive for illicit trade. The West Coast of the country for decades had been regularly supplied by smuggled goods from Gulf Ports, North East, as well as parts of Northern border have always been attractive markets for smuggled goods. Most of the towns along the border have what are popularly known as "China Bazaar". Now that restrictions have gone, these goods have been steadily moving into the inland markets. When legitimate imports take place, consequent to the liberalisation, prices are likely to rise, because of customs duty and that should safeguard the threatened industry. It should not be imagined that India after liberalisation would be left without any defence in the practice of international trade. There are number of provisions under the WTO that can be legally used to protect the domestic Industry. If the balance of payments position worsens or if the foreign exchange reserve decline, a country can invoke the protection of Articles XII or XVIII of GATT and reimpose quantitative restrictions to the extent necessary. India has already raised the tariffs at the beginning of the year in anticipation of increased imports. The current rates are 37.70% for processed food products, up to 60% for dairy and poultry products, 35-50% for fruits and food grains, 35-40% for domestic appliances, 35% for consumer electronics, watches, toys, 35% for textiles and garments and 105% for automobiles.

(iv) Agriculture and Small Scale Sector

Historically, the GATT rules have never been applied to agriculture trade with the same stringency as in the case of manufactured goods. The developed countries have used the GATT loopholes for decades to restrict the imports of agricultural goods into their territories. The developed countries have been protecting agriculture by high domestic support, export subsidies and denial of access through various tariff and non-tariff barriers to imports from developing countries. The average producer support for developed countries is more than 60% but it is negligible in India and other developing countries. Inview of this it may not be in India's interest to fight within WTO for greater domestic support to agriculture, especially if it can blunt our opposition to slow reduction in farm support in developed countries. For its growth, Indian agriculture is in need of substantial public investment in irrigation, power, roads, agricultural research and extension rather than subsidies on inputs. There is indeed a consensus among planners and policy makers that decline in public investment in agriculture is basically attributable to mounting subsidies on irrigation, power and fertiliser.

As for protecting through tariffs, India has negotiated tariff binding at the level of 100% for raw materials, 150% for processed agro commodities and 300% for most edible oils. These may be considered sufficient to protect the relevant commodities against cheaper imports sustained by high domestic support in the countries of their origin. There is need for extreme vigilance so as to be able to take timely measures, to arrest heavy import of certain commodities. The average growth of G.D.P. in agriculture and allied sectors slowed down in the post reforms period of nineties when compared to the preceding decade, while the growth of crop output, especially food grains output, decelerated. The experience of the 1990's clearly demonstrates that for from trade liberalisation dampening performance of agriculture, the failure of public investment and effort is responsible for the inability to benefit from trade liberalisation by stepping up and diversifying agricultural output in a cost effective way.

Why Indian S.S.I. products can not compete with Chinese goods, which have been the main source of competition for the Indian S.S.I. sector units? Technology, credit, raw materials etc. have been often highlighted as problems of small scale units. The government decision to reduce customs duties on host of inputs used in the manufacture of final products is expected to improve price competitiveness of the domestic S.S.I. units and help industry to compete against cheap imports from countries like China. The removal of remaining QRS would lead to an anomalous situation in the case of the products reserved for S.S.I. sector as reserved items could be imported freely. Poor infrastructure, high cost of power, high cost of transportation and high cost of capital in India have made S.S.I. products non competitive. Working capital loans being available at rates between 16% and 19.5% Lack of cheap finance also meant that modernisation was not possible. Because of under invoicing of imports, the prices of imported goods are lower. Labour laws prevent modulation of labour force in accordance with the capacity utilisation. Problems of high cost of power can be overcome by increasing the efficiency in power generation and distribution. Other problems like high import duty on raw materials, under invoicing of imports, smuggling of watch and clock movements and plastic goods from China and Nepal can be overcome by reducing customs duties and by checking the smuggling of watch and clock movements and other goods.

(v) IPRs and Developing Countries

Developing countries opposed the inclusion of IPRs in the new GATT treaty on the ground that this would lead to higher prices and detrimental to the development of their domestic, infant, hi-tech industries. Developed countries, however pointed out that stronger intellectual property protection would stimulate research, which would be beneficial to both firms and consumers in the long run in L.D.Cs. With inclusion of TRIPS component in the WTO agreement, developing member countries are committed to making their IPR regimes TRIPS compliant in the near future. For India, with respect to pharmaceuticals, this implies shifting from process patents of seven years duration to one that of product patents for 20 years. The adoption of process patent helped firms in pharmaceuticals in developing countries to specialise in the production of cheap versions of patent drugs for local as well as for export markets. The move to product patents, however, will make such productions and commerce illegal. As a consequence, the price of newly patented drugs is set to rise sharply in the developing countries. There is trade-off between prices and innovations, higher prices now for, new and improved, medical treatment in future. It is argued that the introduction of product patents in L.D.Cs is unlikely to provide any additional stimulus to the development of new drugs, given the relatively small economic size of these markets. The chief impetus to research comes from the rich, patent protected markets of North. A distinction is made by analysts between medical research and development related to global diseases, such as cancer, that have significant presence in both developed and developing countries and research related to country ailments such as T.B, Malaria, AIDS which are found primarily in L.D.Cs. Hence, research on medical treatment for these diseases is likely to continue apace, regardless of the patent regime in place in the developing countries. For poor country specific ailments such as Malaria and T.B., in contrast, there are no significant markets in the North. Consequently, stronger intellectual property protection in the South is likely to be key to inducing new and better treatment for these diseases. But this alone is unlikely to do the trick, because the small, low income markets in the L.D.Cs can not support the price volume combinations needed to make such research and development projects commercially viable. Thus, for global diseases, product patents will imply higher prices for new drugs in developing countries, with little gain, in the form of higher rates of medical research and innovation. In the case of poor country diseases, on the other hand, stronger intellectual property protection, while necessary may not, by itself, sufficient, to induce new, improved and affordable medical treatments. Thus two sets of options are available to the L.D.Cs. The first relates primarily to global ailments, where R & D is already supported by the North and induces options such as compulsory licensing, tiered pricing, national drug price regulation. The second set aimed at creating markets for treatments relating to poor country specific ailments, in manner that allows affordability, without endangering incentives to future research and innovation.

Compulsory Licensing

Article 31 of the TRIPS agreement permits a government to authorise an agent to produce a patented drug, subjected to certain conditions aimed at protecting the legitimate interests of the patent holder. It requires, for example that prior attempt should be made to obtain such rights at reasonable commercial terms from the patentee and where these fail and a compulsory license is issued. These requirements are waived in case of national or other circumstances of extreme urgency. The issue of compulsory license is, of course subject to the WTOs'. dispute settlement mechanism, with the burden of proof resting on the issuing authority.

Tiered Pricing

This means price discrimination based on income. Drug prices should be close to the marginal cost in the least developed countries.

Conclusion

WTO embodies rule of law in the international trade relations. Its agreements and decisions represent a distinct movement towards liberalisation of world trade. The establishment of WTO has resulted in an unconditional application of GATT rules by all members. A comprehensive dispute settlement mechanism was installed. The strengthening of GATT rules pertaining to anti dumping actions, subsidies, customs valuation methods and countervailing measures are important achievements of the Uruguay Round Negotiations. Trade in agriculture goods and textiles had been brought under the purview of GATT rules. New rules were formulated to govern the expanding trade in services. A controversial agreement was formulated to deal with trade related IPRs, particularly patents. The alleged difficulties of our country are not on account of the terms and conditions negotiated in the Uruguay Round but of our own making. India was one of the founding members of GATT, but had not made significant contributions, except in rhetoric prior to 1995. India faced severe crisis of foreign exchange before the close of second five-year plan. It introduced a planned system of import restrictions that gained in intensity and refinements as the years went by. India insulated itself with import substitution policies. The free play of market forces was not allowed. The domestic industry was shielded from competition and they became more and more inefficient. Public sector enterprises were over staffed and there was no shareholder pressure to improve the efficiency of public sector units. They were given budgetary support from the public exchequer. Labour was pampered and protected and assured of wages and perquisites without any linkages with productivity. There was not a sector, whether it was agriculture, export, industry, or services that was denied public subsidy. Protection of the domestic market, unrestrained flow of subsidies has created a huge complex of vested interests. The vested interests have created a nexus between politicians, bureaucrats and producers. Complex negotiations like under the Uruguay Round necessarily involved a certain amount of give and take by every participant. Every country had to concede something in one area and make some gains elsewhere. The final results of the round reflected a deliberate balance of conflicting national interests of all trading countries. No one was a total gainer or loser. That is why forging this gigantic compromise took 10 years to complete. Renegotiation of the commitments made in the Uruguay Round at this stage is neither credible nor feasible. The dismantling of last bastion of protection has attracted criticism from the farmers lobby and domestic producers of the liberalised items. They would not relish the increased competition from better and cheaper products. Political parties of different hues, from saffron to red, have not been able to resist the temptation to fish in troubled waters. The left parties opposed introduction of market forces because they believed in state control and management. All political parties, without exception are interested in collecting brownie points (funds) from vested interests with an eye on the election.

The quota liberalisation is going on progressively during the past four years. The country is not flooded with imports of liberalised goods. During the financial year 1999-2000, when quota on nearly 1400 products were removed, non-oil imports increased marginally by 2.5% over the previous year. In the last financial year, 2000-01 during the period April-Dec, inspite of extensive liberalisation, non-oil imports actually declined by 7% compared with the previous year. The quotas had always been a strong incentive for illicit trade. Now that restrictions have gone, and legitimate imports take place, prices are likely to rise because of the customs duty and that should safeguard the threatened industries. It should not be imagined that India, after the liberalisation of external trade, would be left without any defence in the practice of international trade. If the balance of payments situation worsens again, India can invoke the protection of Article XVIII of the General Agreement and reimpose quantitative restrictions to the extent necessary. If increased imports of a particular product, arising from liberalisation cause serious injury to the domestic producers, India can take recourse to safeguard measures under Article XIX of the General Agreement and either raise the concerned tariff or introduce quantitative restrictions. The major challenge to the viability of agriculture of most developing countries including India, is posed by high domestic support, export subsidies and denial of markets access through various tariff and non-tariff barriers in the developed countries. India has been fighting with other countries in the WTO for the removal of such barriers. WTO permits the imposition of anti-dumping duties to neutralise the cost advantages. A common perception in the country is the threat of cheap imports from China. The principal problem is that with the porosity of the borders Chinese goods evade the customs duty and the resultant price might be injurious. Why Indian goods can not compete with the Chinese goods, which have been the main source of competition in the small-scale sector? The cost of power and capital is very high in India. Labour laws prevent the retrenchment of labour in India. The competition is on account of price not on quality. Therefore, changes in the labour laws are needed to improve labour productivity in the small sector. Developing countries opposed the inclusion of controversial IPRs in the new WTO treaty on the ground that his would lead to higher prices and detrimental to the development of the domestic, infant and hi-tech industries. Developed countries, however, pointed out that stronger IPRs protection would stimulate research and innovation. The stronger intellectual IPRs protection is alone unlikely to stimulate research and development projects in the LDCs with their small economic size of their markets. In the recent debate on the IPRs, the two options such as compulsory licensing and tiered pricing are available to the developing countries.

There could be no doubt that in the longer term the increased competition from the more efficient producers elsewhere would be beneficial for the domestic sector. Under pressure of foreign competition, domestic producers would be forced to improve productivity, use modern technology and make better use of factors of production. There is no point in indulging in irresponsible talk of withdrawing from WTO for gaining political mileage. Instead there should be positive campaign to make India globally competitive.

REFERENCES

1. Sanjay Bagchi "India and the WTO", Economic and Political Weekly, January 13, 2001.
2. Shridhar Krishna "Phasing out of import licensing and Impact on small scale Industries", Economic and Political Weekly, July 7-13, 2001.

3. C.S. Sundaresan, "Multilateral Trade and Dairy Commodity in L.D.C", Economic and Political Weekly, August 25-31, 2001.

4. C.H. Hanumantha Rao "WTO and viability of Indian Agriculture", Economic and Political Weekly, September 8-14, 2001.

5. A. Damodaran "WTO Agriculture Agreement, Common property Resources and Income diversification's Strategy", Economic and Political Weekly, September 22-28, 2001.

4

WTO Policies-Some Challenges for India

Talwar Sabanna and M.S. Kallur

Introduction

Globalisation has been the catchword for international political economy discourses in the 1990's. In other words, this term connotes a process of free trade in commodities and services across the nations coupled with greater mobility of factors of production between nations such that economies of different nations tend to get integrated. In practice, this would involve gradual dismantling of artificial restrictions on trade and investment in different parts of the world. This would also logically require devising of new rules of the game being evolved at the multilateral level to coordinate the increased flows of trade and investment.

Further, globalisation process in the world economy in the form of free flow of goods and services across nations, international movements of finance, capital and labour migration has been strengthened, particularly after the revolution of information technology and concerned global actions to initiate the process of policy reforms based on trade liberalisation, technological collaboration and participation of foreign equity and portfolio investment in different parts of the world.[1] The emergence of WTO at the conclusion of the Uruguay round of trade negotiations of the GATT has marked the beginning of the multilateral surveillance of the trading arrangements that are evolving under the new global order.

Since 1947, India became a major example amongst the developing countries which have engaged themselves in the experimentation of state sponsored economic planning under the framework of democracy. Further, it started to practice, to begin with, the 'mixed economy' principle. Besides this, converting the predominantly agricultural economy of feudalistic design into a socialistic pattern of society was the prime goal of it. Until 1991, India did not witness any major change in its development policy.

In recent years, there have been intense discussions in the academic as well as policy circles regarding the economic reforms introduced in our country. Because, the first generation of economic reforms in July 1991 was initiated as per the conditionalities of the IMF loan that we took at that time to salvage India's credibility in the world financial market, the second generation of economic reforms at the turn of the 21st century has been guided by our compulsions to conform to the norms set by the WTO in matters of trade policy. Many of the changes that are now contemplated in the functioning of the Indian economy are basically the offshoots of the standards and norms prescribed by the WTO, inter alia, adherence of labour and environment standards in the name of safeguarding the human rights of the globalised world. Hence, in this paper we look at the implications and challenges of WTO on India.

WTO Agreements and India

The most avowed goal of the WTO, as set out in the promoting documents, is to create a fair and equitable, rule-based multilateral trade system. The most appealing aspect is that the new multilateral trade regime would be transparent and nondiscriminatory. For the world trading community as a whole, every initiative on trade liberalisation should ensure rewards in the form of large and expanding markets and greater trade flows for all participating members. Let us now look at some of the agreements and impact of these agreements on Indian economy.

Trade Related Intellectual Property Rights (TRIPs)

The subject of trade-related intellectual rights (TRIPs) has always been very controversial. Intellectual property (IP) refers to "a creation of human mind that is a value to the society, while Intellectual Property Rights (IPRs) are rights granted by the state to persons over creation of their mind".[3] In other words, patent owners exclusive property rights allowing them to prevent others from using the inventions covered. Manufacturers wishing to use patened inventions must obtain licences or authorisations from the patent owners, who normally will require them to pay royalties. The areas of intellectual property that the TRIPs agreement covers are:

*Patents

Plant and seed variety; micro organism; copyrights and neighbouring rights; trademarks, including services marks; industrial designs; geographical indications; integrated circuits; and trade secrets.

For each of these, certain norms of protection are prescribed. These norms do not necessarily have to be attained overnight. There is a transition period allowed. Legislations in most of these items are at various stages of formulation and implementation.

Trips and India

In India, the concern for the protection of intellectual property was evident way back in the Design Act of 1911. Later, the patenting system was modified and comprehensive act viz. Indian Patent Act was passed in 1970. Prior to the agreement on TRIPs, India had legal systems of protection for four types of intellectual properties viz. Patent, trademark, copyright and industrial design.[4]

India has agreed the TRIPs applications from January 1, 1995 onwards. The applications will be received in the 'Mailbox' and will be examined only with effect from January 1, 2005. Further, the TRIPs Agreement also makes it obligatory for India to grant exclusive marketing rights (EMRs) to pharmaceuticals and agro-chemicals, which have been given product patents and marketing approval in another member country of the WTO. India's major concerns in the area of IPR are:

1. Granting of product patents to pharmaceuticals and agro-chemicals.
2. Patenting of micro-organisms or life forms, including patenting of products based on our bio-diversity and traditional knowledge in other parts of the world; and
3. Establishing an effective sui-generis system for the protection of new plant varieties, plant breeders rights, which recognise and rewards the traditional contribution of rural communities to the conservation of bio-diversity.

Besides a rich bio-diversity, India has an abundant wealth of agricultural ideas, techniques, products and processes. Being a country with a long and varied past, many of its knowledge and practices relating to agriculture has come down through generations. These traditional knowledge and practice have found many modern applications. India, therefore, is favourably placed to benefit from the conditions of TRIPs.[5]

However, India's rich reservoir of traditional knowledge and practices are under threat from MNCs and unscrupulous elements who are quick to grab the opportunity to patent our knowledge and practices in

Western countries. India needs to put in place effective steps to protect them. Proper documentation of these knowledge and practices should be the first step in that direction.

Trade Related Investment Measures (TRIMs)

The objective of TRIMs is to prevent member countries from resorting to measures that violate (non-differential treatment between domestic and foreign investors) and impose quantitative restrictions on imports and exports. The agreement provides for transitional period for elimination of prohibited TRIMs with effect from January 1, 1995.

TRIMs and India

Before 1991, India used to have local content requirements in the form of the phased manufacturing programme (PMP). But, this has now been scrapped and only exists in the form of memoranda of understanding imposed on automobile manufacturers.

At this stage, it is important to note that as a part of promoting global investment flows, OECD countries have been keen to take up the issue of multilateral agreement on investment in the WTO negotiations agenda.

However, a MAI type of treaty adopted in the framework of WTO might contribute to an even greater marginalisation of the developing countries like India in the inter-country distribution of FDI inflows than at present.[5] Though TRIMs are prohibited under certain conditions, but India still has such a cover and have to scrap various TRIMs measures by 2003.

WTO Agreement on Agriculture

Until 1994 Agriculture was outside of the GATT purview. The original GATT applied to trade in agriculture also, but it allowed various exceptions to the rules on non-tariff measures and subsidies on industrial products. The

GATT rules also allowed countries to resort to import restrictions (e.g. import quotas) in the agriculture sector under certain conditions to enforce measures to effectively limit domestic production. This resulted in a proliferation of impediments to world agriculture trade.

It was felt necessary to reform agricultural policies in order to achieve trade liberalisation in agriculture. The idea was to progressively reduce trade distorting subsidies, improve import access and curb export subsidies in agriculture. These negotiating ideas were further developed subsequent consultations till some broad agreement was hammered out. Under the Agreement on Agriculture (AOA), the main countries would have to drastically reduce subsidies granted to the farm sector and convert them into tariffs. The tariff rates would be reduced and appropriately bound against subsequent increase.

The Agreement on Agriculture contains provisions in three broad areas of trade and agriculture policy viz; (i) Market access, (ii) Export subsidies and (iii) Domestic support.

(i) Market access

Market access for agricultural products states that there can be no restrictions on farm trade except through tariffs. This means that non-tariff barriers were to be replaced by tariffs on imports to provide the same level of protection and then were to be followed by progressive reduction of tariff levels. Tariffs resulting from this "tariffication process" as well as other tariffs are to be reduced by a simple average of 36 percent over six years in the case of developed countries and 24 per cent over 10 years in the case of developing countries.[7]

Market Access and India

In the case of India which had not converted the quantitative restrictions into tariffs, was allowed to have ceiling bindings. India had bound its tariffs at 100% for primary products, 150% for processed products and 300% for edible oils, except for certain items (comprising about 119 tariff lines), which were historically bound at a lower level in the earlier negotiations. Out of these low bound tariff lines, bindings on 15 tariff lines which included skimmed milk powder, spelt wheat, corn, paddy, rice, maize, millet, sorghum, colza and mustard oil, fresh grapes etc., were successfully negotiated in December 1999 and the binding levels were suitably revised upward to provide adequate protection to the domestic producers.[8]

(ii) Export Subsidy

Disciplines in the area of export subsidy required developing countries to reduce, over a period of 10 years, the volume of subsidized exports by 14 per cent in volume terms and 24 per cent in budgetary outlays. Also, developing countries are free to provide certain subsidies such as subsidising of export marketing costs, internal and international transport and freight charges etc.

Export Subsidy and India

Export subsidies of the kind tested in the AOA, which attract reduction commitments, are not extended in India. Further, India is making use of these subsidies in certain schemes of Agricultural and Processed `Food Products Export Development Authority (APEDA) especially for facilitating export of horticulture products.

(iii) Domestic Support

Domestic support measures, according to the agreement, are meant to identify acceptable measures of support to farmers. These measures are targeted largely at developed countries where the levels of domestic agricultural support has risen to extremely high levels. Domestic support is divided into two categories viz., (a) support with no or minimal, distortive effect on trade (known as "Green Box" and "Blue Box" measures) and (b) trade distorting support (as "Amber Box" Measures). Domestic support (called as Total Aggregate Measurement of Support-AMS) given to the agricultural produce in developing countries is allowed. In other words, AMS within this limit is not subject to any reduction commitment.

Domestic Support and India

In India, the product-specific support is negative, while the non-product specific support i.e., subsidies on agricultural inputs, such as power, irrigation, fertilisers etc. is well below the permissible level of 10% of the value of agricultural output. Therefore, India is under no obligation to reduce domestic support currently extended to the agricultural sector.[9]

In fact, certain provisions contained in Annexure 2 of the Agreement (popularly known as the "Green Box") give us the flexibility to provide support for research and extension services, pest and disease control, marketing and promotion services, infrastructure development, payments made for relief from natural disasters, payments under regional assistance programme for disadvantaged regions and payments under environmental programmes.

The WTO does of course, have the potential to bite deep into the material well-being of the Indian agricultural sector, but its main impact still remains to be played out. Following prolonged and often acrimonious negotiations with major trading blocs under WTO auspices, India agreed early last year to phase out all QR's on import.

However, the disquieting feature of the global trade situation in agriculture is the relentless increase in subsidies in the advanced countries. Agriculture was considered a potential "deal breaker" because of fundamental divergence between the EU, Japan and the United States. The compromise involving these three major trading entities, when it was crafted, allowed for a number of exemptions from the subsidy discipline envisaged, which they have since utilised to the hilt.[10]

Apart from these exemptions, the developed countries also benefit from relatively less stringent requirements with regard to the reduction of export subsidies in operation at the conclusion of the WTO agreement are proliferated from introducing them.

This means effectively that the global market continues to be awashed in highly subsidised agricultural products, which could penetrate Indian market with potentially destablising consequences. What this means for Indian agriculture, clearly, is a period of considerable threat and uncertainty.

Impact of WTO on Agricultural Exports

No doubt, after the formation of WTO the volume of total exports has been increasing, but in case of agricultural products, it has shown a declining trend in recent years (table 4.1). After having the share of 20.4 per cent in total export during 1996-97, it came down to 13.5 per cent in 2000-2001.[11]

Table 4.1: India's Agricultural Exports

Year	*India's Total Export*	*Total Agricultural Export*	*Percentage Share of Agricultural Exports to Total Exports*
1996-97	33470	6828	20.4
1997-98	35006	6994	18.8
1998-99	33218	6014	18.1
1999-00	37599	5457	14.6
2000-01	44560	6246	13.5

Source: Government of India, Economic Survey 2001-02, p. 143.

The world market is becoming more protectionist, in the sense that the developed countries are using several trade and non-trade barriers in the name of technical standards, environmental and social controls as well as imposition of anti-dumping duties, countervailing duties, safeguard measures and sanitary and phyto-sanitary measures which have affected market access for exports.

Amongst the domestic factors that continue to hamper our export growth are infrastructural constraints, high transaction costs, quality problems, quantitative ceiling on agricultural exports and constraints in attracting FDI in the export sector remains problematic. India's agri-exports also face certain constraints that arise from conflicting domestic policies relating to production, storage, distribution, food security, pricing concerns etc. Higher domestic prices in comparison to international prices of products of bulk exports like sugar, wheat, etc., make our exports commercially less competitive.[12]

The essential conditions for the growth of export of agricultural products includes (i) vertical integration of the small holdings with appropriate secondary and tertiary organisations for input supply, quality control, marketing and processing; (ii) infrastructural support in terms of communication, transport, cold storage, etc., (iii) increasing production on a sustained basis, rising exportable surplus after catering the domestic needs and quality improvement; and (iv) strengthening the market intelligence and creating awareness in international market about quality of products.

Impact of WTO on Indian Industry

Due to economic reforms and WTO agreements industrial licensing has been abolished; the list of industries reserved for the public sector has been reduced; access to foreign capital and technology has been made free; QRs on imports have been virtually abolished; import duties have also been significantly reduced. The basic idea behind this is lifting of government controls and regulations on production, trade and investment and to improve the efficiency and growth in industrial sector.[13]

However, trends in overall industrial growth suggest an all round slowdown in industrial activity. Industrial production, measured by the index of Industrial Production, registered a significantly lower growth rate of 5.0 per cent in 2000-01 compared to a growth rate of 6.7 per cent in 1999-2000. Growth rates also fell in both the manufacturing and electricity sectors, from 7.1 per cent and 7.3 per cent in 1999-2000 to 5.3 per cent and 4.0 per cent respectively in 2000-01.[14]

Further, WTO agreements and economic reforms pose challenges for the Indian industry. Obviously, challenges are far more serious and striking given the lack of competitive strength of Indian industries. The serious problems are:

1. The industries are victims of high cost and the technology gaps of several years are too glaring. Even more worrisome are the difficulties in securing technology transfers from developed countries;
2. The technical problems of infrastructure bottlenecks and the consequent constraints on global bench marking;
3. Indian products or services are not competitive in terms of price, quality and delivery schedule. Except for computer software, gems and jewellery, garments and to some extent leather and low value engineering goods, not many other Indian products are export competitive;
4. Market access in developed countries is fraught with difficulties since most of them are practicing "neo-protectionism" in various forms (tariff and non-tariff barriers); and
5. India's share of world exports is a meagre 0.5% and her share of trade in world services is even

less; hence it does not command any bargaining strength in WTO level negotiations.

In the background of above mentioned challenges and industrial slowdown, the endeavour should be that the Indian industry must continue to strive to be an efficient and competitive one and able to stand on its own in the face of rising domestic and foreign competition. In order to ensure this, Government on its part must resist any attempts to delay the process of liberalisation and deregulation and continue to deepen the reforms and remove all obstacles and bottlenecks for unleashing competitive forces in the industrial sector. This would entail removal of the remaining infrastructural constraints especially in power, transport and telecommunications; reducing bureaucratic controls in all spheres liberalising the labour and land market and removing other barriers to growth.

Conclusions and Suggestions

Today, the choice India has is either to go along with the international consensus which we should intelligently shape to our advantage in the future, or be forced to quit the WTO because if we refuse to accept the international consensus, the 'retaliation measures' with the WTO are such that we would pay on global history, it would be irrational and impractical to quit the WTO

Because, the WTO is a vehicle to take us on the path of development in the 21st century. To get on this vehicle is not all that easy, nor is it simple to stay on it without losing balance because of the WTO's unique power of "cross retaliation". Thus, implementing the WTO agreements will mean an upheaval in our attitudes to work hard, meet agreed schedules and deliver quality products in far concerns of the earth or perish.

To support the above conclusions, the following suggestions can be made;

- Inadequacy of preparedness has been quite in evidence both in the content of Uruguay round and the various ministerial review meetings held thereafter in Singapore, Geneva, Seattle and Doha. Therefore, the most important requirement of India in the context of the WTO system is that of preparedness for negotiations.
- Measures to be taken to strength the competitive capability of the domestic industry, trade and agriculture by providing suitable infrastructural support and incentives for inducting technological change, and managerial efficiency
- Continued increase in the exposure of domestic agriculture to international unfair competition would imply considerable damage to the domestic agricultural sector. It is, therefore, necessary that an integrated strategy for the agricultural sector is adopted in the context of the new trading system.
- Indian farmers can export, under the new WTO mandate, cereals, fruits, dairy products, vegetables in a big way. Farmers can, thus, earn on an average four times what they would in India and then farmers would not have to beg the government for small increase in purchase prices or subsidies on fertilizers. The increased revenue from exports could then be used for investment in agriculture and this can multiply agricultural output for further export as well as to create abundance within the country with the support of marketing infrastructure.

REFERENCES

1. Chatterjee Biswajit and Sen Rupamanjari, "Environmental Standards, WTO and the Indian Economy", IEA 83rd Annual Conference, Volume, Jammu, 2000, p. 67.
2. Chadha G.K., "Indian Economy under the WTO Regime: Happenings, Non-Happenings and Missing Links", IEA 83rd Annual Conference, Volume, Jammu, 2000, p. 13.

3. Bhandare S.S., "WTO and Indian Industry", Forum of Free Enterprises, Mumbai, p. 12.
4. Kumar Rajender and Philip P.J. "TRIPs and Indian Agriculture", IEA 84th Annual Conference Volume, Vellore Institute of Technology, Vellore, 2001, p. 58.
5. Ibid., p. 63.
6. Kumar Nagesh, "WTO Regime, Host Country Policies and Global Patterns of MNE Activity", Economic and Political Weekly, Vol. 36, No. 1, Jan. 6-12, 2001, p. 45.
7. Mishra R.S., "The WTO Agreement on Agriculture (AOA) and Agricultural Crisis in India", IEA 84th Annual Conference Volume, Vellore, 2001, p. 29.
8. Ibid; p. 29.
9. Ibid., p. 30.
10. Sukumar Muralidharan, "On the World Trade Front", Frontline, February 2, 2001, p. 11.
11. Economic Survey, Government of India, 2001-2002, p. 143.
12. Singh Bishwa Nath, "Globalisation and India's Agricultural Exports: Challenges and Opportunities", Vellore, 2001, p. 44.
13. Chaudhari Sudip; "Economic Reforms and Industrial Structure in India", Economic and Political Weekly, Vol. 37, No. 2, Jan 12-19, 2002, p. 155.
14. Op cit., Economic Survey, p. 164.
15. Ibid., p. 185.

5

The Impact of Anti-Dumping Duties on Developing Countries Under the WTO Agreement-An Abstract

T. Mallikarjunappa

As per the provisions of Article VI of the erstwhile GATT, the member countries of WTO can impose anti-dumping duties on those members who are exporting goods at below the normal value. Therefore, any member can impose anti-dumping duties on the products exported by another member country after fulfilling the formalities prescribed by the WTO. The anti-dumping duty to be imposed by a member country shall not exceed the margin of dumping in relation to such article. The margin of dumping is the difference between the export price and the normal value. For determination of the anti-dumping duties "export price", means the price of the article exported from the exporting country or territory and in cases where there is no export price or where the export price is unreliable because of association or a compensatory arrangement between the exporter and the importer or a third party, the export price may be constructed on the basis of the price at which the imported articles are first resold to an independent buyer or if the article is not resold to an independent buyer, or not resold in the condition as imported, on such reasonable basis as may be determined in accordance with the rules made. The "normal value", means either (i) The comparable price, in the ordinary course of trade, for the like Article when meant for consumption in the exporting country or territory; or (b) the cost of production of the said article in the country of origin along with reasonable addition for administrative, selling and general costs, and for profits, as determined in accordance with the rules. In the case of import of the article from a country other than the country of origin and where the article has been merely transshipped through the country of export or such article is not produced in the country of export or there is no comparable price in the country of export, the normal value shall be determined with reference to its price in the country of origin.

A member country may impose provisional measures if:

(i) an investigation has been initiated in accordance with the provisions of Article 5, a public notice has been given to that effect and interested parties have been given adequate opportunities to submit information and make comments;

(ii) a preliminary affirmative determination has been made of dumping and consequent injury to a domestic industry; and

(iii) the authorities concerned judge such measures necessary to prevent injury being caused during the investigation.

Provisional measures may take the form of a provisional duty or, preferably, a security—by cash deposit or bond-equal to the amount of the anti-dumping duty provisionally estimated, being not greater than the provisionally estimated margin of dumping. Withholding appraisement is an appropriate provisional measure, provided that the normal duty and the estimated amount of the anti-dumping duty be indicated and as long as the withholding of appraisement is subject to the same conditions as other provisional measures. Provisional measures shall not be applied sooner than 60 days from the date of initiation of the investigation. The application of provisional measures shall be limited to as short a period as possible, not exceeding four months or, on decision of the authorities concerned, upon request by exporters representing a significant percentage of the trade involved, to a period not exceeding six months. When authorities, in the course of an investigation, examine whether a duty lower than the margin of dumping would be sufficient to remove injury, these periods may be six and nine months, respectively.

Anti-dumping duty is based on commodity to commodity, and country to country, and supplier to supplier. All member countries of WTO, can impose anti-dumping duties on goods imported into the country provided the country imposing the anti-dumping duties fulfils the norms required to impose these duties under the WTO agreement.

The provisions relating to anti-dumping measures have become one of the most commonly used and abused provisions of the WTO. The developing countries have been on the receiving end with regard to these provisions. Many of the developed countries have developed good documentation system to initiate actions against the goods exported by the developing countries. Therefore, the EU, the US, Canada, Australia and many other countries have initiated a number of cases of anti-dumping. Similarly many developing countries have initiated anti-dumping duties on commodities exported by other developing countries. These cases are growing every day and the WTO would find it difficult to resolve these issues satisfactorily in the years to come.

Therefore, this issue is likely to be one of the most controversial issues in the WTO This paper addresses the issues relating to the provisions of anti-dumping duties, the concerns of member countries about these duties, the likely effect of these controversies on member countries.

6

Advantages and Disadvantages of WTO Policies vis-a-vis India's Basic Problems

D.K. Mohanty

Introduction

History repeats itself. Opening the pages of history would help us in understanding the world better. A day may come when we will wonder whether to go back to primitive society as science has its own limitations and demerits, which we tend to ignore. We have taught ourselves to create and combine the most powerful technologies. We have not taken pains to learn about the consequences. Today, the consequences threaten to destroy us. This is the challenge before the whole mankind. The question is whether WTO takes this significant factor into account? With this concern in mind, the present paper is presented in the context of its relevance to a developing country like India.

WTO Background

Just after the Second World War, the United States was the most fortunate country in the world that had the most advanced technology having a stable political structure; least affected by Second World War and was economically sound. At that time, the US financial strategists had begur to plan for a post war integration of the world economy along lines more favourable to it. At the Bretton Wood conference in 1944, held under US leadership, 44 nations agreed to set up two key integrative structures—the IMF and the World Bank. The World Bank, at first established to provide post-war reconstruction funds to European nations, generally began providing loans to the non-industrial countries too. Immediately after the formation of these two organisations, a third organisation was added to the system. The General Agreement on Tariffs and Trade (GATT) promoted by USA set out to liberalise trade, which had the effect of making it difficult for the poorer, less technologically advanced countries to protect their tiny fledgling industries. The rules for granting loans by World Bank was made in such a way that without joining GATT or abiding by the GATT regulations, no loan would be sanctioned from World Bank. These three interconnected agencies formed a single integrative structure for the world trade. On January 1, 1948, GATT entered into force. But WTO the new form of GATT came into effect much later, on 1st January 1995 as a watchdog of world trade.

WTO Membership

WTO has 144(2003) members, accounting for over 97% of world trade.

WTO's Aims and Objectives

1. Administering trade agreements.
2. Acting as a forum for trade negotiations.
3. Settling of trade dispute.
4. Reviewing of national trade policy.
5. Assisting developing countries in trade policy issues, through technical assistance and training programme.
6. Co-operating with other international organisations.

WORLD ECONOMY BEFORE WTO

Economy during Primitive Society

The first socio-economic formation was the primitive communal system, which has lasted since time immemorial. At first, the people were depending upon the fruits, roots and nuts gifted by nature. With the passage of time, people could discover fire, bow and arrow, and cultivated land, which changed their life style. People were living in groups or communes and organised their economy (hunting, fishing) and preparation of food on a joint basis. There was no exploitation of man by man.

Economy after Industrial Revolution

About 300 years ago, an explosion i.e. industrial revolution was heard that sent concussive shock waves racing across the earth, demolishing ancient societies and creating a wholly new civilisation and changed the way of life of millions. At one level, the industrial revolution created a marvellously integrated social system with its own distinctive technologies, its own social institution, and its own information channels-all plugged tightly into each other. Yet, at another level, it ripped apart the underlying unity of society, creating a way of life filled with economic tension, social conflict and psychological malaise. In the industrial society, which we come across, today there is hardly any human sympathy, family bond, friendship, neighbourly and community ties, since these values are fractured or corrupted by commercial self-interest. Standardisation of the product and services started during industrial revolution. Money in place of barter was introduced. Human labour was replaced by machine. Productivity of labour went up not due to physical labour but due to machine. Cost of production came down due to mass production. The incarnation of large multinational companies were the fruit of industrial revolution. With the rise of number of corporation in each country, the individual companies trapped the international markets.

Between 1750 and 1914 the value of world trade was estimated to have multiplied more than fifty fold, rising from 700 million dollars to almost 40 thousand million dollars. The advantages of this global trade should have accrued more or less evenly to all countries. In fact, the self-service belief that specialisation would benefit everyone was based on a fantasy of fair competition. It presupposed a completely efficient use of labour and resources. But this global trade only helped either Britain or USA or some highly industrialised countries at that time. Placed below are some data, which confirm, how this global trade benefited Britain, for instance, at that time. The yarn and cloth export from Britain was £ 5927831 and £ 16753369 in 1848, which went up to £ 9870875 and £ 42141505 in 1860 respectively. Exploitation of labour was very much evident. How much the industrial revolution really helped the majority of people remains a moot question.

Socialist economy

The negative impact of industrial revolution had given birth to socialistic economy. The Great Russian revolution of 1917 had paved the way for socialistic pattern of society or controlled economy. This economy continued in many parts of the world from 1917-1990 and collapsed after 1990. The collapse can be attributed less to the economic system rather to the greedy and shrewd individuals at the helm of affairs.

Capitalist Economy

In fact, the economy, which prevailed during the period of first civilisation and even just before industrial revolution, was more or less socialist Economy. Capitalism basically started from creation of a market and free competition. Free competition led to ruin some capitalist and some others to become rich and to expand their production. The concentration of production led straight to monopoly. In order to keep their monopoly alive, they formed an association of capitalists in whose hands the production and sales of the overwhelming majority of particular goods were concentrated. Whatever the different forms such associations might take, they all pursued the same goal—earning of maximum profit. Competition forces each capitalist to reduce the price of his commodities and only big enterprises could afford to do this, While small ones couldn't stand up to the competition. So first they went bankrupt and were taken over by the big fish. When these monolithic conglomeration could not find enough opportunity in their own country tried to capture the world market through their patronising Governments, resulting in formation of WTO And interestingly, the man in the street all over the world does not have the time and patience to understand the game plan behind the move.

Mixed Economy

Apart from capitalistic economy or socialist economy, there is a combination of both which is called the mixed economy as we all know. It envisages the existence of both private and public sectors and with a lot of Government control over the private sector.

INDIAN ECONOMY

Indian Economy has been managed on the basis of industrial policy pursued by the Government from time to time. Broadly, there are only two major industrial policy resolutions. i.e. in 1956 (before liberalisation) and in 1991 (after liberalisation).

Before Liberalisation

- 1956 Industrial Policy Resolution—This policy extended Govt sphere into more categories of industries. It emphasised the need for

(1) development of small scale, khadi and village industries (2) indigenisation of ownership and control of industries while recognising the necessity of securing participation of foreign capital without losing control over the industries. It is a fact that private individuals were neither having the capital nor technical know how to establish heavy industries after independence. Within a span of 35 years these influential groups who acquired black money demanded to remove all restrictions on industries so that private investment would go up. So the question is how all of a sudden some people would be able to organise so much capital. Placed below an official statistics on black money will make the picture clear. The black money, which was around Rs. 650 crores in 1962 jumped to Rs. 80,000 crores in 1990 as estimated by Finance Ministry and Wancho Committee appointed by Government of India on Taxation. The National Institute of Public Finance and Policy estimated that Rs. 40,000 crores were being generated every year by the parallel economy. This money requires an outlet and hence led to the demand by the black money holders to open the economy so that this can be converted into white money through the investment route.

After Liberalisation

- 1991 Industrial Policy Resolution—India's financial condition was in bad shape as Government had no control over expenditure, balance of payment position was worse, and there was no enhancement of revenue. Government had no option other than to approach the IMF and World Bank to come to its rescue. Finally, IMF and World Bank came to India's rescue and advised India to liberalise the economy. Accordingly, in 1991 Govt. of India reversed its economic policy.

The Broad Aspects of this Policy Were

1. To remove all control of the Government on industry.
2. To restructure the public sector means to privatise public sector.
3. To allow free entry of domestic industry to all major categories of goods and services barring a few.
4. To allow foreign capital to flow without any restriction.
5. To integrate and transform the Indian economy into a world economy.

ADVANTAGES AND DISADVANTAGES OF WTO VIS-A-VIS INDIA'S BASIC PROBLEMS

Poverty Alleviation and Employment

The wave of globalisation has surfaced a number of redundanceis. Every organisation was found rolling up sleeves to counter the problem of redundancies. The redundancies can be classified in three important forms. Redundant technology, redundant personnel and redundant knowledge. This is a chain reaction involving redundant man as an outcome of redundant knowledge due to redundant technology. But why the sudden upsurge on redundancies? This is due to competition. No economic policy can be of much value if it does not ensure food, shelter, cloth, education and health-the basic necessities of life of the masses. WTO claims that more jobs will be created which will eradicate poverty. In the present scenario of globalisation, when the technology becomes redundant, machinery and personnel based on that technology also become redudant. This will result in unemployment. For example, USA affords to throw to junkyards millions of personal computers every year and thereby creates more avenues for PC manufacturers. Can India afford to do so?

As per official statistics of Planning Commission, overall employment is estimated to have grown only by about 1.0 per cent per annum during the period from 1993-94 to 1999-2000. Employment in agricultural sector also witnessed a slow growth and forget about industry, in which case for public sector it is negative and for private sector, it is nominal. If this is the state of affairs after 10 years of liberalisation, then we may wonder how all of a sudden a miracle will happen. Speaking on Govt. expenditure on welfare the, late Prime Minister Sri. Rajiv Gandhi had once rued that the beneficiary gets only 15 paisa out of one rupee sanctioned. Then who gets this 85 paisa? To rectify this, we have to make out house in order and WTO cannot be blamed. However, the claim of WTO in respect of employment generation is debatable for the reason stated above.

Industry and Agriculture

Being a member of WTO, India has reduced the custom duty considerably to make import cheaper. It is a fact that our industry could not produce the best and cheapest goods during the last 50 years. According to Indian industrialists, they could not do so up to 1990 because of too much Government restrictions. But what happened after 1990? IMF and World bank have never told us to produce sub-standard goods at a higher price. But they have told us to privatise the Government sectors. Most probably they forgot that sickness in private sectors, where funds of public sector financial institutions are also involved is no less. It is a fact that our infrastructure costs are very high. It is a remote possibility that the industry will produce cheaper goods. A World Bank report published sometimes during 1993 said that India would get only 4.6 billion dollar out of 213 billion dollar world trade. Hence Indian industry will not at all be benefitted, rather many industries will be closed down due to cheap availability of imported goods.

In the 'Agriculture field, India requires six lakh tonnes of seed out of which 2.2 lakhs tonnes, are provided by Government agencies and the rest 3.8 lakh tonnes are produced and supplied by farmers. If they will be debarred, then foreign companies may capture Indian market. Recently, world market has consistently rejected genetically-modified (GM) crops, though the Government of India has allowed the foreign companies to enter our market. On the other hand, many scientific journals apprehended grave risk to human health for use of GM products. When the world is discarding use of chemical fertiliser and insecticide but we are trying to increase its use either by installing more plants or importing it. The WTO policy in this regard needs a serious relook in the context of our agriculture.

Social Law and Order Problems

Highly industrialised nations are having prone to high degree of social problems as evidenced from American experience. A Psychologist of National Institute of Mental Health of USA has revealed that almost no family is free from some form of mental disorder and declared that psychological turbulence is rampant in an American Society that is confused, divided and concerned about its future. India is slowly drifting a state of perpetual social tension due to mal-distribution of wealth and growing unemployment. Moreover, the opening up of media, TV, etc. to FDI as per WTO norms is likely to have its adverse effects, with its direct impact on our society.

Standardisation

India, as on date, was not able to produce goods of international standard. If in the coming days, Indian industries will be able to produce quality goods, it is because of WTO, which will help Indian customers. This is the major advantage in the light of India's membership in WTO.

Intellectual Property Right (IPR)

IPR on seeds and plants, animals and human gene are aimed at transforming life into the property of corporations. While false claiming that they have "invented" life forms and living organisms, corporations are also claiming patents on knowledge pirated from the third world. The knowledge of India's mothers and grandmothers is now being claimed as inventions of western corporations and scientists. The seeds and plants of basmati have been claimed as inventions by US Corporation called Ricetec. And this is only one blatant example of bio-piracy, which will lead to the absurd situation where the third world will pay for knowledge that their ancestors evolved cumulatively and collectively.

Environmental Concerns

The very survival of life in the planet is linked with the question of environmental protection. No individual country, on its own, can protect environment. The followings can be described as major global environmental concerns.

1. Global warming 2. Acid rains 3. Disappearance of tropical forest. 4. Marine pollution and 5. Hazardous and Non-hazardous wastes.

Present day economic growth modeles are based on consumption. Abnormal consumption comes out of over use and reckless exploitation of resources resulting in environmental degradation. India is in the net of all the factors of global environmental concerns. It is estimated that by 2080 the temperature of India may rise as much as 7 degree, which would decrease in rainfall and shortfall in food production. Besides above, in Antarctic the icecaps have shown huge cracks and slowly are melting. If they melts fully the financial nerve centres of the world—New York, Mumbai, and other big island cities will perish. Excessive liberalisation, spreading of oil companies, increase in mining activities, and emission by vehicles are adding to the global warming. In this regard, the politicians have totally failed and it is now for the public to take initiatives.

SUGGESTION IN THE LIGHT OF INDIA'S MEMBERSHIP OF WTO

Since India has taken already WTO membership, and hence has no alternative other than taking a tough stand on some issues on its internal front. A few suggestions, which are of paramount importance, are highlighted below:

Population Control

Aristotle, the ancient Greece political philosopher, said that the population must be kept under limits and this can be done by fixing the rate of reproduction by allowing and encouraging infertility among married couples. If no restriction is imposed on the rate of reproduction, says Artistotle, poverty is the inevitable result and poverty produces in its turn, civic dissension and wrongdoing. Unlimited population not only brings about economic ruin but also extinguish democracy, whose backbone is the mass of people. The population of the state must however, be sufficient enough both qualitatively to provide for itself and from its own resources every material and spiritual requisite of a complete and rounded good life. In light of the above, India should immediately introduce compulsory family planning irrespective of caste, creed and religion for all citizens. All political parties, irrespective of their ideological differences, should rise to the occasion and create public awareness against the harmful aspect of population rise.

Bringing Transparency in Entire Government Machinery

If a democracy is to work, citizens and the authorities must trust each other. Such trust can never exist unless the people have faith in the competence and truthfulness of the authorities and the authorities treat the people as responsible adults entitled to be told the whole truth. People should have access to all the information of the Government except those, which are exclusively related to the country's security. In the process, much wrongdoing will be exposed. It will help in bringing down corruption drastically. Therefore, the Official Secrets Act should be amended so that law should protect the people who help in bringing to the books the culprits responsible for working against the interest of the society as a whole.

Elimination of Black Money

The greatest menace before us is the parallel economy. Development work is blocked due to shortage of funds. It is imperative to bring back to mainstream this parallel economy. Hence, steps should be taken to create a data bank in the Super Computer the details of nature of business, employees, all transactions, sales tax, income tax etc. of all types of business organisations right from small shop to big corporation so that cross reference can be made to find out tax evasion. A separate agency may be created to register and give one code number, which shall be used for all tax purposes. It shall help in finding out under invoicing or over invoicing by any party. Of course, Government is planning to implement MODVAT which is a right step in the right direction The rates of taxes should be brought down and stringent action should be taken against the tax evaders. Law should be framed to confiscate the properties unlawfully acquired by any citizen.

Electoral Reforms

The Centre for Media Studies estimated that the total expenditure incurred by political parties in 1999 Lok Sabha election was Rs. 2500 crores. On an average a candidate had spent Rs. 2.5 crores. Where from they get it? Officially, no body gives them. They have to collect funds from private people lobbies and in return they have to oblige them in case they come to power. The final consequence of this event is unlawful outflow of crores of rupees from the public exchequer in various forms. To stop this practice Government should bear all election expenses not exceeding a certain limit. Any candidate spending more than this ceiling shall be deemed disqualified. There should be an upper age bar for exit and minimum qualification for politicians to elected bodies. Politicians with criminal record should be debarred from contesting the election. All candidates should disclose their assets before the Election Commission.

Increasing the Power of Regularity Agencies

In USA, for instance the Security Exchange Commission is more powerful than the Indian counterpart. So, in similar line, all the regularity bodies should be given the requisite teeth to function fearlessly and without any political or bureaucratic interference, so that the law evader shall be dealt sternly.

Conclusion

India cannot remain isolated from the world. Even if, India has lost a lot after liberalisation, but it has to remain in the main stream. Further more, India is countered with inside and outside threats. Inside threats are from growing population, unemployment, industrial sickness, rising poverty, communalism, and, environment. The outside threats are from cross border terrorism, WTO, and environment. So, it has to strike a balance between these two threats. Firstly, India should not blindly follow the WTO. Secondly, it has to set right its internal problems like population control, elimination of black money, improvement in quality of life of the common man etc. At the same time, stringent action must be taken against the errant multinational companies who violate the law of land so that their misdoings will be thrashed. Further more, no development should be done at the cost of eco-system. Last but not the least, if WTO means business, then defence expenditure of all member countries must be drastically reduced, so that this fund can be diverted for developmental works, which will increase people's purchasing power and in turn, increase world trade. India must take the lead to achieve this.

7

The Strategy and Critical Issues of the Doha Ministerial Agenda: Lessons and Policy Perspectives for India

Dr. U. Arabi

Introduction

WTO negotiations have occupied the centre stage in today's world trade order not only due to their far - reaching implications but also due to the fact that countries have started formulating their trade and economic policies to fall in line with the agreements.

Implementation of WTO agreements is very crucial for the effective functioning of any country. There are serious problems in the implementation of the WTO agreements especially from the perspective of India. The main issue in implementation from the angle of India is related to the question whether the WTO agreements are development friendly. It is well known that the WTO led trading system has failed to deliver the promised expansion in market access for exports from developing and Less Developed Countries (LDCs). The developing world has been pressured to liberalise trade, investment and financial flows. On the contrary, in order to ensure that the LDCs get a fair share of the growth in international trade, the moot question to be answered is, whether the agreements are fair and conducive to the development LDCs. Above all, a serious question arises namely, whether the LDCs have the necessary capacity and resources to implement the agreements within the time limits prescribed.

Free and fair trade is supposed to be the fundamental guiding principle behind the multilateral trade practices to be persued under the GATT/WTO framework and presumed to lead to an increase in global welfare. It is well known that, in the absence of a regulatory mechanism for multilateral negotiation, a nationalistic behaviour of trade policy adopted by all the trading partners tend to result in a war like situation in imposing tariffs, providing subsidies, indulging in dumping activities, retaliating by countervailing duties and so on. As if not enough, many countries further tend to restrict the free flow of trade by means of various "non-tariff" and even "non-trade barriers".

Earlier WTO Ministerial Meet

When we look at the earlier WTO ministerial rounds, one gets a fairly good idea of how the WTO is evolving. The WTO ministerial meet at Marrakesh held during April 1994 formally concluded the results of the Uruguay round of GATT. It also established WTO as an organisation and highlighted the importance of special and preferential treatment for the LDCs.

The first WTO ministerial meet held in Singapore during December 1996 focussed on further liberalisation of trade and implementation of commitments already made. At the same time however, it also pushed new issues such as investments, competition and trade facilitation and working groups were set up for study of such new issues. The information technology agreement was also signed during this meet.

The second WTO meet at Geneva held in May 1998 was a sort of home coming for the WTO as it marked the completion of 50 years since GATT was established in 1948. The agreement on services such as telecommunication and financial services were also duly finalised on this occasion. For the first time, E-Commerce issue came into the picture. The general meet also renewed its implementation thrust.

The third WTO ministerial meet held at Seattle (USA) in December 1999 ended as a miserable failure. There were wide scale protests, particularly by NGOs on the controversial issues such as labour, agriculture subsidies TRIPs etc. The process of green room negotiations sharply divided the developed countries VS LDCs. The Seattle meet marked the lack of active participation by Developed Countries and LDCs thereby leading to an atmosphere of mistrust among the WTO member nations.

The last, fourth WTO Ministerial meet held during November, 2001 at Doha round was held amidst tight security. It was characterised by the active participation by Developed Countries and LDCs. India played a significant role and made substantial contributions to the outcome of this meet.

The Strategy and Critical Issues of the Doha Ministerial Meet

The situation prior to the fourth ministerial round at Doha was extremely critical. The failure at the third Seattle Round weighted very much on the minds of the member nations. The recession in the USA, which happens to be the growth engine for the world trade and economy was confirmed. Inspite of this, after two years of back room argument, 142 member countries of WTO finally agreed to launch a new round of trade talks that keep the global economy on track towards free trade and investment. In an atmosphere of confrontation and uncertainty, the Doha meet deliberated the issues related to:

1. TRIPS and Public Health.
2. Investment and Competition Policy

3. Trade and Environment,
4. TRIPS and Bio-diversity
5. Agriculture,
6. Labour Standards.

However, between now and 2005 there will be negotiation on

1. Implementation,
2. Agriculture,
3. Services,
4. Industrial Tariffs,
5. TRIPS,
6. Anti Dumping,
7. Relationship between RTAs and the WTO
8. Dispute Settlement Understanding,
9. Trade and Environment.

Broadly speaking, the principal agenda on which the Advanced Countries and which were primarily concentrated on the subject of agriculture-related subsidies and trade in services. Negotiations were included to frame rules on phase out of agriculture export subsidies and restraint in challenging measures notified under the 'Green Box' by LDCs to promote rural development and address the food security concerns.

Ministers from WTO member countries approved a 'work programme' called "broad and balanced" which includes negotiation on a range of subjects and other tasks for the coming years. The main agenda of declaration which spelt on intellectual property (TRIPS) and Public Health and one decision on implementation - difficulties of LDCs in implementing current WTO agreements. More Specifically, the Doha Agenda included cutting Tariff on industrial goods, phasing out farm subsidies, reducing barriers for foreign investment and limiting the use of anti-dumping laws. All these issues had hard bargaining between the rich LDCs and developing countries. An important aspect of Doha deliberations was that, France, the world's second largest agricultural exporter next to U.S.A. was not prepared to accept the cutting of the agricultural subsidies. On the other hand, the EU expressed to take some environmental issues as an agenda for discussions instead of the agricultural subsidies. In contrast to these, the LDCs disliked reference to environmental protection because such standards could be used as a cover to keep their goods out of the EU. The agreement to include anti-dumping laws to combat foreign companies that sell steel in the U.S. at low prices. However India, certainly made substantial gains in terms of the agreements on TRIPS and agriculture, even though in the area of textiles India could not get what it wanted. Interestingly, India also made a strong plea for labour issue to be dealt with by the ILO, which was duly accepted.

The health considerations prevailed an edge over the trade related intellectual property rights (TRIPS) at Doha, which recognised the WTO member governments to frame health policies that ensure access to affordable medicine. An important advantage of compulsory licencing rules which allows the member countries to produce patented drugs during national emergency seems to be substantially gain to Indian Pharmaceutical Industry.

The beneficiary of compulsory licensing could be the Indian Pharmaceutical Industry, since it makes generics (Unbranded formulation) that are vastly less expensive than patented drugs produced in developed markets. Indian drug manufacturers stand to gain if more governments grant compulsory licences because only India, Brazil and China have the ability to produce cheap generics.

The Ministerial declaration says that, the mandated negotiation would aim at substantial reductions in market access, reduction of all form of export subsidies, and substantial reductions in trade distorting domestic support. This will help greater agricultural exports from India, as presently because of the heavy subsidies in this sector given by the EU and other developed countries make the Indian agricultural products uncompetitive in the international market.

India's last stand involved pushing back the start of negotiations on investment and Competition policy by two years rather 2005 than to 2001. The extra year would give India more time to ease restrictions on foreign investment in some protected sectors.

Lessons and Challenges for Developing Countries like India

Before counting the lessons and challenges of DCs & LDCs in view of ongoing different WTO's ministerial meets at different venues, it is really become invitable to underline the special problems of the LDCs such as the concentration of exports on primary commodities, the lack of autonomous and indigenous industrial base and hence extreme dependance on both industry and agriculture upon imported inputs, capital and intermediate goods and spare parts, the lack of effectively working markets, financial institution and fragmentation of economic activity etc., So it now becomes necessary to identify and understand the special problems of LDCs work out viable strategies for successful negotiation for a equitable multilateral trade regime in WTO.

The major challenges for LDCs would be:

1. Understanding of the full text of the earlier agreements,
2. Fear of loss of trade gains/concessions,
3. TRIPS and Public Health Services,
4. Industrial Tariff etc.,

An important feature of the Doha-negotiating strategy was undoubtedly the serious efforts of the LDCs to undertake steps to implement the earlier agreements. In essence, the execution of any agreements naturally found to cause both pain and pleasure to member countries. In other words, in order to minimise the trade losses, the member countries prepared for an arrival of a flexible approach towards various issues. In such cases, for e.g. if India was not seen as opposed to the new rounds of talks at Doha, India might have been in a better position to seek concession from other countries on other issues.

However, when we look into the strategies of different countries that has been adopted by different countries at Doha, China's pressure in the WTO appeared as if, the Chinese Foreign Trade minister admitted obviously the substantial impact of Chinese economy and trade and also expressed the willingness for the adoption of a wide range of legal reforms. It is highly significant to note that, for China which adopted the privatisation process since 1970s, had a remarkable impact on the trade and economy, in particular shipping and postal services in the country. China looks at WTO more as an opportunity as well as a challenge, whereas the Indian Commerce Minister has voicing at Doha, that WTO was the 'necessary evil'.

It should also be noted that China is not afraid of negotiations on all fronts including Investments. Infact, the Chinese are the ones who have effectively used foreign investment of export development and India can learn many things from their approach towards trade and export development and trade and investment.

The Doha declaration, as it is well known, the aim is to address their marginalisation in international trade and to improving of their effective participation in the multilateral trading system. There were three main texts agreed at the end of the Fourth WTO Ministerial meet at

Doha, like, the Ministerial Declaration, the Declaration on Implementation Related issues and concerns and the declaration on the TRIPS agreement and Public Health.

Besides trade competition from China and other similar Countries, India's biggest challenge could be seen in the area of subsidy component; i.e. of export subsidies. Because the export subsidies have the effect of leading to artificially cheap prices for food exports, which can trigger import surges which under-cut and destroy the livelihood of third world farmers. The U.S.A.'s, for instance, most favourite instruments-export credits and food aid also be brought under all form of export subsidies as envisaged encouragingly by European Union; besides applying to substantial trade reduction in trade-distorting domestic 'support'. The special and differential treatment for LDCs is also worthy to note here. As it is evident, most of the LDCs were asking for preferential tariff treatment and specific measures for small scale agriculture through a special chapter in the Agriculture Agreement. This demand was put forth as the concern of the "Development Box'.

The non-tariff trade barriers which are difficult to quantify owing to lack of transparency and problem of identification, include quantitative restrictions, orderly marketing arrangements, voluntary export restraints, non automatic licensing, quotas and prohibitions and price controls i.e. anti dumping and countervailing duties, public procurement policies, administrative procedure and technical studies are more severe and biting in nature as compared to tariff. These barriers though under the UR have been committed to be reduced progressively but still are highest in U.S.A. and Canada in the case of semi and finished manufactured goods as compared to the raw materials; agriculture, forestry and fishing. There is practically little or no change in the case of Japan even after the signing of "WTO agreement". Even the rates of tariff except in case of E.U.; are still the highest on the finished and semi-finished products as compared to other countries. And these barriers tend to reduce significantly the export opportunities of South and India by raising prices to the consumer and thereby restricting the demand. The "low wage argument" advanced in favour of such barriers, seems to be totally unconvincing because, (a) Wages are only one element in total costs. (b) the competitive advantage in the different sectors of industries depend as much on such other determinants of costs as the state of their technological advance, capital stock, gains of economies of scale and the price of raw inputs and (c) the relative advantages resulting from the low wage paid are in general, more than offset by the low level of productivity of labour so that labour cost per unit of output may in fact, be higher as compared to rich countries. Besides this, there has been a rising trend of anti-dumping and countervailing measures and voluntary export restraints (VER) arrangements particularly after 1995.

Policy Perspectives for India

Regionalism, Multilateralism and further development in regional trade arrangements among or between countries is the good positive sign of improvement in the liberalised global trade markets across the world. Indian economy has shown a high degree of interdependence and integration with the world economy in recent times. The Fourth Ministerial meet held at Doha has turned to be an important event in the ongoing process of multilateral trade negotiations. The analysis of the contentious issues, both quantitative and qualitative require detailed analysis and appropriate action keeping in view the required of 'sustainable development' as well as those of "sustainable development Policy".

Most of DCs are predominent in agriculture and see free trade in agricultural product as their best hope in benefitting from world economic integration. So, it now becomes necessary to identify understand the special problems of developing countries, work out viable strategies for successful negotiation for a equitable multinational trade regime in WTO.

The special problems of many of the LDCs are; the concentration of exports on primary commodities, the lack of autonomous and indigenous industrial base and hence extreme dependence of both industry and agriculture upon imported inputs, capital and intermediate goods and spare parts, the lack of effectively working markets, financial institutions and fragmentation of economic activity, studies on TRIPS and FDI have indicated, while there is no positive evidence of flows of either technologies or FDI as a consequence of adopting TRIPS regime, negative impacts like increase in financial and administrative costs are certain and increase in prices of patented products.

Indeed, the Doha meet is indication of strategies that developing countries should now pressure. The deferment of the four Singapore issues of competition, investment, transparency in govt procurement and trade facilitation, Concessions on TRIPS, tariff, reductions for non-agricultural exports, creation of scope for further negotiation on implementation issues pertaining to textiles, clothing, counter ailing measures, dumping, deferment of social clause, provision for setting up of working groups, debt finance and technology transfer explicit consensus as modality of negotiation for WTO forums, extension of periods for adjustment to developing countries, for the imposition of sanitary and phytosanistary specification and technical specification which can serve as barriers to trade, the possibility of extending geographical applications to goods other than wines and spirits - such as Indian basmati, Darjeeling tea etc., have become possible because of more effective strategies of the developed countries. The most contentious issue is anti-dumping. The US, feels that the D.Cs apply these laws don't have the same transparently information standards of analysis and method of service, thus there is need to discipline antidumping.

Whether in US, Europe or Japan, it would be politically inexpedient to reduce subsidies and other form of supports for their farmers. However it is done. But the developing countries are not convinced that the developed countries are genuine in their commitment to free trade that is beneficial to all. European Union, Japan on one and US on the other still want to improve breadth and depth of any new trade agenda. US wants focus on agriculture, services, market access as well as developing countries issues. E.U. and Japan want broader agenda including investment, antitrust rules, new disciplines on the use of anti dumping laws. Mechanism of implementation and safeguards are often beyond the resource capabilities of many LDCs and this may prove a handicap in the long run.

Emergence of trading bloc like NAFTA has serious implication for exports of developing countries. An open and stable multilateral trading system as well as progressive elimination of developed countries protectionist bias against exports from developing countries can benefit the countries both of north and south.

In more than 80 countries around the world, farmers are facing devastation due to dumping of cheap agricultural goods that the European and the US are exporting. The developed nations spend close to I billion dollars a day to subsidise farmers. The efforts of these countries, however to incorporate this initiative in the final ministerial declaration failed. However, a group called the "Friends of the Development Box" succeeded in taking birth to press forward the inclusion of the 'Development Box' at the next round. India is noticeably missing from this group.

Evidence Tending Towards Formation of New Regional Trade Arrangements

As the world tending towards a new trading alliance and direction at different 'stages of growth of trade sectors among different countries, the evidence of formation of a new regional trading bloc also seems emerging. This would be possible primarily due to several kinds of trade agreements that tend to evolve since the formation of the WTO.

India at this time, possibly can make trade alliance group with African nations most of what are members of G.77 and also looking for concessions from the WTO on similar grounds. The benefit of the common agenda if it all discussed, on issues such as anti-dumping, competition, investment and agreement such as GATS. Further, if India tries to stimulate trade relation with many of the African countries certainly such a move may encourage among African countries, whom might feel to control trade exchange with U.S.A., or other similar countries who continuously dump cheap agricultural goods in African countries. In otherwords, if this new regional trade arrangement seen effectively, then trade gains would be more both to India and African countries. If this could be seriously taken up, it could be an emerging trade arrangement similar to U.S.A.which influenced Latin American and South trade arrangement.

India's strategy has been to form an alliance of developing countries, as in the case of the Like minded group at Seattle. This group again has included Pakistan and goes to the extent of cooperation between the two countries at the WTO. Other natural allies of India have included such countries as Egypt, Cuba and South Africa. An important point of noticeable feature of such alliance is India's negligible volume of trade and India enjoys a definite trade surplus. As it appeared, the strategy of India to move closer to developed world as it contended for incooperation into clause of Green Room in any future negotiation on agriculture almost clear, as this issue more explicitly pronounced by Uganda as, "The inflex of food imports is the result of unfair practices of the developed countries" which needs to be addressed with a two pronged approach.

1. Raising tariff on food imports.
2. Negotiating with the developed countries for the phased removal of their subsidies.

At the Doha round, the E.U rescinded to reducing tariff. However, the European Trade Commissioner stated to the whole group as the deal was off", which conveyed U.S. considering allies in the developing world, making India, with a rapidly liberalising economy, and a comparatively flexible political class, fixes perfectly into the US scheme of things.

Between Asian and African Countries, the point of conflict was seen at the begining of Doha meet, where African Countries suggested for taking up new rounds of negotiations, which was not accepted by India and Pakistan which had a firm stance of implementing issues as the first priority at Doha.

An important critical issue in the Doha-agenda as it appeared i.e. the issue of agricultural and food subsidisation policies. The major option of different countries were, whether the agricultural subsidies need to be phased out completely as the European Union expressed or it should be reduced or increased so as to boost agricultural production and to facilitate agricultural trade further. As dialogue continued, the members from different developing countries expressed their concern over their small poor farmers the need to protect them from flood of subsidised imports from Europen Union (EU) and the US.

The "Third Force Group" consisting of the Ministers from various third world countries demand for a pro-poor on agriculture. which is among the most contentions issues at the conference. These issues have been brought together in the proposal for a "Development Box".

It might even be desirable to consider the idea of having a 'preferential trading agreement, or regional trading bloc between China and India. Both countries have extremely large domestic markets and their coming together can certainty lead to the expansion of the markets by achieving the economies of scale. It should be noted that, both India and China are not members of any regional trading blocs.

Conclusion

To conclude, the forgoing analysis reveals that, India is a marginal player in the global trade arena. The recent changes in the country's foreign trade policies reveals that, India is committed to integrate with the world economy's trade markets as a sign of the globalised trade practices. India being a member of WTO or a part of any regional trading arrangement is bound to have certain trade distortionary effects. This trade distortion arises because of the discriminatory treatment advanced to the non-members of the regional trading arrangement or the members. This discriminatory treatment arises because of the increased market access granted to the members of the same. The multilateral trading system allows the formation of regional trading arrangements on the logic that they would facilitate the creation of a liberalised multilateral trade regime.

REFERENCES

1. Bishwajit Dhar, *Doha: A Developing Countries Perspective*, Economic and Political Economy, Nov. 24, 2001.
2. Upali Wickramasinghe: *"Preparing for Doha WTO Meeting: Development as Central Theme,"* Economic and Political Weekly July, 14th 2001.
3. Seminar Report on *Negotiating Technique in the area of Trade and Investment Liberalisation,* Indian Institute of Foreign Trade, New Delhi, 2000.
4. Bernard Huckman and Will Martin, (ed.) *Developing Countries and the WTO: A Pro-active Agenda*—Blackwell Rbbshem, Oxford (UK) 2001.
5. H. Ashoka Chandra Prasad, *WTO Negotiation: Some Important Issues and strategies for India*-Commonwealth Publishers, 1999.

6. *Focus WTO,* Vol. III, No. 3, Sept-Oct. 2001. IIFT, New Delhi.

7. *Focus WTO,* Vol. II July-Aug., 2001, IIFT, New Delhi.

8. *Seminar Papers Vol, I and II, National Seminar on WTO and Allied Issues,* Conducted at Indian Institute of Foreign Trade, New Delhi February, 2-3, 2002.

9. WTO and Allied Issues: Seminar Papers Vol. I and II, conducted at I.I.F.T, New Delhi February, 2-3, 2002.

Part—II
WTO and Indian Agriculture

8

WTO—Agreement on Agriculture Agenda for Reforms in Indian Agriculture

K. Nageswara Rao

After the Great Depression in 1930s, the leading countries, in order to prevent another global recession, proposed to lower the trade barriers permanently. This attempt paved the way for the establishment of GATT in 1947. Though the code on subsidies was moved in the seventh round of GATT at Tokyo in 1979, trade negotiations in the area of agriculture were initiated in the 1986 Uruguay round. USA was instrumental in forcing trade negotiations in agriculture because USA economy was in recession in 1980, USA was losing its dominance in the area of agriculture because USA export markets in agriculture were threatened by the heavily subsidised agricultural sector of EU more specifically by France. Hence, USA proposed to reduce the practice of subsidising farm exports and open the EU to USA farm products. Though the cut in agricultural subsidies was opposed by EU, USA managed to push through its proposal in Uruguay round. Inspite of several global changes and frozen negotiations, Dunkel Draft was prepared by 1991 and EU agreed on its comprehensive reform of agricultural policy in 1992 and created the conditions for settlement. The Dunkel Draft, with a view to promote the trade of agricultural products between countries, proposed for the allowance of import of agricultural products from other countries to some extent, estimation and gradual reduction of subsidies to agriculture sector. It was stipulated that the governmental support to agricultural products in developed countries not to exceed 5.0 percent and in developing countries not to exceed 10.0 percent of its share to non-agricultural products.

Agreement on Agriculture (AOA)

As per the negotiations mandated under new GATT in April 1994 at Marrakesh—Agreement on agriculture and Global Agreement on Trade Services (GATS)—India has to implement the terms of AOA by the end 2000. The objective of the negotiations under AOA is to put trade in agricultural goods on the same basis as trade in other goods and establish a fair and market oriented agricultural trading system which corrects and prevents restrictions and distortions. WTO's AOA implies the opening up of the world market for agricultural products. The negotiations under AOA relating to developing countries like India may be classified as under:

(a) All non tariff barriers are to be converted into tariffs and a ceiling is to be placed on tariffs. Import duties are to be reduced at least by 10% on all tariff levies and 24% on simple unweighted average over a period of 10 years from 1995 to 2004.

(b) Trade relations are to be conducted under a system of transport tariffs. This facilitates the import of unlimited quantity of commodities by paying the applicable duty.

(c) Minimum market access for agricultural commodities is to be ensured. For the commodity, which is staple in the diet, with 1.0% share of the base level consumption is to be raised to 2.0% by 1999 and to 4.0% by 2004.

(d) QRs on the import of agricultural commodities are to be withdrawn. Infact, India has to withdraw

QRs on 1429 commodities in all. As a result, the imports go up by 2.7%.

(e) Export subsidies to agricultural products are to be reduced. Developing countries have to cut the value of export subsidies by 24% over a period of 10 years. Agricultural commodities other than specified in a member country's list, receive no export subsidies in India.

(f) Domestic support (economic help) to farm sector is to be kept with in limits. The Aggregate Measures of Support (AMS) is to be reduced if it is greater than 10% of the value of agricultural production over a period 10 years.

The agreement on agriculture is expected to give a new impetus to agricultural trade in the international market. The developing countries like India too will benefit provided the developed countries adhere to all the provisions of the agreement, especially those on tariff reductions and removal of non-tariff barries. The ability to take advantage of these opportunities would depend upon the structural strength of the agricultural sector. India's gains depend upon the level and type of technology used and the size of the market developed for agricultural commodities apart from the level of inflation in relation to other countries. Unfortunately, the first phase of economic reforms did not address the crucial and strategic issues of Indian agriculture. As a result, the domestic agricultural sector is becoming weak and getting marginalised and thereby aggravating the problems of poverty, unemployment and rural deprivation.

Strategic Issues for Agriculture Sector

Several crucial issues have surfaced the agriculture sector which need immediate attention and debate with in the country to enable India to take a realistic stand at the mandated negotiations under agreement on agriculture. The following are some of the strategic issues that will have a major bearing on the future of agricultural activities.

1. The transitional period available for India to implement the provisions of agreement on agriculture need to be extended by another five years.
2. The conditions, terms and structure of tariffs that enhance India's access to other markets are to be specified.
3. The domestic support measures shall ensure food security and distribution to all areas at reasonable or affordable price.
4. Indian Government has to restructure the export subsidies to ensure Indian exports to be competitive in world market.
5. The safe guard provisions that impose import restrictions under certain conditions are to be considered discriminatory against India and other developing countries.
6. India has to study the impact of phasing out of QRs on the basis of her balance of payments problems.
7. India has to expand its access to cost effective modern technologies particularly the agricultural bio-technology to make a major impact on the cost of production and prices of agricultural commodities.
8. Favourable (negative) aggregate measure of support is to be maintained to derive the benefits from across the broad commitments for tariff reduction in agricultural trade.
9. Equally important for India is the full utilisation of special and differential treatment provisions available to developing countries.

10. India has to study and assess the possible ramifications of settlements under the mandated reforms process on agricultural production and distribution.

Addressing of these issues immediately assumes immense importance in the context of the outcome of the negotiations held in Doha in November 2001. The items of investment, competition policy, transparency in government procurement and trade facilitation have been placed on the agenda for Doha meet and the Indian delegation negotiated very hard on the implementation issues. Ultimately, a trade negotiating committee has been established to supervise the overall conduct of the negotiations scheduled to be concluded by the end of 2004.

Agenda for Reforms in Agriculture Sector

In view of WTO stipulations and the Doha declaration 2001 Indian Government has to review its policies on agriculture, specifically relating to self sufficiency in food grains, poverty, unemployment and the burden of subsidies. The agriculture development strategy should aim at increasing the value added per hectare, improving the productivity of agricultural inputs and irrigation water, prevention of environmental and ecological degradation and supporting the farmer self help institutions.

All the states in Indian Union must evince keen interest in implementing the reforms in agriculture sector as agriculture is primarily a state subject. In view of low value of agricultural production more investment need to be injected into this sector to raise productivity. Contract farming is to be encouraged to raise high value crops on small farms. Production and processing of high value crops are to be separated and the value addition in processing is to be organised by the farmers cooperatives.

In order to keep the aggregate measure of support the distortions in the agricultural price policy are to be eliminated. New agricultural price policy shall ensure that minimum support prices cover only the variable cost of crop production and to be applied only to high risk crops. Minimum support price and procurement price are to be distinguished and the continuous rise in the later is to be arrested. The cost of procuring and distributing food grains is to be lowered by decentralising the food corporation of India and making public distribution system the responsibility of state governments. Procurement operations should aim at purchasing minimum stocks necessary to influence the open market prices by releasing the food grains. Such commitments falling under the Amber Box measures will minimise the distortive effects and facilitate domestic support favourable to agriculture.

Review and rationalisation of agricultural inputs subsidies is to be the major concern at present. Subsidised inputs are not contributing to productivity and hence bad subsidies are to be given up. Subsidies are to be withdrawn progressively and the amount saved is to be used to strengthen the rural infrastructure and extension. Commitments like income support to farmers and safety net that fall under Blue box measures are to be taken care by the adjustment strategy through diversification of region specialised agriculture. Minimum support should be extended through crop insurance for a limited important crops and all high risk crops.

Full utilisation of Green box measures is necessary to enhance the ability of Indian agriculture to drive home the gains from the AOA. Investing in the Research and Development activities to invent the low cost high yield technologies including the pest control measures in agriculture. Reasonable level of support is to be extended to flood control and disaster relief measures.

The domestic support to agriculture is to be quantified by Aggregate Measure of Support (AMS). Any developing country whose product specific and non-product specific

AMS does not exceed 10.0 %of the total value of agricultural products need not lower its domestic support commitment. India has to maximise its advantage as the domestic support in terms of AMS is negative. Since the obligation is on total AMS, greater care is to be exercised in utilising the "flexibility" margin to choose products covered and extent of support measure and quantity of products that benefit from them. Further, it is necessary to maintain the gap between fixed external reference price and the applied administered price to keep the market price support within limits.

In the area of export competition agricultural commodities receive no export subsidies in India. Hence, India has the right to ask for compensation from subsidy giving exporting countries for the potential loss of her markets. Further, India, a non subsidising country has to take advantage of the right to impose counterveiling duty equivalent to the export subsidy by exporting nations.

REFERENCES

1. Gulati, Ashok, Kelly, Tein, Trade liberalisation and Indian Agriculture, Oxford University Press, New Delhi, 1999.
2. Gulati, Ashok, Mehta, Rajesh and Narayanan Sudha, From Marrakesh to Seattle, Indian agriculture in Globalising World, EPW Volume XXX IV October 9-15, 1999.
3. V.S. Vyas, Lecture delivered at 83rd annual conference of India Economic Association at Jammu, December, 2000.
4. S.S Bhandare, Forum of Free Enterprise, Mumbai, 24-1-2001.
5. Muchkund Dubey, Implications of Doha for India, the Hindu Daily, dated 24.12.2001 and 25.12.2001.

9

WTO and Indian Agricultural Exports Opportunities and Challenges

A.C.K. Nambiar

The world economies are now getting integrated with the adoption of globalisation policies. Trade liberalisation is the important instrument to this. The philosophy is that trade liberalisation lead to the maximisation of the global welfare through efficiency gains. Thus multilateral trade promotion policies were negotiated and evolved for almost half a century under the GATT which was set up in 1947. Though it was comprehensive enough to cover every aspect of foreign trade the mandate was extremely limited and has been confined to broader measures such as tariffs. However the WTO which came into existence on January 1, 1995 is far reaching as a large number of agreements are implemented and member governments are required to act in conformity with these agreements regardless of the fact whether they might conflict with the short term and long term objectives of the member countries. It is also an open ended one as it can take up any specific issue which the member governments think should be brought under multilateral trade discipline.

An issue that gave rise to intense debate on the trade liberalisation front is the opening up of the agricultural sector. Though even under the GATT a beginning was made to liberalise the agricultural trade the WTO has adopted sweeping policy measures with the signing of the AOA by the member countries. The goal is removal of trade distortions resulting from different levels of input subsidies, price and market support, export subsidy and other kinds of trade distorting support across countries. There is wide spread apprehension about the impact of this on the third world agriculture, its economy and people. Thus an intense debate is going on all over the world. In this context this paper makes an attempt to examine the various facets of Indian agricultural exports. Specifically the future opportunities, the present agricultural export pattern and the future challenges.

Opportunities

On the impact of trade liberalisation there is serious concern among the developing countries in general. Here it can be said that given a level playing field the third world countries in general can improve their export performance. This is on account of the fact that support given to agriculture was found as negative in developing countries whereas most of the developed countries were found as heavily subsidising their agriculture. Thus the reduction in support under the WTO's AOA in the developing countries would raise the international prices of agricultural commodities paving the way for the export prospects of developing countries. India too can stand to benefit from this. However, much depends upon how we reform the agricultural sector to strengthen its competitiveness. To make a brief comment on this it can be seen that the agricultural policies and programmes since independence were governed by the overriding objective of maintaining food security—i.e. domestic production and availability of food grains at reasonable price. Thus, the provision of agricultural subsidy, the public distribution system, trade policy, public investment, price, marketing controls etc. was all evolved to accomplish this. This has led to considerable inefficiency in resource use and distortion in the allocation of resources in the agricultural sector. Further, to a certain extent even the scope for competitive domestic market price realisation was prevented, as some of the above policies were quite repressive in nature. The insulation of agriculture from foreign competition also meant denial of world market price. Here, it is estimated that taking all crops together farmers were getting in the early 1990's 16 to 25 per cent less than what they would have in the world market (Vaidyanathan 2000:1738). If we assume that the domestic market got aligned with the world market there would have been a significant gain to the farming community in India. To cite the magnitude of denial if we assume that if price difference were 20 per cent in 1998-99 the agricultural community was deprived Rs. 96566 crores of income as the total income originating from the agriculture and allied activities was Rs. 482832 crores in the year (RBI 1999:9). The measure can trigger a chain developmental effect. High farm income will lead to higher private investment in agriculture and this in turn lead to higher productivity and growth of the farm sector. In the non-agricultural sector too the impact will be felt. High rural income generates higher demand for non-agricultural products, which in turn lead to an expansion of the non-agricultural sector. Though income accrue to the better off sections within the agriculture it can indirectly help the poor as tight labour market given the expansion of the agricultural and non-agricultural sectors can lead to a rise in employment and wage. Thus, agricultural trade liberalisation can be said as capable of giving a boost to the economy in general and the rural economy in particular. On several other considerations too, it can be said that the Indian agriculture can reap large benefit by trade liberalisation. Compared to many other developing countries India is favourably placed as far as many of the resources are concerned. Vast under and unutilized land and water resources with varying agro-climatic and soil conditions suitable to grow varieties of crops, cheap labour, somewhat developed indigenous farm technologies, institutional network for farm research, development and extension etc. are our capabilities. If properly deployed they can lead to substantial quantum jump in the production of a variety of agricultural products for export. In many crops it can reasonably be expected that we have comparative advantage. Further, this gives huge opportunities for the development of agri-business and scope for the export of high value added agricultural products. WTO reports that since mid 1980's trade in processed and other high value added agricultural products have been expanding much faster than trade in basic primary products such as cereals (See Thamarajakshi 2002:23). This in turn too can generate substantial rural income and employment opportunities. Also from the domestic point of view as income rises we can expect a relative decline in the importance of cereal production compared to items such as fruits and vegetables, milk and milk products, meat and meat products, poultry etc. tending to the growth of agro-processing industries providing assured demand and good prices and scope for diversification. In addition to all this, it is also to be recognised that India is rich in genetic resources. We did not allow patents on seeds or plants and had no system for protecting plant varieties. The conclusion of the TRIPS agreement under WTO stipulates that all member countries must grant IPR protection for plant varieties. The Convention on Biological Diversity abandons the common heritage frameworks and asserts that plant genetic resources are the sovereign rights of nations in which they originate. This goes well with India's interests as this can regulate bio-piracy. Besides rich bio-diversity, India is endowed with abundant wealth of agriculture ideas, techniques, products and processes. They have come down through generations. These traditional knowledge and practices have many modern applications. What is required is transformation of these wealth into commercial products through scientific experiments and innovative actions.

While these are some of the beneficial impacts it also needs to be mentioned that there are dangerous effects too. The most important of all is the threat to food security. Instability in prices and the impairment of the capacity of domestic food grain production is one such consequence. A country like India with vast population and sisable population in poverty will face acute problems on extreme dependence on external markets for food. Here, we have to safeguard our interest and we make a pointed reference to this later. So also it is being argued that WTO and similar other trade liberalisation measures threatens the national sovereignty. Here again it has to be argued that for that matter any international agreements infringe upon the sovereignty of the countries parties to it. Thus, technically speaking, there are costs and benefits. If the benefits exceed the costs we have to opt for it. Further, it has to be reckoned that India cannot walk out of WTO, as bilateral and trilateral agreements are difficult to strike. In this predicament, the best course that India can follow is to equip our agriculture to travel along the road of liberalisation with our own built in checks and balances for which policies and programmes have to be carefully crafted. This is indeed a challenging job. So also there are a number of asymmetries and inequities that now inhibits the smooth transition to free trade on the international plane and this too needs to be addressed by developing countries unitedly. We now address to some of these challenges. Before that let us examine in brief the growth and structure of agricultural exports from India.

Growth and Structure of Agricultural Exports

The development strategy followed by the country for a long time was inward looking in nature, as the export orientation of the domestic economy was less. This was particularly so of the agricultural sector. Though this approach is considerably modified now as per the WTO agreements, agricultural exports have not shown any dynamism even after liberalisation. Table 9.1 clearly indicates this. As is observable from the table while the share of agriculture in exports was 30.65 percent in 1980-81, the highest ever share during the two decades the share declined to the lowest ever share of 15.09 per cent in the

Table 9.1: Indian agricultural exports (Rs. crores)

Year	*Total exports*	*Agriculture/exports*	*Col 3 as % of Col. 2*
80-81	6711	2057	4.41
81-82	7806	2221	28.45
82-83	8803	2258	25.65
83-84	9771	2622	26.83
84-85	11744	2997	25.52
85-86	10895	3018	27.70
86-87	12452	3422	27.48
87-88	15674	3504	22.35
88-89	20232	3723	18.40
89-90	27681	4879	17.63
90-91	32553	6317	19.40
91-92	44042	7878	17.88
92-93	53688	9457	17.61
93-94	69751	13021	18.67
94-95	82674	13712	16.58
95-96	106352	21138	19.88
96-97	118817	25040	21.07
97-98	130107	25419	19.53
99-99	139753	26104	18.68
99-00	162955	24576	15.09

Source: Economic Survey (various issues)

year 1999-2000. Over the years, the share was almost on the decline. Till 1986-87, agriculture constituted more than a quarter of the total exports. When as in the later years the share stood considerably low and ranged from 15.09 per cent to 22.35 per cent. Further, it was found that while the share of agriculture and allied activities was 24.55 per cent on an average during the first 11 years in the following nine years the average share declined to 18.33 per cent. It is thus, very conspicuous that despite agriculture trade liberalisation the Indian agricultural exports have not shown any sign of improvement. Whereas the liberalisation era is clearly marked by declining share of agricultural exports. To further highlight this, the share of Indian agricultural

Table 9.2: India's share in the world exports of selected agricultural commodities(%)

Items	*1980*	*1985*	*1990*	*1995*
Meat and meat preparations	0.4	0.04	0.2	0.1
Fish and fish preparations	2.0	2.4	1.6	2.6
Cereal and cereal preparations	0.5	0.6	0.6	0.6
Vegetables and fruits	1.1	1.4	0.8	1.0
Sugar, sugar Preparations	0.3	0.0	0.1	0.2
Coffee and coffee substi.	2.1	1.9	1.7	2.4
Tea and mate	27.7	26.2	22.1	11.2
Spices	14.5	19.3	7.7	8.3
Unmanufactured Tobacco	4.4	3.0	2.1	2.2
Feeds of Animals	1.6	1.5	2.2	3.5

Source: Economic Survey (various issues)

trade in the world exports is analysed. The share in respect of some of the important commodities, is shown in Table 9.2. The result too paints a very distressing picture. In the case of most of the commodities it was either marked by stagnation or decline and in the case of some of the products there was perceptible decline in the share. In particular, mention may be made about the behaviour of the commercial crops such as tea and spices. India had a dominant presence as the country accounted for 27.7 per cent of world trade in tea in 1980, which declined to 11.2 per cent by 1995. In the case of spices, the share slipped from 14.5 per cent to 8.3 per cent. Though the export of fish and fish preparations and feed of animals more or less showed marginal improvement, the share of India was pretty low. On the whole, thus it emerges that the Indian agricultural sector has failed to show the much needed resilience in exports.

Let us also focus on some of the other features of agricultural exports. The commodity composition of exports in the pre and post-liberalisation period is shown in Table 9.3. A few observations can be made from the table. While in the pre-liberalisation period tea and tea mates accounted for the largest share as a single commodity, 18.56 per cent it was taken over by the fish and fish preparations, 18.41 per cent. To some extent, it can also be seen that in the post-liberalisation period the commodity concentration ratio has somewhat increased as the share of the three major agricultural commodities increased to 44.39 per cent of total exports in the post-liberalisation period as against 41.24 per cent in the pre-liberalisation period. In the post-liberalisation period rice export has gone up as its share, which was 8.22 per cent rose to 14.86 per cent. This was followed by fish and fish preparations (from 14.46 per cent to 18.41 per cent) and oil cakes (from 7.68 per cent to 11.12 per cent). There was notable decline in the export share of tea and raw cotton in the post liberalisation period. This

Table 9.3: Structure of agricultural exports

(Rs. crores)

Items	*1980-91 Value*	*%*	*1991-00 Value*	*%*
Coffee	2655.6	7.17	10024	6.02
Tea and tea mates	6872.5	18.56	12333	7.41
Oil cakes	2845.6	7.68	18491	11.12
Tabacco	2034.0	5.49	5536	3.31
Cashew kernels	2747.0	7.42	11695	7.03
Spices	2312.76	6.25	8687	5.22
Sugar and molasses	489.0	1.32	3217	1.93
Raw cotton	1903.89	5.14	4171	2.51
Rice	3043.56	8.22	24722	14.86
Fish and fish Preparations	5353.2	14.46	30634	18.41
Meat and meat Preparations	955.6	2.58	4847	2.91
Others	5805.07	15.68	31988	19.22
Total	37017.80	100.00	166345	100.00

Source: Economic Survey (various issues)

is less encouraging a phenomenon as India, which enjoyed a significant role in the export of tea, is losing the position. Now let us consider the growth in exports. The commodity wise value of exports is shown in Table 9.4. Compared to the pre-liberalisation period invariably the export value of all the agricultural commodities increased. Thus, in the first five years of reform (1991-95) the average annual value of exports commodity-wise, the growth ranged from 71.71 per cent to 591.02 per cent compared to the average annual export value of 1980-91 period. Though subdued the average value of annual exports went up in the following four years in the case of all commodities. Quite paradoxically thus the WTO era was characteri,ed by

Table 9.4: Growth of agricultural exports

Items	*Annual value (Rs. crores)* 1980-91	*91-96*	*96-00*	*%increase in 91-96 over 80-91*	*%increase in 95-00 over 91-96*
Coffee	241.42	762.00	1553.50	215.63	103.87
Tea and mates	624.77	1073.80	1734.75	72.67	60.80
Oil cakes	258.69	1787.60	2618.75	591.02	46.19
Tobacco	184.90	402.8	895.50	117.84	122.31
Cashew kernels	249.72	990.00	1686.25	296.44	575.25
Spices	210.25	547.00	1486.75	160.17	171.80
Sugar and molasses	44.45	251.40	490.00	465.57	94.90
Raw cotton	173.08	297.20	371.25	71.71	24.91
Rice	276.68	1758.60	3982.25	535.61	126.44
Fish and fish preparations	486.65	2531.20	4494.50	420.13	77.56
Meat and meat preparations	86.87	352.60	771.00	305.89	118.66

Source: Economic Survey (various issues)

deceleration in the growth of Indian exports. In this context, it is also significant to note that this is despite rise in the value of export price realisation (Table 9.5). Accordingly, compared to the 1990-91 export price the average price realised during the first five years of reform increased and commodity wise the increase ranged from 5.30 per cent to 275 per cent. In the case of most of the commodities there was marked rise in price realisation. Though subdued the price continued to rise in the following four years (except raw cotton) and commodity wise the price rise ranged from 20.53 per cent to 145.69 per cent compared to the price realisation in the first five years of reform. At the same time, as evident from the table the quantity of export growth has not at all kept pace with the increase in price and this indicates that the Indian agriculture is less oriented to respond to the world market prices.

Table 9.5: Size of export price* and export quantity increase commodity wise

Items	*Increase in 91-95 over 90-91*		*Increase in 95-96 over 91-95*	
	Price	*Qty.*	*Price*	*Qty.*
Coffee	113.05	42.33	42.41	42.94
Tea and tea mates	18.25	–14.73	49.29	7.79
Oil cakes	72.00	68.56	60.46	–7.39
Tobacco	29.13	–3.36	145.69	43.14
Cashew kernels	80.49	22.74	116.52	42.14
Spices	52.81	29.76	27.76	145.63
Sugar and molasses	275.00	54.46	22.67	80.46
Raw cotton	5.30	–66.60	–40.76	279.84
Rice	23.07	210.13	20.53	87.51
Fish and Fish preparations	62.41	62.33	26.40	12.41

*The price is worked out from the data of quantity and value published in the Economic Survey (various issues).

Challenges

The agriculture package of WTO on domestic support and export subsidies provides for complex classification of support and subsidies in agriculture, some of which are totally exempt from reduction commitments. This classification favours developed countries particularly EU, US, Canada and Japan, which are able to maintain very high level of support for agriculture in the exempt category. The level of non-exempt subsidies in developed countries remains awfully high even after meeting the reduction commitments. These empower developed countries to cause distortions in the international trade and protect domestic producers from competition. Compared to this the level of support in developing countries is so low that a level playing field in agricultural trade is only a far cry. This phenomenon needs to be rectified by the collective effort of developing countries where the reduction commitments have to be fixed in such a way as to permit at least the principle of comparative advantage to govern the agricultural trade if not a favoured treatment to developing countries.

History is replete with instances when developed countries blatantly violated the principles as and when their general and sectoral interests get adversely affected. Also, when developing countries emerged as competitors in some of the products the developing countries did not hesitate to abandon the principle of free non-discriminatory multilateral trade. For e.g. the textile trade regime was derogated from the GATT as early as 1962 and only under the Uruguay round has been brought it under the multilateral trade regime. It is also significant to note that even today a large number of products of interest to developing countries are subject to high tariffs in developed countries. All this can happen in the case of agricultural trade too. These unscrupulous practices should go.

Trade and environment is another contentious issue. The current mood in WTO is to legitimise the environmental concerns of members and hence time is not far to allow the use of environmental protection goals by unilateral trade measures and to include the subject of environment in the next round of trade negotiations. This is a clear move away from the understanding that GATT/WTO rules should not regulate process and production methods is as opposed to product characteristics. Each nation has its own environmental protection measures and the trade has to be permitted to take place within that framework. Also the labour issue and other non-tariff measures are real challenges faced by the developing countries. Unless these are addressed properly the trade and development of the developing countries would suffer in a big way.

Some of the rules and regulations of the WTO too have large implications. Under the present Dispute Settlement Undertaking Panel, Appellate Body reports are adopted by the negative or reverse consensus principle, which assures their automatic adoption by the WTO dispute settlement body. That is to say as long as even one member state in the DSB wants a panel or an appellate body report to be adopted it will be so adopted. This principle gives enormous power authority to the panels and appellate body. Their interpretations of the existing agreements can be used to create new rules and also to pre-empt the scope of future negotiations in new subject areas. The appellate body reports in turtle shrimp case clearly established this that the trend of WTO dispute settlement bodies is to legitimize through the backdoor the subject of trade and environment. This too needs to be properly addressed.

While these are some of the serious common issues that have to be addressed collectively by the developing countries there are problems that has to be addressed on the domestic front in India. We now turn to highlight some of the important issues.

Input use efficiency and productivity is very much low in India. There are reasons to this. Main agricultural inputs viz. water, electricity, fertilizers and credit are all being supplied to farmers at prices, which do not cover costs. This unrecovered cost is rising at a faster rate. Under pricing of inputs is a major cause of indiscriminate and wasteful use of these inputs, raising the cost of production and contributing to the degradation of land, pollution of water resources and over exploitation of ground water. There should be efficient and sustainable use of resources. Over a definite period of time input subsidies may be brought closer to the real costs. Another distressing phenomenon is the perceptible decline in real public investment in agriculture as against the increasing role of public decline in real public investment in the new era. Thus, the development of infrastructure like irrigation, rural electrification, roads and markets has come to suffer. No surprise crop productivity is the lowest in India in the case of most of the crops. Thus, any future increase in agricultural production has to come from rise in productivity. This yield increase also mainly have to come from the rain fed areas for which technological packages for sustaining high growth of agriculture in these regions have to be evolved. Another avenue is biotechnology. All this underlines the significance of public investment in irrigation, research, extension training etc. Also there are big gaps in post harvest technology and in respect of management like cold chains, the adoption of food safety measures and irradiation techniques to extend the shelf life of produce. So also there is the need for the adoption of organic farming, integrated nutrient supply, pest management, superior quality and in all this farm research and extension is important. Public investment again assumes significance in all these areas.

The agricultural sector in India is not fully equipped to compete in the world market. The negotiated tariff bindings are reasonably adequate to protect against cheap imports. Hence, protection should be extended to the agriculture. However this should not continue for long. The agriculture must be open to competition time bound by phasing out protection. A road map for this may be drawn and the farmers must be educated and kept informed of the time bound plan to get themselves adapted to the new environment.

Attainment of reasonable level of food security must form an integral part of our agricultural policy. Thus reasonable level of domestic production of food grains, holding of buffer stocks and provision of food grains at reasonable rate at least to the weaker sections targeted through public distribution system must be ensured. However all this has to be done much more efficiently and cost effectively.

Agri-business needs a big boost for which comprehensive measures may be taken. Technology up-gradation should be promoted for which import duty concessions on capital imports may be provided and FDI liberalised. Import duty concessions for the import of other materials too may be provided. Also the existing plethora of controls and regulations on food processing industries should be rationalised.

Protection and commercial exploitation of the genetic resources, agriculture ideas, techniques, process and products must get added emphasise in the emerging era. Apart from protective legislation the agricultural research establishments have to experiment and perfect some of the ideas, processes and products by closely working at the grass root level communities.

In view of all these, in conclusion it can be stated that India has to remain within WTO and strive to fight for its own genuine causes and also for the genuine courses of fellow the developing countries collectively.

REFERENCES

1. Ministry of Finance, Economic Survey (various issues), Govt. of India, New Delhi.

2. Reserve Bank of India (1999), Handbook of Statistics on Indian Economy, Mumbai.
3. Thamarajakshi R (2002), Doha Declaration and Agriculture in developing Countries, Economic and Political Weekly, Jan. 5.
4. Vaidyanathan A (2000), India's Agricultural Development Policy, Economic and Political Weekly, May 13.

10

Ailing Indian Agricultural Sector and WTO

C.K. Renukarya

It is claimed that, reforms in general have improved the situation of agriculture in many countries. Often examples of Chile, China, Ghana, Uganda and Vietnam are quoted in this regard. Following table from World Development Report (2000-2001) is used extensively to substantiate this point of view.

Table 10.1: Percentage Change-Five-Years Post Reform Period Compared With Five Years Pre-Reform Period

Country	*Real Agri-cultural Price*	*Real Exchange Rate*	*Real G.D.P. Growth Rate (%)*	*Agri-cultural Output*	*Agri-cultural Productions Growth(%)*
Chile	120	105	2.8	40	8.2
Ghana	5	230	3.9	50	12.2
Hungary	–10	–23	—	–15	25.4
Indonesia	20	75	–0.6	42	2.3
Madagascar	11	94	2.0	15	2.9
Mexico	–24	22	–3.7	14	1.3
New Zealand	–31	–2	0.4	5	0.8

Sources: Meerman 1997.

It is argued that, "Under inward-oriented models of development the structure of tariffs and non-tariff barriers and often the exchange rate were biased against agriculture. Market-oriented reforms that reduced this agriculture bias- and dismantled various forms of state intervention (Price supports, input and credit subsidies, support for marketing products have generally increased agricultural growth. Policy reforms such as privatisation, reduced regulation, and trade and price liberalisation have had a positive impact for many countries". As agricultural output and productivity growths have generally risen in the countries, which have adopted reforms, it is believed that reforms can benefit farm sector in developing countries. Reforms are also believed to improve the conditions of poor. It is pointed out that, case studies of Chile, China, Ghana, Uganda and Vietnam show that reforms, have helped raise producer prices for small farmers by eliminating marketing boards, changing real exchange rates, through broader economic reforms, lowering tariffs, and eliminating quotas" (W.D.R. 2001).

On this score, more and more reforms are advocated. Pointing to the fact that barriers to trade tend to be highest in agriculture and services, it is said that reducing tariffs on agricultural commodities would do good to developing countries. As things stand now, the average tariffs on agricultural imports are in the range of 15-20%. In many developing countries, it exceeds 100% for some commodities. Compared to agricultural commodities the tariff levels are low for manufactured goods. Tariffs imposed on agricultural commodities by developed countries, on the imports of developing countries are estimated to be 15.6%. This however, works to be 20.1% for developing countries. Patterns of tariff barriers in different regions are shown in Table 10.2.

As such it is evidenced by studies (Martin and Winters 1996) that, all developing regions barring some middle eastern countries that developing countries have stood to gain, by reducing tariff levels on imports of agricultural commodities.

Table 10.2: Protection for Agriculture (1995)

	Importing High Income	*Region Developing*
Exporting region.		
(Implied Tariff paid) (US $ 6n)		
High Income	17	20
Developing	16	14
World	53	34
Import—weighted average tariffs (%)		
High Income	15.9	21.5
Developing	15.1	18.3
World	15.6	20.1

Sources: Hertel and Martin (2000)

Hence, many researchers such as Anderson, Hoekman and Strut (2001) suggest that in WTO rounds of talk, the priority should be on reducing import barriers on agricultural commodities and bring them on par with import tariffs of manufactured goods. They go to the extent of recommending eliminations of exports subsidies on agricultural commodities.

The Indian Position

In the post-reform period, the growth of agricultural value added averages to around 3.2%. This is actually slightly lower compared to 3.6% during eighties. In fact, there has been dismal performance between years 1997-2001, when the average growth rate of agricultural value added works out to 1.2%. Following table 10.3 presents the growth of food grains and non-food grains for pre and post-reform periods.

Table 10.3: Growth Before And after 1991

Period	*Food Grains*	*Non-food Grains*
1949-50 to 1964-65	2.93	3.54
1967-68 to 1969-70	2.74	2.72
1970-71 to 1979-80	2.08	1.66
1980-81 to 1989-90	3.54	4.84
1990-91 to 1997-98	1.66	2.36

Sources: Government of India, Economic Survey (Different Issues).

As such there is no evidence to show, as propounded by reformers that growth in agricultural sector has improved due to reform efforts. In fact it has been the other way round. Though, it cannot be argued that reforms have brought down agricultural growth rate in India, there is no evidence that reforms have any impact on agricultural growth rate of the economy. In fact, more than external factors, particularly WTO factor, seven internal factors account for the slow down of agricultural output in the country. They are (i) Fall in public investment during the period 1994-95 and 2000-2001 (ii) Poor operational and maintenance system of irrigation in states (iii) most unsatisfactory infrastructure in villages (iv) Inadequate and non-respective agricultural research, development and extension service (v) inappropriate increase in procurement prices for wheat and rice (vi) subsidisations for fertilisers which has caused overuse of fertiliser and determination of soil fertilising and (viii) continuous fragmentation of land holding.

Clearly above factors have little correlation with WTO agreements hence, blaming WTO for the ills of Indian agriculture will be misplaced. This however, does not mean that we can ignore WTO. The emphasis is only on the fact that we should set our house right as early as possible to compete with other nations of the world. As has been rightly maintained by Alagh (2001). "Preparation for a specialised agriculture, which can import substitute efficiently and also produce for exports would begin in practice, rather than in globalisation slogans. It would also bring out inherent strengths of India's farming communities, as high light, also how the problem lie elsewhere, outside the agricultural sector in banking practices, weak support systems, misguided subsidies, businessmen and traders intent on making a fast back and laws which let them do so". Thus, if India wants to take advantage of reforms in agricultural sector, it is imperative that internal problems of this sector are sorted out in with short a period as possible. Then only, any negotiation as the WTO table can be made advantageous to the Indian Economy.

REFERENCES

1. Alagh K.Y., Globalisation debates IEA 84, Conference Volume 2001 pp. 1-10.
2. Hertel T.W. et al, Developing countries and a new round of WTO negotiations. *Research observer* volume 17. Number 1 spring 2002, pp. 113-136.
3. Meerman Jacob: 1997, Reforming Agricultural, The World Bank goes to market. Washington D.C. World Bank, operations evaluation department.
4. Pulapre Balakrishnan, Agriculture and Economic Reforms, Growth and Welfare, E.P.W. March 18, 2000 pp. 999-1004.
5. Shankar Acharya, India's Medium-Term growths prospects, E.P.W. July 15, 2002. pp. 2897-2906.
6. World Bank, World Development Report 2000-2001, pp. 65-70.

11

WTO and India's Small Farmers

A.R. Padoshi

Introduction

Under the policy of economic globalisation—or WTO—the internal as well as the international trade in all agricultural commodities is to be made free i.e. without any legal restrictions on the movement of commodities. The farmers—under the provisions of WTO—are free to produce any commodity/commodities that they want to produce and also sell their produce in any market either inside the country or outside. All the QRs on the imports and exports of the agricultural commodities are to disappear albeit in a phased manner. Similarly, the restrictions like import duties and export duties, if any, are also to be abolished or reduced significantly in a phased manner. The internal (i.e. within the country) and the international market for the agricultural commodities is to be completely free and fully integrated. There are no restrictions on the farmers as regards the production and sale of their produce. Thus, the farmer is totally free and the only decision maker about his own production and sales policy. There would not be (and should not be) any intervention especially from the government in his production plans or sales plan. Thus under the provision of WTO, the agricultural trade in general and the international trade in agriculture in particular is to be made totally free. Thus the WTO provides for an 'Export led strategy of growth for the agricultural Sector'.

Several advantages are expected to flow from the WTO strategy of growth. They can be mentioned as under:

(a) **Market Access:** This is an obvious and extremely important advantage for the farmers. Under the restrictive policy of agricultural growth followed in India till recently, the farmer did not have the much needed freedom of sale, for his commodity. There were—and even are at present—several restrictions imposed especially by the state governments upon the movement of farm products. As such the market for agricultural products is not fully free and integrated. As a consequence, the farmer is put to great inconvenience and loss of income because he is not free to sell his products in the most remunerative market. WTO seeks to abolish all this. Under WTO, the farmer will have free access to the market—whether internal or external—of his choice.

(b) **Efficient Production:** With the total freedom of sale (and exchange) it will be possible for the farmers to produce that commodity or commodities for which their resource position is especially suitable and efficient. (And purchase of the commodity/commodities from the market for which their resource position is not suitable and efficient). Thus, the farmers would be able to reap the advantage of their 'Comparative Cost' position. There would national—or possibly international—specialisation of production. The production would be based on the 'Comparative Cost' principle and as such it would be more

efficient in terms of resource use and cost than what it is today.

(c) **Consumer's Gain.** Under WTO, with agricultural production following the principle of Comparative Cost', the average cost of production and hence the prices of the agricultural commodities are almost sure to fall. Lower prices of agricultural commodities will be a great boon to the Consumers in general and poor in particular. (And as the average cost also would be lower, the price cost equation would not be unfavourable to the farmer). Thus, the consumer will gain without any loss to the farmer.

(d) **Economic Development with Social Welfare.** Free sale of agricultural commodities and the comparative cost advantage in production will ensure larger volume of production for the country and possibly for the world. The world will be richer and as such greater social welfare will also be ensured. Also with growing specialisation of production there would be great boost to the volume of trade, commerce and exchange of commodities. The inter-dependence of the people will also increase. And this will ensure a higher level of economic development. Because, "economic development stands for a transformation from (a state of) meagre self sufficiency to (a stage of) prosperous interdependence".[2] The interdependence would increase (but) so will the prosperity the world. The doctrine of self sufficiency (which India followed till recently) ensures a lower and poor standard of living while the doctrine of interdependence and exchange (under WTO) ensures a prosperous life for the people, and greater economic welfare.

The success of WTO provision in India lies in making available the advantages of WTO to the small farmers of the country.

In the following section, we examine the importance of the small farmers for the agricultural sector of India.

II

Importance of Small Farmers in India's Agriculture

The concept of a small farmer as used in the present discussion is any person or family 'who *operates* (i.e. not necessarily owns) less than two hectares of agricultural land'. The main characteristics of the class of the small farmers can be mentioned as under: (Here we make an assumption that each operational holding is operated by one family. Its head is a small farmer).

(*a*) **Numerical domination:** The class of small farmers shows a clear numerical domination by them of the Indian Agrarian scene. Thus the percentage of the small operational holdings increased from 63 in 1960-61 to 81 in 2000-01[3]. Thus, a very large percentage of the total operational holdings in India is accounted for by the small operators or small farmers.

(*b*) **Uneconomic Cultivation:** The percentage of land operated by the small farmers/operators has increased from 19 in 1960-61 to 39 in 2000-01. In the Indian context an operational holding of less than two hectares is generally deemed as uneconomic. It thus means that, in India, the percentage of land uneconomically cultivated has been increasing in the past forty years or so. This is a very serious trend.

(*c*) **Domination of Food Crops[4]:** The cropping pattern of the small farmers seems to totally dominated by food crops. Thus, in 1991-92, the small operators allocated 75 per cent of their land for the cultivation of food grains which is 'least paying' of all agricultural crops.

(d) **Needs of Consumption:** The fact that small farmers allocate most of their land for the production food grains, of even after, knowing that it is 'least paying' shows that the need of home consumption forces them to do.

(e) **Greater use of owned (i.e.) family inputs:** It has been observed by researchers that small farmers use owned inputs to a greater extent than other cultivators. Thus, even in 1995-96, the percentage of cost (of one hectare of paddy cultivation) accounted for by family inputs was 50 for operational holding of less than one hectare, 42% for operational holding of 1-2 hectares, (38% for holdings of 2-4 hectares, 35% for holdings 4-6 hectares and 33% for holdings above six hectares). Interestingly, it has also been noted that the total cost of one hectare of paddy cultivation was higher (i.e. Rs. 4889) on small holdings than that (Rs. 4457) on large holdings.[5] But still the small holders continued to allocate more land for food grains due to their greater use of family inputs (i.e. family labour, owned animals, own seed and organic manures) and thus less need of direct cost to be paid in cash out of pocket.

(f) **Wide Spread Poverty:** Authorised statistics in India reveal that the problem of poverty in India is mainly that of rural poverty. Similarly according to the available official statistics the category of 'self employed in agriculture' which includes almost wholly the small farmers accounts for over 28 per cent[6] of total poverty in India. Thus, a very important characteristics of the class

of the small farmers is the wide spread poverty among them.

(g) **Net Buyers of food grains:** This is perhaps the most important characteristics of the class of the small operators (i.e. small farmers) of India. Though their cropping pattern is dominated by the cultivation of food crops, the small farmers, by and large, are unable to produce sufficient foodgrains even for their own household consumption. And most of them are forced to purchase[7] some food grains from the market or from the Public Distribution System to supplement their production to take care of the household consumption. *Naturally, there is no question of any marketable surplus* from the small farmers.

III

Small Farmers and WTO

In the above sections, we have examined the expectations and hopes about the benefits from WTO and also the characteristics of the class of the small farmers of India. Now, we examine in this section as to how far will the small farmers will get the expected benefits from the WTO.

When we examine the possible benefits from the WTO on the background of the conditions of the small farmers we are constrained to conclude that 'The small farmers of India are not likely to get benefits from WTO. In fact, they may suffer due to WTO. This conclusion is in escapable owing to the following reasons:

(a) **Absence of Marketable Surplus.** As we know, the most important benefit of WTO for the farmers is the market access and the freedom to sell the produce. But unfortunately, small farmers of India do not have any marketable surplus. And, therefore it would not be possible for them to reap the benefits of the WTO. In fact, it has been observed that India's small farmers by and large have not been able to get any benefit from the 'Minimum Support Price (MSP)' of the Government of India due to their inability to have any marketable surplus.[8] Thus, it should be clear that the benefits of the WTO are only for the large farmers with some marketable surplus and not for the small farmers.

(b) **Perpetuation of traditional cropping pattern:** It appears that the provision of WTO would force the small farmers to perpetuate the unremunerative food grains dominate cropping pattern. This is because, as we have seen above, the small farmers allocate more land for foodgrains (*despite the higher cost*) due to the considerable use of "on farm" inputs (family labour etc.) where direct payment of cost is not involved and as such food is artificially cheaper.

(c) **Food Prices with WTO:** It is expected and hoped that full provisions of WTO may cause fall in food grains prices. However this depends on the actual, availability of food grains at home. If, unfortunately, growing agricultural exports create a fall in food availability at home there is a possibility that food prices might rise in the country. And most small farmers being 'Net buyers' of foodgrains they are likely to suffer. This will be due to the WTO.

(d) **Poverty:** As noted above, the small farmers account for a sizeable portion of poverty in India. The inability of the small farmers to benefit from WTO and/or a rise in food prices will perpetuate their poverty. This does not augur well.

IV

What can be done?

We examine in this section as to what can be done so that the expected benefits of WTO become actually available to the class of the small farmers of India. As the analysis so far suggests, the difficulty of the small farmers is three fold: (a) The necessity to allocate more land for food grains which is not remunerative and yet essential to take care of home consumption though insufficiently. (b) The inability of the small farmers to produce sufficient marketable surplus. And (c) The resultant inability of the small farmers to allocate sufficient land for high value, saleable products or cash crops. Any suggestion/s, ought to address the three difficulties above. (However, while making any suggestion about extending the benefits of WTO to the small farmers it MUST NOT be forgotten that the first requirement of small farmers is availability of cheap and adequate food). With the above background in mind, we offer the following suggestions.

(a) **PDS of food grains for small farmers and farm workers only:** The PDS of food grains in our country has been found wanting on several counts. It has not delivered the expected results. Inclusion of the non-Poor is a serious shortcoming of the PDS. This is due to the inability of the government machinery to correctly identify the poor mainly due to the use of income as the criterion (which can easily be hidden or under reported) for the identification. Therefore, it is strongly suggested that income as the criterion for the identification of the poor be replaced by "Profession" or "means of livelihood" as the criterion for the identification. It is further suggested that, since over 70 per cent of the Indian poverty is accounted for by the classes of small

farmers and landless farm workers they be accepted (by definition) as poor and the PDS be made available to these two classes only. It will solve the problem of giving cheap and adequate food grains to these vulnerable classes. With the huge food stocks of over 60 million tonnes the job is not difficult.

(b) **Shift from food crops to high value crops:** With their food problem solved in the above way, the small farmers can be encouraged to allocate more land for cash crops/high value crops like horticulture, floriculture etc. which are marketable and high income yielders.

(c) **Marketing through Co-operatives:** It is equally necessary that adequate transport, marketing services be made available to the small farmers in order to take care of the sale of their produce. The co-operatives can go a long way in making these services available to the small farmers. This will also ensure higher incomes for the small farmers and a possible solution to the problem of their poverty.

Conclusions

From our above analysis, the following broad conclusions can be drawn.

(a) In the existing agricultural set up in India, benefits from WTO appear unlikely for India's small farmers. They might even suffer due to WTO.

(b) In order that the benefits from WTO become actually available to small farmers it is necessary to make them free from the compulsion of growing food crops.

(c) Freedom from the compulsion of growing food grains is possible if PDS is kept reserved for the

classes of small farmers (and landless farm workers) and if cheap and adequate food is supplied under it.

(d) This will enable the small farmers to grow cash crops etc. produce marketable surplus and reap the benefits of the provisions of WTO.

Notes and References

1. Naik S.D. "Agenda for Agricultural Reforms" in 'Business Line' 26-01-2002.
2. Johnston and Kilby, "Agriculture and Structural Transformation" O.U.P. 1975.
3. Jha, Dayanath, "Agricultural Research and Small Farmers" in India Journal of Agricultural Economics' January/March 2001.
4. Jha Dayanath: *"Ibid"*
5. Jha Daynath: *"Ibid"*.
6. N.S.S. 50th Round.
7. Millor John W.: "Function of Agricultural Prices" in Indian Journal of Agricultural Economics" Jan/March, 1968.
8. See Economic Times 26.01.2002.

12

WTO and Sustainable Agricultural Policies

Suchitra Krishnakumar

Let us begin by addressing the question—How will the WTO sustain agricultural development? For this, we need to know what exactly sustainable agriculture means.

World trade involves a number of complex transactions which cross national borders. Thus, the nature of the transactions is such that more than one national law applies on the transactions. Uniform laws on trade transactions are a must in todays world where goods worth 5.5 trillion are exported. Moreover, international trade facilitates efficiency. Hence, each country should specialise in the production of those goods and services in which it has abundant factor endowments.

The WTO agreements, negotiated and signed by the main trading nations provide the legal ground rules for international commerce.

Upto 1995, GATT rules were largely ineffective in disciplining agricultural trade. In particular, export subsidies came to dominate many areas of world agricultural trade whereas the disciplines on import restrictions were often flouted. The Uruguay Round succeeded in changing that. The trade is now within the multilateral trading system.

The AOA formed a part of the final Act of the Uruguay Round of multilateral trade negotiations, which was signed by the member countries in April 1994 at Marrakesh, Moracco and came into force on 1, January 1995. The Uruguay Round Agreement sought to bring order and fair competition to this highly distorted sector of world trade by establishment of a free and market oriented agricultural trading sector.

The root cause of international trade in agriculture had been the massive domestic subsidies given by the industrialised countries to their agricultural sector over many years. This in turn led to excessive production and its dumping in international markets as well as import restrictions to keep out foreign agricultural products from their domestic markets. Hence, the starting point for the establishment of a fair agricultural trade regime has to be the reduction of domestic production subsidies given by industrialised countries, reduction in the volume of subsidised exports and minimum market access opportunities for agricultural producers world wide.

The obligations and disciplines incorporated in the AOA therefore relate to:

(i) Market Access

(ii) Domestic subsidy or domestic support

(iii) Export Subsidy

It is necessary to define sustainable agriculture before going into the discussion on the policies and programmes for sustainability of agriculture.

It is very difficult to define sustainability even though it is relatively easy to describe goals for a more sustainable agriculture. According to Francis Hildebrand, everyone assumes that agriculture must be sustainable. But we differ in the interpretations of conditions and assumptions under which this can be made to occur.

Since the Brundtland Commission's definition of sustainable development in 1987, there have been at least seven more definitions constructed, each different in subtle ways, each emphasising different values, priorities and goals. But precise and absolute definitions of sustainability and therefore of sustainable agriculture are impossible. Sustainability itself is a complex and contested concept. To some it implies persistence and the capacity of something to continue for a long time. To others, it implies resilience and the ability to bounce back after unexpected difficulties.

Sustainable agriculture is not a model or package to be imposed. It is more a process of learning. Definitions of sustainable agriculture are generally concerned with the need for agricultural practices to be economically viable to meet human needs for food, to be environmentally positive and to be concerned with quality of life.

These objectives can be achieved in a number of different ways. Sustainable agriculture is not linked to any particular technological practice. Nor is sustainable agriculture the exclusive domain of organic farming. This is because sustainable agriculture is thought of in terms of its adaptability and flexibility over time to respond to the demands for food and fibre, its demands on natural resources for production and its ability to protect the soil and the resources. This requires an efficient use of technology in a manner conducive to sustainability. Since agriculture is affected by changes in market and resource decisions in other sectors and regions, it is important that these changes do not provide a rationale for depleting the agricultural resource base locally.

The WTO Agreement in its preamble recognised the special economic and developmental needs of the developing countries and incorporated a host of special and differential measures.

Special and Differential (S & D) provisions in the Uruguay Round Agreements fall under two main categories.

(a) Lenient provisions in the form of longer transition periods, more favourable thresholds in the application of countervailing measures and for undertaking certain commitments and greater flexibility with regard to certain obligations.

(b) Clauses providing for specific, although undefined, action by developed countries under certain agreements, while dealing with developing countries.

In AOA developing countries enjoy special and differential treatment in three main areas of agreement. That is market access, domestic support and export subsidies.

I. **Market Access:** On market access the agreement has two basic elements:

(a) Tariffication of all non- tariff barriers

(b) Tariff rate quotas -Minimum access opportunities

Tariffication of all Non-Tariff Barriers

In the area of market access, non-tariff border measures are replaced by tariffs that provide substantially the same level of protection. Tariffs resulting from this tariffication process as well as other tariffs on agricultural products are to be reduced by an average 36% in the case of developed countries and 24% in the case of developing countries. Reductions are to be undertaken over six years in the case of developed countries and over ten years in the case of developing countries. (see Table 12.1)

Table 12.1: Reduction Commitments for developed and developing countries

Tariffs	*Developed Countries 06 years (1995-2001)*	*Developing Countries 10 years (1995-2005)*
Average cut for all agricultural products	36%	24%
Minimum Cut Per Product	15%	10%
Domestic Support total AMS cuts for sector (base period) (1986-88)	20%	13%
Support Subsidies (value of subsidies)	36%	24%
Subsidised Quantities (base period 1986-90)	21%	14%

With India being under Balance of payment cover (which is GATT consistent measure) India had not undertaken any commitments with regard to market access. The only commitment India has undertaken is to bind its tariffs on primary agricultural products at 150% and edible oils at 300%.

Tariff Rate quotas—Minimum access opportunities: The second element relates to setting up of a minimum land for imports of agricultural products by member countries as a share of domestic consumption. Countries are required to maintain current levels (1986-88) of access for each individual product. Where the current level of import is negligible, the minimum access should not be less than 3% of the domestic consumption. This minimum level is to be raised to 5% (by the year 2001) in case of developed countries and 2005 in the case of developing countries. However, special safeguard provisions allow for the application of additional duties when shipments are made at prices below certain reference levels or when there is a sudden import surge. The market access provisions however, does not apply when the commodity in question is a traditional staple of a developing country.

II. **Domestic Support:** Provisions of the agreement regarding domestic support have two main objectives:

(a) To identify acceptable measures that support farmers and

(b) To deny unacceptable, trade distorting support to the farmers. These provisions are aimed largely at the developed countries where the levels of domestic agricultural support have risen to extremely high levels in recent decades.

All domestic support is quantified through the mechanism of total Aggregate Measurement of Support (AMS). AMS is a means of quantifying aggregate value of domestic support given to each category of agricultural product. Each WTO member country has made calculations to determine its AMS. Wherever applicable commitment made requires a 20% reduction in total AMS for developed countries over six years. For developing countries this percentage is 13% and no reduction is required for the least developed countries. The base period external reference price on which the reductions were calculated was 1986-88.

AMS consists of two parts—product specific subsidies and non-product specific subsidies.

Product-specific subsidies refer to the total level of support provided for each individual agricultural commodity essentially signified by procurement price in India.

Non-product specific subsidies, on the other hand refer to the total level of support for the agricultural sector as a whole i.e., subsidies on inputs such as fertilisers, electricity, irrigation, seeds, credit etc.

There are three categories of support measures that are not subject to reduction under the agreement and support within specified de-minimum level is allowed. These three categories of exempt support measures are:

1. Measures which have a minimum impact on trade and which meet the basic and policy specific criteria set out in the agreement (Green Box measures). These include Government assistance on general services like:

   (i) Research, pest and disease control, training, extension and advisory services

   (ii) Public stock holding for food security purposes

   (iii) Domestic food aid

   (iv) Direct payments to producers like government financial participation in income, insurance and safety nets, relief from natural disasters and payments under environmental assistance programmes.

2. Developing country measures, otherwise subject to reduction which neat the criteria set out in paragraph 2 of article 6 of the agreement (special and differential treatment or S & D box). Examples of these are:

   (i) Investment subsidies which are generally available to agriculture developing countries.

   (ii) Measures to encourage agriculture and rural development in developing countries.

   (iii) Direct payments under production limiting programme which confirm to the requirements set out in paragraph 5 of Article 6 of the Agreement (Blue box measures).

GEEN BOX

This includes expenditure on:

- Support for Research

- Control of Pests and Diseases
- Training, Extension and Advisory Services
- Public Stock for Food Security
- Direct payment to producers
- Farm Income Insurance
- Disaster Management
- Government Financial Participation in Income, Insurance, and Income Safety Nets Programme.
- Extension, Advisory, Marketing and promotion and Infrastructural Services, and
- Investments Subsidies and Agricultural Input Services to Resource Poor Farmers.

The Green Box subsidies are those subsidies which are supposed to have no or minimal trade distorting effects. They are exempt from reduction commitments. To be regarded as Green Box, support measures must meet certain criteria. A major requirement is that any exempt measure shall be part of the publicly funded government programmes not involving transfers from consumers and shall not provide price support to producers.

Amber Box subsidies are considered to be trade distorting and come under progressive reduction commitments. The three types of Amber Box measures exempted from reduction are de minimis support. The de minimis levels at which support is regarded as having minimal effects are defined for developed countries as support not exceeding 5% of the value of production of individual products of the value of total agricultural production. For developing countries the de minimis level is 10%.

Certain measures to encourage agriculture and rural development in developing countries including generally available investment subsidies to low income producers and support to diversification away from growing illegal narcotic crops and certain direct payment under production limiting programmes are dubbed as Blue Box.

BLUE BOX

The components of Blue Box are:

- Direct payments under production limiting programmes
- Certain government assistance measures to encourage agricultural and rural development in developing countries,
- Decoupled income support,
- Structural adjustment assistance provided through produces retirement programmes,
- Payments under environmental, regional assistance programmes, and
- Other support measures which make up only a low proportion (5 per cent in the case of developed countries and 10 per cent in the case of developing countries) of the value of production of individual products or, in the case of non-product specific support, the value of total agricultural production.

In the case of developing countries, the reductions are two thirds those of developed countries over ten year period (with no reductions applying to the least developed countries). These are subject to certain conditions, that there are no commitments on subsidies to reduce the costs of marketing exports of agricultural products or internal transport and freight charges or export shipments. Where subsidised exports have increased since 1986-90 base period, 1991-92 may be used. In certain circumstances, as the beginning point of reductions although the end point provides for some limited flexibility between years in terms of export subsidy reduction commitments and contains provisions aimed at preventing the circumvention of the export subsidy and sets out criteria for food aid donations and the use of export credits.

III. Export Subsidy

The AOA lists several types of subsidies to which reduction commitments apply. However such subsidies are virtually not existent in India as exporters of agricultural commodities do not get direct subsidy. It is also worth noting that developing countries are free to provide three of the listed subsidies viz. reduction of export marketing costs, internal and international transport and freight charges.

The Agreement on Agriculture bans the use of subsidies other than those which fall under one of the four exceptions. The exceptions are:

(a) Export subsidies subject to reduction commitments in part IV Section II of a members schedule of commitments attached to Marrakesh Protocol.

(b) Export subsidies by developing countries consistent with the Agreement provision for S & D treatment in their favour.

(c) Spending on export subsidies or quantities on subsidised exports than exceed those limits specified in a members schedule provided the excess is covered by the agreements downstream flexibility' provisions.

(d) Export subsidies not covered by reduction commitments, provided they confirm to the agreements anti-circumvention disciplines.

The agreement on subsidies and countervailing measures is intended to build on the Agreement of Interpretation and application of Articles VI, XVI and XXIII which was negotiated in the Tokyo Round. This Agreement contains the definition of subsidy and introduced the concept of a specific subsidy. Only specific subsidies would be subject to the discipline set out in the agreement.

There are three types of subsidies:

(a) Prohibited Subsidies

(b) Actionable Subsidies

(c) Non-Actionable Subsidies

Prohibited Subsidies: Prohibited Subsidies are those contingent (in law or in fact, whether solely or as one of several other conditions) upon export performance and those contingent (whether solely or as one of several other conditions) upon the use of domestic over imported goods. Prohibited subsidies are new to dispute settlement procedures. The main features include an expedited time table for action by the dispute body, and if it is found that the subsidy is indeed prohibited, it must be immediately withdrawn. If this is not done within the specified time period, the complaining member is authorised to take counter measures.

Actionable Subsidies: As per the Agreement, no member should through the use of subsidies cause adverse effect to the interests of other signatories (i.e. serious prejudice to the interests of another member injury to domestic industry or another signatures, nullification or impairment of benefits accruing directly or indirectly to other signatories). Members affected by actionable subsidies may refer the matter to the dispute settlement body. In the event that it is determined that such adverse effects exist, the subsidising member must withdraw the subsidy or remove the adverse effects.

Non-Actionable Subsidies: This could either be non-specific subsidies or specific subsidies involving assistance to industrial research and pre-competitive development activity, assistance to disadvantaged regions or certain type of assistance for adapting existing facilities to new environmental requirements imposed by law. When another member believes that a non-actionable subsidy results in serious adverse effects to a domestic industry, it may seek a determination and recommendation of the matter.

Countervailing Measures: One part of the AOA concerns the use of countervailing measures on subsidized imported goods. It sets out disciplines on the initiation of countervailing cases, investigation by national authorities and rules of evidence to ensure that all interested parties can present information and argument. Certain disciplines on the calculation of the amount of a subsidy are outlined, as is the basis for the determination of injury to the domestic industry. The agreement would require that all relevant economic factors be taken into account in assessing the state of the industry and that a causal link be established between the subsidised imports and the alleged injury. Countervailing investigations shall be terminated immediately in cases where the amount of a subsidy is less than 1% ad valorem or where the volume of subsidised imports, actual or potential or the injury is negligible. Except under exceptional circumstances, investigations shall be concluded within one year after their initiation and in no case more than 16 months. All countervailing duties have to be terminated within five years of their imposition unless the authorities determine on the basis of a review that the expiry the duty would be likely to lead to continuation to recurrence of subsidisation and injury.

The Agreement recognised that subsidies may play an important role in economic development programmes of developing countries and in the transformation of centrally planned economies to market economies. Least developed countries and developing countries that have less than $ 1000 per capita GNP are thus exempted from disciplines on prohibited export subsidies and have a time bound exemption from other prohibited subsidies. For other developing countries, the export subsidy prohibition would take effect years after the entry into the force of the agreement establishing the WTO and they have a time bound (though fewer years than for poorer developing countries) exemption from the other prohibited subsidies. Countervailing investigation of a product originating from a developing-country member would be terminated if the overall level of subsidies does not exceed 2% (and from certain developing countries 3%) of the value of the product, or if the volume of the subsidised imports represent less than 4% of the total imports for the like product in the importing signatory. For countries in the process of transformation from a centrally planned into a market economy, prohibited subsidies shall be phased out within a period of seven years from the date of entry into force of the agreement.

Peace provisions are also given in the agreement. These include on understanding that certain actions available under the subsidies agreement will not be applied with respect to Green Box policies. Similarly, domestic support and export subsidies maintained in conformity with commitments would be the requirement. There is an understanding that due restraint will be used in the application of countervailing duty rights under the General Agreement and setting out limits in terms of the applicability of nullification or impairment actions. These peace provisions will apply for a period of nine years.

The agreement provides for setting up a committee that will monitor the implementation of commitments, and also monitor the follow-up to the decisions on measures concerning the possible negative effects of the reform programme on least developed and net food importing developing countries. The package is conceived as part of a continuing process with the long term objective of securing substantial progressive reductions in support and protection. Further negotiations in the fifth year of implementation are to be called for. These negotiations along with an assessment of the first five years, would take into account non-trade concerns, S & D treatments for development countries. The objective is to establish as fair and market oriented agricultural trading system and other concerns and objectives noted in the preamble to the agreement.

Implications of the Agreement

Implications of the agreement would differ from country to country and would depend largely on the overall agricultural scenario in the country. Indian agriculture is characterised by a preponderant majority of small and marginal farmers holding less than two hectares of land, less than 35.7% of the land is under any assured irrigation system and for the large majority of farmers, the gains from the application of the science and technology in agriculture are yet to be realised. Farmers, therefore, require support in terms of development of infrastructure as well as extension of improved technologies and provisions of requisite inputs at reasonable cost. India's share of world's agricultural trade is of the order of 1%. There is no doubt that during the last 30 years, Indian agriculture has grown at a reasonable pace, but with stagnant and declining net cropped area it is indeed going to be a formidable task to maintain the growth in agricultural production. The implication of the agreement thus have to be examined in the light of the food demand and supply situation. The size of the country, the level of overall development balance of payments position, realistic future outlook for agricultural development structure of land holdings etc. are the other relevant factors that would have a bearing on India's trade policy in agriculture.

Implications of the AOA for India should be gauged from the impact it will have on the following

1 Whether the agreement has opened up markets and facilitated exports of our products and
2. Whether we would be able to continue with our domestic policy aimed at improving infrastructure and provision of inputs at subsidised prices for achieving increased agricultural production.

Short Term Implications

Regarding opening of markets and impact on trade in agriculture it may be noted that the share of developing countries in world exports of food remained at 44% and of agricultural raw materials increased from 32% in 1994 to 34% in 1996. The average growth of developed countries imports of agricultural products increased by just 1% during 1994-96. Agricultural exports of 10 Asian developing countries increased from US $ 49252 million in 1994 to US $55902 million in 1996. India's share in total agricultural exports from developing Asia is 8% behind China's 19% Thailand's 17% Malaysia's 14% and Indonesia's 10%. India's exports of agricultural products have increased from US $ 4151 million in 1993-94 to US $ 7054 million in 1997-98. No tangible opening of markets have been noticed so far.

Regarding freedom to pursue our domestic policies, in the short run India will not be affected by WTO Agreement on Agriculture. India has been maintaining quantitative restrictions on import of agricultural commodities. Within the provision of GATT Agreement India has bound tariffs at high levels of 100%, 150% and 300% for primary products processed products and edible oils respectively.

Long Term Implications

For large majority of farmers in different parts of the country, the gains from application of science and technology in agriculture are yet to be realised which would require infrastructural support, improved technologies and provision of inputs at reasonable cost. The Agreement on agriculture recognised this and developing countries have been given the freedom to implement such policies under Article 6 relating to S & D but any attempt in future to dilute provisions relating to S & D for developing countries could affect us adversely.

Regarding the impact of liberalisation of trade in agriculture in the longrun, Indian agriculture enjoys the advantage of cheap labour. Therefore, despite lower productivity a comparison with world prices of agricultural commodities would reveal that domestic prices in India are considerably less with the exceptions of few commodities (oilseeds). Hence, imports to India would not be attractive in the case of rice, tea, sunflower oil and cotton. On the whole, large scale import of agricultural commodities as a result of trade liberalisation is ruled out. Even the exports of food grains which are cheaper in the domestic market but are sensitive from the point of view of consumption by the economically weaker sections are not likely to rise to unacceptable levels because of high inland transportation cost and inadequate export infrastructure in India. Through proper tariffication we will have to strike a balance between the competing interest of 10% farmers to generate marketable surpluses and consumers belonging to the economically poorer sections of the society.

The nature and character of state intervention and state support will have to undergo qualitative changes in order to realise the opportunities for exports and also to cope with the implications of agriculture of developing countries in order to come into increasing alignment with the international market place.

REFERENCE

1. Goyal Arun Edited (2000) - WTO in the New Millenium, World Trade Centre, Mumbai.

2. Pursell Garry (1996) India Trade Policies Since the 1991-92, Reforms, Draft Paper International Trade Division, World Bank, Washington.

3. Srinivasan P V and Shukha Jha (2000), Impact of Recent Policy Changes and globalisation on the Agricultural Sector and Agricultural Research in India, Project Report No. 40 Indira Gandhi Institute of Development Research, Mumbai.

4. Martin, Will and Alan Winters (1998): The Uruguay Round and the Developing Economies World Bank Discussion Paper No. 307, World Bank, Washington.

5. Gulati, Ashok, Rajesh Mehta and Sudha Narayan (1999), from Marrakesh to Seattle Indian Agriculture in a Globalising World, Economic and Political weekly Vol. 34, No. 41 October 9-15.

6. Sen, Sunanda and V Upendra Das (1992): Import Liberalisation as a tool of Economic Policy in India since Mid-Eighties. Economic and Political weekly Vol. 27, No. 12, 21st March.

7. Celeste Richard WTO after Seattle Times of India 10-12-1999.

8. Narsalay Raghav Developing Countries and WTO Business Line 10-10-2000.

9. Padmanabhan, Anil 'Sleepless in Seattle' Business Standard 11-12-1999.

10. Nair M D 'WTO Agreement on agriculture'—Strategic issues for India' 14-12-2000.

11. Moore, Mike 'The lessons from Seattle' The Hindu 25-12-1999.

13

WTO Regime and Its Implications for Indian Agriculture

T.S. Raghavendra

Introduction

The main objective of WTO treaty is to reform highly distorted world trade because of direct and indirect subsidies. The world trade treaty, aimed at opening up international markets was finally signed in April 1994. India is one of the signatories to this treaty. One of the major agreements concluded in the Uruguay Round of negotiations was the Agreement on Agriculture. Accordingly, the on-going policy reforms in India aimed at correcting the anti-agriculture' bias, thus leading Indian agriculture towards globlisation. The Government of India initiated various measures to make agricultural exports more viable. These measures have opened up significant vistas for agricultural development in India.

It is against this background that this paper makes an attempt to study the performance of Indian agriculture under the WTO regime. Thus, section II concentrates briefly on WTO agreement on Agriculture, Section III examines the development of agricultural sector in India and Section IV tries to draw some conclusions.

II

WTO Agreement on Agriculture

The Uruguay Round of trade negotiations, which paved the way for the establishment of WTO, for the first time brought agriculture into the sphere of GATT. One of the most important goals of WTO's Agreement on Agriculture has been the removal of trade distortions resulting from different levels of input subsidies, price and market support, export subsidy and other kinds of trade distorting support across countries. The broad areas envisaged under AOA are discussed briefly in the following paragraphs.

Market Access

One of the main features of the AOA is to replace all quantitative restrictions on agricultural commodities by an appropriate amount of tariff. All member countries are expected to move towards" tariffs only" regime. In other words, there can be no restrictions on farm trade except through tariffs. This means that non- tariff barries such as quantitative restrictions namely quotas, import restrictions through permits, import licensing etc. were to be replaced by tariffs on imports to provide the same level of protection and then were to bc followed by progressive reduction of tariff levels. The stipulated process of tariffication is gradual and gives ample scope for adjustment. The ceilings on tariffs proposed by India and accepted by WTO are fairly high — 100 per cent on primary products, 150 per cent on processed products and 300 per cent on edible oils.

Domestic Support

The domestic support is quantified through the aggregate measure of support (AMS). The domestic support is classified into five categories.

(a) Aggregate measure of support which includes product-specific and non product - specific support.

(b) Green Box support.

(c) Blue-Box support.

(d) De minimus support and

(e) Special and differential treatment box.

Among these, the WTO agreement requires a reduction only in AMS and export subsidies, whereas support under all other categories is exempted. Domestic support measures are meant to identify acceptable measures of support to farmers. They include:

(a) The sum total of subsidies on inputs such as fertiliser, water, credit and power, and

(b) Market price support measured by calculating the difference between domestic administered market price and world price multiplied by the quantity of production eligible to get applied administered price. Domestic support which includes both product specific and non-product specific support given to the agricultural sector up to 10 per cent of the total value of agricultural produce in developing countries is allowed.

In fact, certain provisions under Annex 2 of the Agreement known as the "Green Box" encompasses different forms of support such as direct payment to producers, infrastructural services, pest control, environmental programmes, inspection and market intelligence, relief in terms of natural disasters, payment under regional assistance programme for disadvantaged regions which are all exempted from reduction commitments. However, most of the developing countries were familiar only with support in the form of input subsidies and price and market support but the green-box measures are very great in all the developed countries. It is said that the expectations about reductions in domestic support, subsidies prevailing in the developed countries at the time of conclusion of AOA have not materialised. The opportunity of getting market access to all the developing countries has thus been effectively denied.

Export Competition

In the area of export subsidy WTO agreement emphasises reduction of direct export subsidies to a level of 36 per cent below the 1986-88 level in the case of developed countries over a period of six years and 24 per cent for developing for the same period. The developing countries are free to provide certain subsidies such as those of export marketing costs, internal and international transport and freight charges etc. The least developed countries are not subject to any reduction commitment.

III

THE FARM SECTOR OF INDIA

Growth

For all the concerted efforts of industrialisation for over five decades in independent India, agriculture still remains the backbone of its economy. The agricultural sector of the economy feeds the entire development process of the country. The performance in agricultural sector during the last two decades has been reasonably satisfactory. The growth of output around three per cent per annum in this period against the one per cent per annum during the first half of the tewentieth century is impressive. Output growth has been well ahead of the rate of population growth which has been 1.6 per cent per annum. In recent years, expansion of cultivated area has virtually come to a stop. Growth in yields per hectare of cultivated area has become increasingly important and is now the predominant source of agricultural growth. Even Indian agriculture has travelled a very long distance from the night-marish 'begging-bowl' status to that of 'self-sufficiency. It can be seen in the virtual elimination of food grains imports. The green revolution spread to new regions and there was diversification into oil seeds, horticulture and live stock. An efficient diffusion of technology has been the main instrument of agricultural development and has made India self sufficient, and a leading producer of several agricultural commodities in the world. The growth of agricultural sector owes much to a conscious and proactive policy of Government for promoting agricultural development. The well known policy measures include massive public investments in the irrigation works, rural electrification, nation wide network of specialised research stations, development of rural credit system, expansion of transport network which have contributed significantly in raising productivity. However in the light of the experience of the post-reforms period (Table–13.1) experts are of the opinion that the 'composition' of economic growth must be shifted in favour of agricultural and rural sector (Bhupat Desai 2001). If India could streamline its domestic policies it has the potential of achieving higher productivity in the near future and thereby come out of the present crisis.

Table 13.1: Annual compound Growth of Crop Agriculture

(per cent)

	1980-81 to 1991-92	*1992-93 to 1999-2000*
Crop Agriculture	3.4	2.2
Food Grains	2.9	2.0
Non Food Grains	4.3	2.4

Source: Economic Survey 2000-2001

Investment

Since reforms-philosophy considers direct public intervention less important than creating a favourable climate for private investment, public sector investment has declined continuously. (Table–13.2) Although real gross capital formation by the private sector has increased, that by the public sector has continued to dwindle significantly, as a result of which the total gross capital formation has declined continuously during the reforms period. In fact, terms of trade in agriculture did improve during the 1990's and private investment increased. Despite this, however, post-reform agricultural performance has been disappointing (Abijith Sen, 2001).

Table 13.2: Gross Capital Formation in Agriculture (at 1993-94 prices).

Year	*Per cent Share*		*Investment in Agriculture as*	
	Public	*Private*	*Per cent of GDP*	*Per cent of Current Expenditure*
1993-94	33.0	67.0	1.6	3.4
1994-95	33.0	67.0	1.6	3.3
1995-96	30.9	69.1	1.6	2.8
1996-97	28.9	71.1	1.5	2.3
1997-98	24.9	75.1	1.4	1.7
1998-99	23.5	76.5	1.4	1.4
1999-2000	25.0	75.0	1.5	1.4

Source: Economic Survey 2000-01.

In this respect, the effectiveness of the investments also needed higher attention. However, fragmented planning, poor design, over-capitalisation, inordinate delays in completing works and large-scale corruption the well-known banes of public investment in India, have played havoc again.

The observed decline in investment unless reversed, may slow down the future growth of output in the agricultural sector. In China, a big spurt in agricultural output over a long period following the opening up of the economy could largely be attributed to the high rate of investment in agriculture, over at least three decades. The gains from the rise in the productivity of resources were thus considerable following structural adjustment in agriculture over there. In India, on the other hand, the rate of investment in agriculture rose for only a decade following the green revolution, and the development of human capital has been painfully slow. (C.H.H. Rao and Gulati, 1994)

Subsidies

Subsidies in general, and agricultural subsidies in particular, have assumed greater significance because of two reasons: (a) fiscal imbalance, and (b) WTO negotiations. The agreement seeks to reduce domestic support exceeding the de minimus exempt level. A Study by Gulati and Sharma (1995) came to the conclusion that Indian agriculture is not 'net subsidised' but 'net taxed'; that over valued exchange rate and high protection to industry have discriminated against agriculture; that subsidies on key inputs have lost their rationale and are now crowding out productive investments, damaging environment, accentuating inequity and promoting inefficient cropping pattern; that raising prices is only a partial solution to the ills of the input sectors and that these sectors must experience institutional reforms to make the entire agricultural system sustainable. On the contrary, the developed countries were found to be heavily subisdising their agriculture. Therefore, it was expected that implementation of the AOA would result in increased prices of agricultural commodities and thus improve export prospects for India and other developing countries. However, international agricultural prices in the post- WTO period have declined sharply, and agricultural exports from developing countries such as India have declined.

Table 13.3: Major Input Subsidies

(Rs. in Crores)

Year	Fertili-sers	Electri-city	Canal Irriga-tion	Total Subsidy	GDP in agri-culture	Col.5 as Per-centage of Col.6
1	2	3	4	5	6	7
1990-91	4,389	4,605	2,505	11,499	1,35,162	8.51
1991-92	4,800	5,889	3,109	13,798	1,62,317	8.50
1992-93	6,136	7,335	3,420	16,891	1,84,536	9.15
1993-94	4,400	8,966	3,880	17,246	2,06,322	8.36
1994-95	5,241	10,941	4,502	20,684	2,39,159	8.65
1995-96	6,235	13,606	5,253	25,094	2,55,613	9.88

Source: S.S. Acharya Agu. 2000

Exports

The recent trend in agricultural exports indicates that the WTO failed in its attempt to provide level playing field to developing countries Though India is a very minor player in the world market, it is now recognised that, in the case of some staple commodities (like rice) India's entry in a bigger way would make a significant impact; and that this possibility should explicitly be taken into account in revising trade policy and tariff structures (Vaidyanathan, 2000). With a determination to orient agricultural production to exports on the basis of comparative advantage principle, agriculture can contribute substantially to foreign exchange earning and can introduce 'value-added' agriculture even on the small and marginal holdings (Vyas, 2001).

It was found that the classification of subsidies under agricultural package of WTO favoured developed countries, particularly EU, the US, Canada and Japan which are able to maintain very high levels of support for agriculture in the exempt category. The heavy subsidy exemption

Table 13.4: India's Export of Agriculture Products

(US$ million)

	1996-97	1997-98	1998-99	1999-2000
1. Total Export	33,470	35,006	33,218	35,822
2. Total Agri-Export	6,828	6,594	6,039	5,608
3. Per cent of Agri-Exports to Total Exports	20.4	18.8	18.2	15.2

Source: Economic Survey 2000-01, 2001-02.

empowered the developed countries to cause distortions in the international market and protected their agriculture. To achieve a level playing field, distortion -free trade and efficiency require that high level of subsidy and support must be reduced considerably by developed countries (Ramesh Chand et. al,. 2001). For this, all kinds of subsidies to agriculture should be clubbed in one category and then reduction principle should be applied.

IV

MAIN CONCLUSIONS

From the preceding analysis it may be concluded that the primary purpose of the AOA is to promote global trade by removing various trade distortions at the international level. In fact, aggregate measure of support to Indian agriculture, calculated by various scholars, did not suggest any gross distortion either in positive or in negative terms. The inter-sectoral terms of trade were gradually improving in favour of agriculture. It is very clear that Indian system is addicted to subsidies. But it is very essential to restructure the subsidy regime entirely and carefully so that the productivity of such inputs would increase continuously. Therefore, in order to reap these benefits of globalisation the following suggestions can be looked into:

1. The process of liberalisation in the domestic market should be accelerated.

2. Public Investment in agriculture should be stepped up to create needed infrastructural facilities.
3. A more dynamic strategy is very important to attract foreign customers. The need of the hour is to work out a long-term export strategy for commercial crops.
4. Emphasis must be given to value addition with encouragement to agro-processing industries.
5. A massive food-for-work programme would help clear the heavy stock-up of grains in our godowns.
6. Credit for agriculture has to expand at a faster rate than before because of the need to step up agricultural growth to generate surpluses for exports.
7. Effective diffusion of technology across unfavourable agro-climatic regions is essential for sustaining high growth, improving the efficiency of resource-use etc.,
8. The public sector organisations involved in the development of infrastructural facilities need to be restructured so that they are conducive to efficiency and accountability.
9. All restrictions on agricultural trade, marketing and processing within the country should be removed. It requires major reforms in governance and institutions at the state level.
10. Any deviation from the main objective of WTO should be challenged effectively and India should take initiative in organising other developing countries for the same purpose.

India can benefit from the changing world economic scenario by accelerating the growth in the agricultural sector. The major reforms in agricultural sector will lead to greater employment, regional and sectoral equity, poverty reduction, more efficient resource use and overall progress of the entire economy.

REFERENCES

1. Acharya S.S. (2000) "Subsidies in Indian Agriculture and their Beneficiaries", Agricultural Situation in India, August 251-260.
2. Chand, Ramesh et. al. (2001) "Subsidies and Support in Agriculture: Is WTO Providing Level playing Field?" *EPW*, Aug 11-17, No 32
3. Damodaran A. (2001)" WTO Agriculture Agreement, Common Property Resources and Income Diversification Strategy", *EPW, Sept22-28,* No 38
4. Desai, Bhupat M. (2001), "Policy Frame Work for Reorienting Agricultural Development" Presidential Address 61st Annual Conference, ISAE, Gulburga, Dec 27,29.
5. Government of India, Economic Survey, 1998-99,2000-200,2001-2002.
6. Gulati, Ashok and Anil Sharma (1994) "Agriculture under GATT: What it Holds for India" *EPW*, July 16, No. 29.
7. Gulati, Ashok and Anil Sharma (1995) "Subsidy Syndrome in Indian Agriculture", *EPW*, Sept. 30, No. 39.
8. Gulati, Ashok et. al (1999) "From Marrakesh to Seatle; Indian Agriculture in a Globalising World", *EPW*, Oct. 9-15, No. 41.
9. Mishra R.S. (2001), "The WTO Agreement on Agriculture (AOA) and Agricultural Crisis in India", IEA 88th Conference Number, Vellore.
10. Hanumantha Rao C. H. (2001), WTO and Viability of Indian Agriculture", Sept. 8-14, No. 36.
11. Sen Abhijith (2001), "Agriculture: A Long Road Ahead", *The Hindu* July 19.

12. Vaidyanathan A. (2000), "Indias Agricultural Development Policy" *EPW*, May 13-19, No. 20.

13. Vyas V.S. (2001), "Agriculture: Second Round of Economic Reforms", *EPW,* March 10-16, No. 10.

14. ————(1998), "Freeing Trade in Agriculture: Implications for Resources use Efficiency and Cropping Pattern Changes", EPW, Dec. 27, No. 52.

14

WTO and India's Agricultural Exports Problems and Prospects

P.A. Rego

Sustained export of agricultural commodities encourages modernisation of production, post harvest processing and marketing system in agriculture. It not only helps to earn foreign exchange but also competitiveness in production, productivity, cost effectiveness and quality compared to its potential of competitive countries in the global market.

However, the terms of trade for agricultural sector have been unfavourable for India compared with Industrial sector. Now under the changing world economic scenario as well as global trade agreement and development of institutions like WTO the emerging world trading system may claim to change the terms of trade in favour of agriculture and trade goods from India. Being a member of WTO we have several commitments to the provisions related to QRS, TRIPS, patent, trade marks etc. and these provisions are likely to harm the cause of our agricultural growth and export unless we correct ourselves in the global market. India cannot ask to dismantle all the trading blocks. It has to take it as a challenge to make the efforts to derive the maximum benefits from the process of globalisation and get the status of a most favoured nation. The process of globalisation is a reality which cannot be derived and should not be avoided. It provides a wide range of challenges and opportunities as far as Indian agriculture is concerned. It calls for drastic changes from subsistence type of farming to commercialisation of agriculture, development of agro-based and agro-processing, allied activities, diversification of agriculture generation of large surpluses so as to compete with several allied countries of the world.

Present Scenario of Agricultural Exports

During 1980-81 to 1991-92 the percentage share in the growth of agricultural export is 24.2 while manufactured sector is 62.6. During 1992-93 to 1999-2000 it was 18.3% and manufactured sector 76.6%. The world market is becoming more protectionist because several countries specially developed ones are using several trade and non trade barriers like technical standards, environmental and social controls, high tariffs, qualitative restrictions quota, strict hygienic restrictions, package standards, labelling requirements etc. which have been discouraging our exports. Eg: Floriculture products, marine products and basmati rice to European Union, Mushroom export to U.S.A.

Among the domestic factors that continue to hamper our exports growth are infrastructural constraints, high transaction costs, quality problems, processing of agriculture goods pricing etc.

The Exim policy of Government of India 2002 has emphasized the importance of agricultural exports and nexus between export and openness which promotes GDP, domestic competition, cost control, effective resource use, removal of QRS, transport subsidy etc.

Thus, even after setting up of the WTO, Industrialised and developed economies as have several weapons for their advantage which are threats to poor nations. Though these are challenges and problems, we have opportunities to improve our agricultural exports also. They are enumerated as given below.

1. A sizeable and growing demand for the exportation of crop products like basmati rice in recent years.
2. There exists a good demand for drum type of wheat in Egypt and West Asian market.
3. India can boost export of best quality cotton to world market.
4. There are bright opportunities for the exportation of spices from India.
5. A very good scope for the export of fruits, vegetables and flowers throughout the year. Hi-tech method of producing fruits, vegetables and flowers will be resulted in cost effectiveness and promotion of India's diversified exports.

Therefore, to reap the benefits of globalisation and move into the international marketing on lines with WTO we can suggest the following measures.

1. Huge investment in agriculture to boost the productivity and production of selected export oriented agricultural crops.
2. Reforms in agricultural marketing particularly measures for the promotion of value added products through modern methods of processing, grading, packaging, storage etc. with quality assurance.
3. Encouragement to the exports of agricultural commodities which are unique in the world (due to geographical features).
4. Setting up of export oriented farms for selected agricultural crops and spices by offering incentives to different farm groups.
5. Special encouragement by the Government to 100% export oriented units by way of duty free importation of capital goods to such units.

6. Encouragement for the expansion of agro processing Industries.
7. Air-cargo transportation facilities have to be stepped up to perishable items like fruits, vegetables and flowers.
8. Popularisation of attractive and quality assured storage and packaging methods.
9. Systematic Planning for the exportation of agricultural products.
10. Dissemination of knowledge about the recent changes/development which are taking place in the area of agricultural exports to the farmers and the public.

Besides these, a holistic approach by the Government and the people is required to take advantage of the changed circumstances in the promotion of India's agricultural exports after the formation of WTO.

REFERENCES

1. Bhattacharya B. "Exim Policy"—2001-02, Yojana Vol. 45, May.
2. Government of India, Economic Survey 1999-2000.
3. Gulati A "Effective Protection and Subsidies in Indian Agriculture—A Case of Wheat and Rice 'EAE' Vol. 24, October-December.
4. Rao C.H. Hanumantha Agriculture Growth, Rural Poverty and Environmental Degradation in India, New Delhi.
5. Ninth Five Year Plan-Government of India.

15

Globalisation of Indian Agriculture

Shripathi K.P.

Though the economic reforms initiated in 1990 focussed mainly as industrial, fiscal, financial and external sectors, it was anticipated that market determined exchange rate regime, removal of restrictions on agricultural exports would benefit the agriculture sector. It was also expected that the Agreement on agriculture would enable India to increase her share in world exports of agricultural and agro-based products.

With the establishment of WTO, the external environment has changed. For the first time, agriculture and textiles and clothings have been included under the multilateral trade discipline. Increasing foreign direct investment and raising India's share in the world exports are essential, if India wants to achieve a sustainable GDP growth of seven per cent. This indicates that India has no option but to globalise. Success of globlised economy is in its ability to sustain competitive efficiency. Competitive efficiency can be enhanced through right reform measures. The right reform measures of liberalisation would provide stimulus to agriculture to improve its productive efficiency. Such improvement would enhance value addition activities through agro-processing and exports of agricultural and agro-based products. These activities, in turn, would increase income and employment in the industrial processing sector. Agriculture would also benefit through better returns to its produce owing to increase the demand. Hence globalising agriculture through liberalisation has the potential to transform the subsistence agriculture in to commercialized agriculture and to improve the living conditions of the rural community.

Though the WTO Agreement on Agriculture (AoA) came into force in 1995 several concerns have been raised only after the virtual removal of the quantitative restrictions (QRs) on agricultural imports with effect from 2001-2002. To a large extent, these reactions explain the hike in customs duties on a wide range of agriculture products in the union budget for 2001-2002. It is also note worthy that the Exim Policy of 2001-02, despite removing QRs on practically all agricultural commodities, had sought to hedge this liberalisation with its own systems of 'checks and balances'. Meanwhile, India has also taken up certain important concerns, relating to food and livelihood security in the current round of negotiations on the AoA.

Agricultural Exports and Imports: During the Reform Period

India's share of world trade at the time of independence stood at two per cent, but gradually went down to 0.4 per cent by the mid 90's. Right now, this stands somewhat corrected at 0.7 per cent.

India faced a critical year in 1998-99 when export growth declined to 5.1 per cent. However, there was a sharp turnaround in 1999-2000 when exports grew 13.2 per cent. During April-December 2000-01, exports recorded a 20.63 percent growth in dollar terms, against 10.3 percent during the same period of the previous year.

The value of agricultural exports at current prices increased from Rs. 79 billion in 1991-92 to Rs. 252 billion in 1998-99. As a percentage of the total exports, the share of agricultural sector increased from 17.9 in 1991-92 to 20.5 in 1996-97 and declined to 17.8 in 1998-99. Relaxation of control on export of non-basmati rice resulted in its large exports. However, the value of rice export has been fluctuating over a period of time for two reasons. First, India has a relatively large share in world rice exports and hence her export volume would have effect on the world price. Second, world border price of rice is subject to price fluctuations. India's export potentials are high in fruits and vegetables, processed vegetables, floriculture products and meat products but to realise this potential, investments in post-harvest and processing technologies and storage and efficient transportation arrangements are necessary.

India's import of agricultural products in 1998-99 was only Rs. 101 billion as against its export value of Rs. 252 billion during 1998-99. It may be noted that the value of edible oil import alone amounted to 71 per cent of the value of agricultural imports in 1998-99, otherwise our import dependence on agriculture is lower.

There is some concern about whether India can increase its share in world exports from 0.6 to 1.0 per cent or more by export led growth in agriculture and other sectors. The prospects of growth in agricultural exports depend partly on our policies and partly on the removal of protectionist policies pursued by developed countries.

An export target of four per cent of world exports is achievable if the government creates and enabling policy environment for our exporters and bargains effectively in multilateral trade negotiations. It is believed that India has a comparative advantage in many agricultural and agro-based products. This advantage is yet to be fully exploited. It may also be noted that the import intensities of these sectors are low compared to other products and services and hence, most of the export earnings from these sectors are available to finance other external payments.

Even we are leading in the production of many crops in the world, for most of the crops India's average yield rates are below the world average yields and far below the highest yield rates obtained in some countries. Further, within India itself we observe large variations in average yields rates among states. Even within a state we observe large inter-farm variations. Most farms do not operate on their production frontiers due to various reasons. India's agricultural trade policy regime in the past was dualistic. Exports of plantation crops and a few commercial crops were free from export restrictions, but exports of essential commodities, particularly food products were subject to bans, quotas and other restrictions. Complete removal of quantitative restrictions by end of March 2001 will provide an opportunity for our farmers and agro-based industries to tap the world markets.

Trade liberalisation also provides many other benefits such as scale economies because of increase in market size; knowledge of demand characteristics in foreign markets; information about new technologies, processes and products; and cost reductions and quality improvements in products because of international competitiveness. Thus, opportunities do exist. Also, in the Indian context, the gains from trade can arise because of (a) movement to the existing production possibility frontiers (due to technical efficiency), (b) movement along the existing frontiers (because of new trading opportunities), and (c) upward shifts of the frontiers (due to learning, application of improved technologies and adoption of better farming practices).

Conclusion

WTO dictated globalisation is a challenge to policy makers in the sense that there is need for a change from the inward looking and state directed policy regime to an out-word oriented ward oriented and market driven policy regime. Food security and environmental sustainability have

Table 15.1: Commodity Composition of Agricultural Exports

(Rs. crores)

Commodity	*1991-92*	*1992-93*	*1993-94*	*1994-95*	*1995-96*	*1996-97*	*1997-98*	*1998-99*
Rice (Basmati)	499	801	1,061	858	851	1,248	1,674	1,866
Rice (Others)	256	175	225	323	3,717	1,925	1,600	4,335
Wheat	127	10	—	31	367	698	—	3
Pulses	—	53	74	90	132	132	355	219
Groundnut	7	8	171	99	231	326	557	122
Cashew	672	745	1,045	1,242	1,236	1,285	1,384	1,610
Sesame and Niger Seeds	102	116	74	142	257	275	334	325
Cotton Raw and Waste	306	182	654	141	204	1,575	840	224
Fruits and vegetables	349	312	414	489	569	621	622	590
Processed vegetables	—	—	—	79	143	117	109	164
Floriculture products	15	15	19	29	60	63	78	103
Sugar and Molasses	157	354	178	62	506	1,078	248	23
Spices	372	393	569	612	794	1,202	1,408	1,617
Coffee	332	376	546	1,052	1,503	1,427	1,622	1,703
Tea	1,212	977	1,059	975	1,171	1,037	1,876	2,302
Meat and preparation	231	257	345	403	627	709	803	760
Poultry and Dairy products				49	59	124	107	99
Total agri. and allied products	7,878	8,770	12,609	13,269	20,442	24,363	24,626	25,224
Total Exports	44,042	53,688	69,749	82,673	1,06,353	1,18,817	1,30,100	1,41,604
Share of agricultural export in total exports	17.9	16.3	18.1	16.0	19.2	20.5	18.8	17.8

Source: CMIE, 1998.

Table 15.2: Commodity Composition of Agricultural Imports

(Rs. crores)

Commodity	1991-92	1992-93	1993-94	1994-95	1995-96	1996-97	1997-98	1998-99
Wheat	—	710	126	5	10	404	971	940
Cereal preparation	162	182	110	83	69	83	90	32
Pulses	255	334	567	593	686	890	834	404
Cashewnuts	267	376	483	691	760	688	744	693
Edible oil	248	167	167	624	2,262	2,929	2,733	7,131
Spices	—	—	76	55	74	97	103	127
Total agricultural products	785	1,701	1,335	3,967	3,685	4,865	6,228	10,137
Total Imports	47,851	63,375	73,101	89,971	1,22,678	1,38,920	1,51,554	1,76,099
% of agriculture in total imports	1.64	2.68	1.83	4.41	3.00	3.50	4.10	5.76

Source: CMIE, 1998.

Table 15.3: India's Shares in World Exports: Agricultural and Agro-based Products

Commodity	*1990*		*1995*		*1996*		*1997*	
	US$ million	*Share (%)*	*US$ million*	*Share (%)*	*US$ million*	*Share (%)*	*US$ million*	*Share (%)*
Meat and meat preparations	77	0.2	183	0.4	195	0.4	196	0.4
Fish, crustaceans and molluscs and preparations	521	1.6	994	2.1	1,111	2.3	1,116	2.3
Cereals and cereal preparations	285	0.6	1,576	2.7	1,244	1.8	1,250	2.1
Rice	254	6.4	1,362	18.6	894	12.1	898	12.6
Vegetables and Fruits	400	0.8	682	1.0	666	0.9	668	0.9
Sugar, sugar preparations and honey	21	0.1	156	0.8	308	1.6	309	1.6
Coffee, tea, co-coa, spices and manufactures	842	4.0	973	2.9	939	2.8	944	2.7
Feeding stuff for animals	336	2.2	706	3.4	997	4.1	1,002	4.0
Tobacco and tobacco manufactures	145	0.8	113	0.5	186	0.7	187	0.7
Oilseeds and oleaginous fruits	83	0.8	158	1.2	188	1.2	189	1.1
Leather, leather manufactures and dressed for skins	832	6.3	716	3.1	616	2.5	618	2.5
Textile yarn, fabrics. made-up articles	2,180	2.1	4,360	2.6	4,937	3.0	4,959	2.9
Total exports	18,143	0.5	31,108	0.6	32,704	0.6	32,636	0.6

Source: Economic Survey, 1999-2000, pp. S-95 and S-96.

to be safeguarded. Globalisation of Indian agriculture would provide an opportunity to India to increase her share in world exports. For this, the requirement is to increase the productions of Indian agriculture with low cost technology adoption. Policies strengthening the two way linkages between agriculture and industries would help to make the sector more dynamic. The need of the hour is to explore the opportunities in the globalised context.

REFERENCES

1. *K.P. Kalirajan, G. Mythili, U. Shankar (2001)* "Accelerating Growth through Globalisation of Indian Agriculture—*MacMillan, New Delhi.*
2. *A Damodaran*—"WTO Agriculture Agreement, Common Property Resources and Income Diversification Strategy"—*Economic and Political Weekly, September 22, 2001.*
3. *Baldev Raj Nayar* "Opening Up and Openness of Indian Economy". Economic and Political Weekly, September, 15, 2001.
4. Chandan Sengupta—*"Conceptualising Globalisation: Issues and Implications"* EPW, August, 18, 2001.

16

WTO and Indian Agriculture–Abstract

A.R Viswanath

Abstract

WTO aims at creating a liberal and open trading system, under which business enterprises from member countries can trade with each other, under conditions of fair and undistorted competition. Accordingly, the 'Agreement on Agriculture' under WTO provided for a liberal approach to export and import of agricultural commodities. As per its provision, India has already removed the quantitative restrictions on the import of various agricultural commodities.

Under this scenario, some of the far reaching implications on agriculture are highlighted below:

1. The Indian market has faced with the problem of low cost import of most of the agricultural commodities from several countries, which has caused considerable anxiety among the domestic producers.

2. The gradual reduction in subsidies in a developing country like India as against the high level of subsidies provided by developed countries, results in high costs of production for comparable agricultural crops and affects adversely the growth of agriculture and allied exports in India.

3. Liberal import of agricultural commodities may create difficulties for supply-demand balance for essential commodities, especially foodgrains, in a developing country like India in the event of natural calamities like flood and drought.

4. The shift in cropping pattern from subsistence farming (labour intensive) into commercial or export-oriented farming (capital intensive) will adversely affect the employment opportunities in India.

5. Finally, increased investment in modernised and export-oriented agriculture would require reallocation of financial resources, which would pose a problem to our policy makers and planners, as they are already facing the fiscal deficit in their budgets.

Future Approach

1. The farmers', particularly small and marginal farmers, interests must be protected by providing infrastructural facilities such as cold storages, warehouses and testing laboratories for maintaining quality, etc.

2. Conducting marketing research, evolving a system of appropriate quality standards for major exportable agricultural commodities and pass them to the producers along with other marketing intelligence on a regular basis.

3. A careful strategy of agricultural development, i.e. modernisation of agriculture on the one hand and creation of more employment opportunities on the other hand, is the need of the hour in a developing country like India.

4. Last, but not least, a programme to revitalise the cooperative marketing system through a proper management and constitution with genuine growers

participation, both in management and decision making process, is necessary. This will go a long way in interacting with the market with better information on prices, purchase terms and market practices.

17

Karnataka's Agriculture and WTO An Analysis of the Position of Agriculture, Horticulture and Animal Husbandry

K.M. Veeraiah

A. Agriculture

Agriculture plays an important role in Karnataka's economy. It is contributing a substantial part to the state domestic product (about 28.2%), it is the largest source of employment (about 67%). Karnataka is the eighth largest state having 190.5 Lakh hectares, out of which cultivated area is about 108 lakh hectares. Agricultural crops constitute about 89% of the total cropped area. About 24% of gross area under agricultural crops irrigated and the remaining area of 76% is cultivated under rainfed conditions.

Karnataka has an advantage in agriculture due to the existence of ten agro-climatic zones, different soil types, bimodal rainfall pattern and irrigation potential. It has potential for growing varieties of crops. There is a tremendous scope for watershed management. Strong public and private sector network for input supply is available.

Karnataka has achieved self sufficiency in food grains, cotton and sugar production. There is a marginal shortfall in oil seeds production and only about 50% of requirement of pulses are produced. According to 2001 census, the population of the state is 5,27,33,958. State has developed a professional extension service and pioneered technology of watershed development model for the whole country. Inspite of all these achievements there is a big gap that still exists between research potential and present productivity levels.

Increasing trends in area and production has been observed in case of rice, maize, sugarcane and tobacco. Especially, in case of maize about 100% jump in area and 20% increase in yield has been observed. Even though fluctuations in area in case of jowar, ragi and wheat has been observed, production has been maintained due to increase in yields.

About 95 lakh hectares of the gross cultivated area is rainfed. Tremendous scope exists for sustaining and increasing agricultural production on a long term basis through watershed approach. So far only 13 lakh hectares have been treated under watershed development programmes. Financial resources needed for watershed development projects are considerably low compared to development of irrigation facilities. Irrigation development at a greater pace may help increase irrigated area from the present level of 29 lakh hectares to maximum potential of 49 lakh hectares.

Average size of holding which was 2.41 hectares in 1985-86 has reduced to 1.95 hectares in 1995-96. It is difficult to sustain production and productivity levels in these holdings due to their uneconomic size.

Agricultural statistics of 1996-97 indicate that state contributes about 4.6% of total food grains to national food basket. In case of pulses, oil seeds, cotton, sugarcane and tobacco the contribution towards national production is about 5.1%, 7.2%, 8.9%, 10.3% and 9.7% respectively.

In case of rice, the yield in the state is above the national average on par with Andhra Pradesh and below Tamilnadu yield levels. State's average yields of jowar, bajra are above the national and neighbouring state's averages. Karnataka occupies the first position in the productivity of maize in the country. In case of sugarcane and cotton the yields are above the national levels. In case of pulses and oil seeds yields state is lagging behind the national average. Food production in the state has increased from 71 lakh tons in 1989 to 100 lakh tons in 1999.

B. Horticulture

Karnataka endowed with varied topography, agro-climatic conditions and enterprising farming community has been in fore front in respect of horticultural development in the country. Horticulture sector which includes fruits, vegetables, mushroom, floriculture, medicinal and aromatic plants has established its credibility for improving productivity of land, generating employment, raising economic status of farmers and entrepreneurs, enhancing exports and above all providing nutritional security to the people.

Most of the developments that have taken place in this sector have been in the last 12 years. Their impact has been visible in terms of increase in area, production and export of fruits, plantation, floriculture and spice crops. Between 1987-88 and 1997-98 the areas under horticultural crops has increased from 11.56 Lakh hectares to 17.18 Lakh hectares.

C. Animal Husbandry

The bountiful and diversified agro-climatic conditions prevailing in Karnataka have rendered a decisive advantage for the successful adoption of animal husbandry activities. Livestock rearing plays a vital role in the state's rural economy in supplementing family incomes and providing employment to rural poor. Animal husbandry sector has achieved a great success since independence.

Impact of WTO on Agriculture in Karnataka

World Trade Organisation came into existence on 1st Jan. 1995. Since it's inception it spreads both desirable and undesirable effects on Karnataka's agriculture. Agriculture and allied activities like horticulture and animal husbandry have been by and large protected from outside market forces through import and export restrictions. However, under new global agreement this scenario cannot continue. As India is committed to lift restrictions under the WTO agreement, time bound removal of quantitative curbs on import of agricultural, horticultural and animal husbandry products and other barriers to domestic market access will takes place sooner or later. This will require domestic products to compete with imported items. It is therefore necessary to ensure that not only production should continue to grow, but do so in cost effective manner.

Implications of WTO agreement on the livestock sector in Karnataka due to its congenial agro-climatic conditions, the poultry industry would attract the entry of well-known brands of Kentucky and McDonalds much more aggressively. Such fast food companies naturally steadily change consumers preferences in urban areas and influence integration of poultry industry.

It is feared that farmers will not be in a position to compete with external world as their competitive strength is low. This is likely to manifest itself in terms of low agricultural prices. Alternately there may be a shift from food production to commercial production resulting in shortage in food products and food crops and also affecting the food security for vulnerable sections of people. Since western agriculture enjoys high element of subsidy vis-a-vis India. It is likely that a dumping process may set in Karnataka.

Farmers Suicide and WTO

The researches indicate that there is no definite correlation between farmers suicides and WTO agreement. The farmers suicides are mainly due to inherent weaknesses of farmers. To mention a few of other reasons the incomplete land reforms, inadequate supply of credit to farmers, poor electricity supply, inefficient marketing facilities, lack of storage facilities, and above all conspicuous absence of crop insurance are bogging Karnataka's agriculture. In fact, there is no scientific agricultural policy as such in Karnataka which can effectively help agriculturists to become competitive. The agricultural policy which exists does not address the basic issues of farmers. Much less said about National agricultural policy is better. This is being so attributing WTO policies to the suicides of farmers proves totally misfounded. Rather, it may be well established that the disarray of governments attitudes and measures are responsible for increasing farmers suicides.

Suggestions

To protect the agriculture from the threats of WTO following suggestions are offered.

1. Participation of the state in policy discussions at the centre and preparation of a similar policy in the state government with full participation from district levels.

2. Seeking of funds under EXIM policy from the centre for development of complementary export related infrastructure such as roads connecting the production centres with ports, research and development of cold chains for agro-exports, development of minor ports.

3. Maize, groundnut seeds, nigar seeds, chillies, mangoes, pomegranates, grapes, lime, flowers, garlics, cashewnuts, coffee, onion, potato and vegetable seeds have been identified as requiring special attention on market channelling and processing.

4. Steps to be taken to educate the exporters in terms of the requirements under special safeguard measures and plug to sanitary measures from the view of destination countries.
5. Utilisation of bounded duty provisions to our advantage.
6. Urging government of India to take into account the domestic cost of production of crops and agricultural commodities while fixing the import tariff.
7. Establishment of a nodal agency at the apex level of the Ministry of Agriculture, Government of India and another at each state head quarters, linking the export houses in each of the state with that at the Agriculture Ministry.
8. Comprehensive Crop Insurance scheme has to be introduced to cover all crops.
9. The sound agricultural policy has to be formulated which addresses the issues of the farmers.
10. Correct price policy has to be formulated to protect farmers from price collapse.

Part—III
WTO and Indian Labour Service Sector Industry

Part—III

WTO and Indian Labour Service Sector Industry

18

WTO and India's Perspective on Labour Standards

D. S. Leelavathi

Since the inception of World Trade Organisation (WTO) International Labour Standards (ILS) have become a bane of contention between the developed and developing countries. ILS as such are unopposed and hardly there is any controversy relating to freedom of association of labourers, right to collective bargaining, prohibition of forced labour, equality of treatment and non-discriminations in employment, minimum age of employment etc. However, the ILS issue became controversial when a few rich developed countries try to impose such standards on developing countries through WTO forum. Imposing of sanctions against noncompliance with such standards, has made the situation much worse. However, these standards have human rights dimension and also constitute the fundamental framework for the exercise of labour rights.

The objective of the paper is to analyse the Indian perspective of WTO's social clause particularly of labour standards. However in general, it speaks of the thinking of all developing countries of the world regarding ILS. As a prelude to the discussion of labour standards, a brief understanding of both WTO and International Labour Organisation (ILO) is very much essential.

World Trade Organisation

Next to new economic policy, WTO is the most widely debated and highly politicised issue since its inception on Jan. 1, 1995 in Marrakesh, as a successor of GATT. The overriding objectives of WTO are to help trade flow smoothly, freely, fairly, predictably and transparently. Thus, WTO is based on the principle of comparative cost advantage which ensures optimum utilisation of world resources and enabling the consumers world over to choose the best quality goods at affordable prices. It incorporates Dunkel proposals in respect of international trade and trade related matters. WTO has 144 members, including China and accounting for 90% of the world trade. All WTO decisions are taken by the entire membership, typically by consensus. Though, a majority note can be taken, it has not happened since WTO replaced GATT. The top decision making level is the ministerial conference which happens once in two years and the coming will be at Mexico. At the heart, of the system—known as the Multi Trading System—are the WTOs agreements negotiated and signed by the members. The complete set of rules runs into 30,000 pages and consists of 60 agreements and commitments which are technically called as schedules.

WTO and India

No doubt, as a member of WTO, India has certain benefits but there are several serious short comings too. Some issues have still remained unresolved and on several lines, India still need to make efforts to maximise gains from new trade order. Trade in agricultural goods and services is to be brought within the scope of negotiations with the aim of eliminating barriers to trade on these sectors. The inclusion of trade related matters such as in respect of domestic investment measures and intellectual property rights makes trade transactions to influence domestic policies of India. In this wake, top world MNCs entered India, demanding a liberal treatment. Trade without barriers is expected as a result of which the quantitative restrictions have gone from April 1, 2001 and a sort of market-led globalisation is operating at present. India is benefitted from the expansion of export sector and increasing exports of some services. However, WTO still demands competitive efficiency and efficient resource management from India. But, with regard to trade in services, the developed countries have a competitive edge.

With regard to multi-fibre agreement, India has a comparative advantage in textiles and clothing, but quota restrictions on export adversely affect Indian exports. The current efforts of developed countries to link some social issues with trade adversely affect the exports of India. Similarly, insufficient provision for agricultural subsidies, small farmers and the poor, inappropriateness of patenting living organisms, unequal competition etc. have neutralised the spread effects in India.

International Labour Organisation

ILO is one of the oldest organisations which came into existence in 1919 for improving labour standards throughout the world and for uniting the world labour force. With the birth of UNO in 1945, to maintain world peace, security and social justice, ILO became much more powerful and active. Today, it has emerged as one of the strongest branches of the UN tree. The preamble of the constitution of ILO states that universal peace can be established on the basis of social justice and social justice can be established on the basis of international agreement. Humanitarian, Idealistic and Utilitarian standards of thought have combined together to create ILO. The labour standards set by ILO constitute the foundation of labour and social security laws in all its member countries. The famous Philadelphia declaration i.e. "Labour is not a commodity, it has to be handled with utmost care and importance.." is the corner stone of labour laws of the entire world. ILO functions through, International Labour Conference, the Governing Council and International Labour Office.

ILO and India

The relationship between India and ILO dates back to the day of its birth in 1919. The Indian delegation attended the first International Labour Conference at Washington. Since then, India is playing a very active role in the formulation of ILS. India's association with ILO reflects the aspirations of the developing countries in general and the countries within the Asian region in particular. The Indians on the staff of ILO have increased over the years and have been prominent in the inner counsels of the administrative machinery at the ILO heard quarters at Geneva.

The impact of ILO on evolving the labour code in India is quite significant since all the major labour laws in India date from 1919 onwards. Similarly, the influence of ILO on the Indian Trade Union Movement is also significant and it coincided with the birth of ILO. Thus, since its inception, ILO has been involved with a wide range of activities on the Indian soil like productivity movement, abolition of child labour, protection of unorganized labour, poverty alleviation, technical cooperation activities, employment programmes, protection of women workers etc. Even in the present context of liberalisation, ILO is playing a very useful role of diffusing labour tensions and in advising and assiting the government in formulating effective and feasible labour policies. Infact, ILO has a tremendous potential in smoothening the process of labour restructuring in the context of structural adjustment programme. Its role in providing the safety net to the affected workers and their rehabilitation can never be underestimated.

Of 175 conventions adopted by the ILO so far India has ratified only 35 conventions. Although, the record is not quite impressive, the extent of country's compliance with ILS cannot be measured in terms of formal ratification alone, while ratification is important, inability to ratify a convention in all its details may often be due to difficulties of technical or administrative nature. Further, it needs to be stated that, some of the conventions are enshrined in the Indian constitution and are also recognized to a greater extent by the legal provisions in the respective labour laws.

The Singapore meet of ILO in 1996 set aside the social clause and declared that all nations should accept the basic ILO standards. This was agreeable to India and it has ratified already some of the core ILO conventions

International Labour Standards

ILS setting and their observance are the most important among the activities of ILO. They are generally in the form of conventions and recommendations adopted by the apex body of the organisation namely international labour conference, while conventions are the basic standard setting instruments, the importance of recommendations cannot be over looked for these provide guidance for national action. These standards endeavour to help the member countries develop socio-economically, in a manner conducive to the promotion of social justice and improvement of the quality of life of the working population.

ILS are adopted by the tripartite constituents and technical and advisory services are also available to member countries which wish assistance not only for implementation but even at the standard setting stage. The labour standards cover many areas of labour policy of relevance to member countries and ought to be seen as a set of goals for achievements. These standards provide a stimulus to national action in formulating labour and social security policy and bringing about improvements in the existing labour and social laws. They have been a source of inspiration to governments employers and employees associations and the NGOs. The member countries are free to select the standards which are relevant and useful for them in promoting social and labour welfare.

ILS evolved on the basis of International Conventions have the force of international law of the ratifying countries. The system has weathered the challenges of the great depression, the rise of fascism, II World War, decolonisation of the developing world and more recently the collapse of communism. Although conceived in the colonial era, it has evolved into a system with universal coverage that is reflected in the ILO's present membership size. At present, ILO is focussing on rationalising its operations and setting new priorities to rejuvenate its efforts at making ILS enforceable. To this end, ILO would concentrate on building pressure on government to implement their obligations under various conventions they are party to it.

Major ILO conventions which have formed the base for ILS include:

1. Right to form trade unions. Convention No. 87.
2. Right to collective bargaining. C.No. 38.
3. Prohibition of bonded labour and forced labour—C.No. 29 and 10 respectively.
4. Prevention of discrimination in employment—C.No. 111.
5. Equal pay for equal work—C.No. 100.
6. Abolition of child labour—C.No. 138.
7. Defining worst form of child labour—C.No. 182 etc.

However, of all the conventions, C.No. 138 and 182 are most widely debated ones under the banner of social clause of WTO. These have been ratified by relatively a few governments and none of the countries of Asia, including India has ratified this convention. Obviously, in these countries child labour is of very serious magnitude and its abolition in one stroke is almost impossible.

In tune with a shift in the development paradigm since 1980, and the emergence of WTO there has also been a change in the nature of debate concerning ILS. In the context of increasing globalisation along with flexibalisation of labour market, ILS have assumed added significance on account of the following reasons:

1. There are still pockets of poor and morally unacceptable labour conditions in low income countries. Where the primary agenda of labour is unfulfilled.
2. ILS are to be seen in a much more dynamic context of human rights.
3. The revolution in the global communication system has created an awareness among the public regarding the appalling conditions of child and women labour, especially in the export processing zones.

In brief, both public awareness and political pressure have contributed to the raising of the issue of social clause in the international trade agreements by some developed countries. Thus, WTO provided a channel for linking trade with labour standards, especially under the leadership of Uncle Sam.

WTO and Social Clause

The group of 24 especially USA has been repeatedly demanding since the beginning of eighth round of GATT, inclusion of "Social Clause" in the WTO negotiations which may allow them to impose restrictions on the products originating from the countries which don't comply with a specified set of minimum core labour and environmental standards. The developing countries, however, are forcefully opposing these demands as they represent for them a new form of disguised non-tariff barriers which would be very harmful to their exports, in which they possess comparative advantage due to the availability of cheap labour. There is nothing wrong in improving labour standards to a level approved by ILO, but these must not be used by the developed countries as an excuse for imposing restrictions to protect the inefficiencies of some of the sectors. After WTO has emerged the issue of trade and the enforcement of minimum labour standards was taken seriously by the north due to frequent occurrence of structural crises and unacceptable high levels of unemployment in their economies, which have been attributed wrongly due to the unfair relative advantage enjoyed by the developing countries. The aim of this demand is to prevent social dumping and is now being pushed with great vigour by major industrialised countries. But WTO is not the right platform which should enforce social laws and labour standards and is also impossible to equalise labour standards when the levels of productivity and culture differ markedly between nations and within a nation at different stages.

Globalisation is not a matter of capital alone but is also influenced by the conditions of business operations. The developed countries argue that, the developing countries keep prices attractive and low usually through minimisation of labour cost rather than maximising the skill of labour, which amounts to exploitation. In the expanding export sector, more labour intensive production methods are used since the employees subcontract part of their production to small units where cheap labour is employed. Therefore, their natural argument is minimum labour standards should be set in the light of a more liberalised international policy.

Labour standards are endogenous to individual economies. They are culture specific and would be difficult to arrive at a universal moral consensus that could underpin a set of ILS. In the absence of this imposing labour standards, which evolved in the west, would constitute, political and cultural imperialism. Each country has an optimum level of labour standards within the given constraints. In such cases universalising labour standards would imply sub-optimal outcomes. At the same time, we should remember that member countries of ILO have almost accepted the universality of labour standards, but not willing to accept the same in the form of non-tariff barriers.

Similarly, labour standards are mainly a function of culture, degree of democracy and particularly the level of development. Low level of development is positively correlated with lower labour standards. And any effort to harmonise the labour standards at global level, without raising the level of development will erode the competitive advantage and hence gains from trade of developing areas. Infact, economic progress precedes social progress. Trade policy can be the second best or even the third best policy in this regard.

Paradigm of Social Clause

The idea of introducing social clause under WTO, is to achieve a set of ILS environmental concerns and human rights. However, realising ILS is as old as ILO itself, but what is new at present is politicisation of social clause for protectionist purposes under non-tariff barriers. The adherence to ILS would increase the cost of labour in labour surplus developing economies and thereby reduce their competitive efficiency. On the contrary, the proponents of social clause believe that it reduces exploitation of labour and provides for human rights. However, the developing countries suspect the ulterior motives of the rich countries in pushing ILS through social clause under WTO. Thus, the debate has laid the theoretical foundation for the critical analysis of ILS in the present day context.

The proponents of social clause in trade agreements argue that:

1. The linkage between labour standards and international trade reinvokes the ILS through trade sanctions.
2. Such links enable fair trade by eliminating unfair trade competition arising from labour exploitation.
3. It represents a moral concern over child labour and other exploitative labour conditions.
4. The existing system of ILS is inadequate in the context of globalisation.
5. It shows that not only the end result but even the means of production are also equally important.
6. Harmonisation of labour standards across the countries is necessary to ensure fairness and a level playing field in international trade relationship.
7. Unless, a strong public opinion is created against exploitative labour conditions, the labour standards in LDCs will never improve.

However, the developing countries including India oppose linking of trade with labour standards on the following grounds:

1. It would reduce the competitive edge of developing countries.
2. It is a disguised instrument of protectionism followed by rich countries.
3. It would violate the sovereignty of developing countries.
4. It is blind towards the ground realities of the pre-requisites to comply with ILS.

5. It is immaterial for the developed countries to worry about the source of relative cost differences.
6. There is no strong evidence to show that developing countries are actually keeping labour costs artificially low through the repression of labour standards.
7. The rich countries also have a comparative advantage with regard to capital, economies of scale, technology, a well developed infrastructure and market etc.
8. None of the concerns of the labour of developed countries are reflected in the core standards like jobless growth, increased casualisation of labour, reduction in social security, flexible work hours scarcity of decent jobs etc.

The above debate found its ugly expression in the Seattle negotiations in the fag end of 1999, which failed miserably on account of two issues namely labour and environmental standards.

Seattle and Labour Standards

The government prepared well for the Seattle show from November 30, to Dec. 3, 1999. But the negotiations failed miserably on account of too much pressure from developed countries to include social clause in the WTO to provide a non-tariff barrier and opposition from developing countries for the same. The assumption of rich countries is that, since ILO is a toothless organisation it cannot effectively implement the ILS through trade sanctions.

In the Seattle negotiation Mr. Bill Clinton stated "We will work with ILO on a new initiative to raise labour standards around the world. And this year (1999) we will lead the international community to conclude a treaty to ban the abuse of child labour in the world". However, the experts feel that the complex problem of child labour cannot be resolved easily by domestic and international sanctions. According to the recent estimate of ILO, approximately 250 to 300 million children work around the world. Of these the largest concentration is in Asia, Africa and Latin America. In India, for example, nearly 20% of the GDP is being contributed by child labour. Poverty is the main cause for child labour, its ban in one stroke would exacerbate the problem rather than helping to find solutions. A more realistic approach would be to create a situation whereby children in the developing countries will no longer have to work, where it would be worthwhile for them to attend the school, where the income of the parents will have to be sufficient to provide for the children. In a similar tone, the United Kingdom states that labour standards can be improved through economic growth and not through trade sanctions.

A recent statement entitled Third World Intellectuals and NGOs Statement against Linkage (TWINSAL) circulated by Prof. Jagadish. N. Bhagawati of Columbia University argues that "achieving trade and improving labour standards are both desirable goals. But assigning them to a single institution namely WTO, is like trying to kill two birds with one stone. Such a strategy is bound to miss both birds except the fluke."

Similarly, the CATO centre for trade policy studies of the United States infers that:

1. The use of sanctions as a means of enforcing social standards would undermine the WTO's central mission of trade liberalisation.
2. Labour and environmental regulations are internal matters that should be left to individual countries to determine.
3. WTO exaggerates the fact that lower labour standards give poor countries a significant

advantage in attracting global capital and gaining export markets.

4. The study emphasises that the new WTO round should not be seen as a system in which countries liberalise not merely to gain concessions from other countries but also to reap the economic rewards of their own liberalisation.

Mr. Ali Taqui, the Assistant Director of ILO while trying to clarify the controversy over social clause stated that low wages constitute a legitimate comparative advantage of developing countries. Further he said that it is impossible to ensure essential social protection to workers in an effective way while removing those constraints upon employers which impede economic efficiency.

The U.S. trade representative has called for a WTO working group on trade and labour, which would examine the issues like the effect of increased international trade on investment, on levels and composition of country's employment, the relationship between economic development, international trade and investment and implementation of core labour standards. If at all, the U.S. succeeds in setting up a working group for labour standards, then the developing countries would be at a great disadvantage. Therefore, the biggest challenge facing them is to keep non-trade issues out of WTO on the one hand and improving labour standards on the other.

Indian Perspective on Labour Standards

India has a fantastic legal frame work for the protection of labour and promotion of their welfare. There are 167 central and another 57 state labour legislations for the purpose. Moreover, ILO since its inception, has tremendous impact on the formulation of Indian labour laws. Therefore, the legal environment of labour is less wanting. Infact, some would argue that on account of too much of state intervention Indian labour market has become more rigid and hence less adaptable to SAP. At the same time our democratic set up and the Directive Principles of the State Policy under the Indian constitution, made the Indian organised labour class quite safe and secure. But the real problem lies in the vast unorganised labour on the one hand and inadequate and inefficient implementation of labour laws on the other. In case of conventions on occupational safety and health, although India has a large body of legislation, main difficulty in the way of ratification has been the lack of statutory cover to the economic activities in the unorganised sector. This problem has been compounded by the requirement of an extensive enforcement agency.

India is one of the first Asian country to ratify convention No. 144, concerning the tripartite consultations in labour matters. However, the socio-economic conditions prevailing in the country do not permit the expansion of social security to the extent prescribed by ILO. But the constitution imposes the duty on both the central and state governments to make effective provision for social security. At the same time, the government reviews the unratified conventions from time to time and examines whether it could be made to conform to the standards embodied in them.

The enforcement of ILO conventions and recommendations is the responsibility of central government, particularly the Ministry of Labour. The State governments, however, are responsible for the administering of labour laws and practice in respect of most of the industries. The enforcement of the labour laws itself comes under constant review by the tripartite machinery set up in various states. At the national level, apart from state Labour Ministers Conference, the tripartite bodies such as the Indian Labour Conference, standing Labour committee, Industrial committees on individual industries etc. have on their agenda an item relating to the review of labour laws. The above facts reveal that India has a very vast and strong legal environment to protect the interest of labour and the role of WTO in this regard through trade sanctions is uncalled for.

We have a reasonable foundation to oppose G-27, which is trying to push through international labour standards through WTO. This can be expressed in terms of the following arguments.

1. India has a very good net work of labour laws and they are good enough to protect the interests of labourers and promote their welfare. Their formulation, objectives, revision procedures are extremely reasonable. However, what we want is just their effective implementation. Therefore, imposing labour standards through trade sanction is an unwanted intrusion in the sovereignty of a nation.
2. Comparative advantage in labour cost is a feature of all labour surplus economies and this need not be construed as a violation of labour standards. Given the constraints, the labour class in the organised sector, is quite allright, although the standards cannot be compared with that of rich countries.
3. As per the demands and requirements of new world trade order we have considerably liberalised on trade and even removed the quantitative restrictions since April 2001. When such is the development, is it fair on the part of the powerful members of WTO to demand for the imposition of sophisticated non-tariff barriers in the name of labour standards?
4. India is the second largest democratic country in the world, with a strong and deep rooted welfare foundation, under several provisions of the constitution and the Directive Principles of the State Policy. Therefore, there is hardly any need

for the super imposition of any welfare measure from the outside element.

5. In India, 90% of the work force is in the unorganised and informal sector and just 10% is engaged in the organised sector. Therefore, naturally, bringing the entire labour force in the network of labour standards becomes too idealistic. However, it does not mean that we should not aim at it.
6. One of the foremost important requirements to cope up with the labour standards is, a higher rate of growth. Therefore, it is clear that if at all the rich are really interested in improving labour standards they should think in terms of helping the developing countries to increase their growth rate, instead of imposing trade sanctions.
7. When there is an international organisation called ILO to exclusively look into the labour standards there is no need to have a parallel organisation to perform the same duty.
8. We believe that gentle persuation, technical, financial, and advisory assistance go a long way in improving labour standards than imposing trade sanctions to conform to the labour standards.
9. With regard to the abolition of child labour, India has one of the best legal frame works, available in the developing countries. Apart from the central legislation, there are very effective measures taken by the state governments to abolish the same and also to protect them whenever possible. The role of NGOs is also quite significant in this regard. Therefore our stand is, WTO need not take unnecessary pains to abolish child labour by linking labour standards with trade.

10. At the same time, we cannot be indifferent towards labour standards altogether. Because, the export sector, which is growing very fast, and which has become a potential job creator, has to observe these labour standards at any cost. If not, they cannot make much head way in the global market.

Conclusion

Poor labour standards are essentially a problem of developing world. Blind opposition to any link between trade and labour standards would in the long long run hurt our interests. Globalisation and labour standards should go hand in hand. At the same time, any attempt to use trade to alter labour standards would necessarily affect developing countries. If India, like any other developing country, thinks that ILS are the domain of ILO, the stronger will be the impression that Indian goods are manufactured under abysmal labour standards. This will affect the brand equity of Indian products. Moreover, the Director General of ILO, has recommended the introduction of global system of "Social Labelling" to guarantee that internationally traded goods are produced under human conditions. Although the U.S. pressure is suspicious, developing countries are too weak to bargain. More than anything else, whether we like it or not, western markets are sensitive to labour standards.

The linkage issue calls for a more complex response than merely refusing to talk, Indian effort must be to ensure that the link does not take on a protectionist lure and in this juncture multilateral agreements need to be encouraged. Labour standards are really ethical questions of economic development but are to be left to individual countries. They can be enforced through national struggle and international solidarity and certainly not by trade sanctions. ILO is the right institutional trigger to let lose a wider consciousness on labour standards together with a strong national movement.

REFERENCES

1. U.N. U.N.O.—Sales No. E90, 1-12, 1990.
2. U.N. Europe Year Book, 1994. Vol. 1.
3. U.N. The Tree of Life—A exhibition of 50 years of the U.N. in India designed by France and France.
4. U.N. World Summit for Social Development, 1995.
5. NLI—ILS. Report of National Tripartite Seminar, New Delhi, 1992.
6. Nandeem and Mohsin-Child Labour and Social Clause; Dilemma in International Trade Agreements—Labour and Development. Vol. 2, No. 1, 1996.
7. Rodrik Dam—Has-globalisation Gone Too Far? Washington DC 1997.
8. Sunil Guha. Towards Industrial Dynamism and Harmony. Oxford and IBH 1994.
9. Eddy Lee—Globalisation and Labour Standards International Labour Review. Vol. 136, No. 2, 1997.
10. Alternate Economic Survey—AES Group, Rainbow Publication, Delhi 2000-2001.
11. Francis Cherunilam. Global Economy and Business environment. Himalaya Publications, New Delhi 2001
12. Lakshmidhara Mishra. Can of Liberalisation and Labour Rights Co-exist. Vol. 44. No. 1, Jan-Mar 2001.

Economic Times

1. 06-12-1999 WTO and Social Clause.
2. 07-12-1999 INT and Child Labour
3. 15-11-1999 The Fear of Labour Standards
4. 17-11-1999 Return to Labour Standards in WTO.
5. 19-11-1999 Too Weak to Negotiate
6. 30-11-1999 Indian Stand on Labour
7. 12-12-1999 Special Report on WTO and Seattle
8. 12-12-1999 No trade in Labour Yet.

19

Self Help Groups—Empowering the Vulnerable-Towards Sustainable Development

A. Jayakumar Shetty

Introduction

With the advent of WTO, there is a pressure on the economic policies regarding public expenditure on social sector and agriculture. In this backdrop, conservatively one can predict that in coming years government involvement in development will be marginalised. Hence, there is need to develop alternatives to prevent the onslaught of WTO implications on people involved in agriculture and allied sectors.

This paper in the context of WTO probes into the fall in social sector investment, credit flow to agriculture, small cultivators approaching money lenders. This suggests that there is a need to voluntary initiation to maintain the sustenance of agriculture and allied activities. Part I deals with social sector expenditure, reduced public investment in agriculture and glaring deficiency in the provision of bank credit etc. Part II deals with micro credit and rural poverty in general and micro credit policy in India. Part III deals with self help groups and progress of Pragathi Bhandhu Groups—a case study.

Part I

(a) Social Sector Expenditures in the 1990's

According to the recent Human Development Reports of UNDP, India has moved from the category of 'low' human development to that of 'medium' human development. Nevertheless, India's performance in the social sector is far from satisfactory (Dreze and Sen, cite in Mahendra Dev). Some people have claimed that one of the aims of the economic reforms is to withdraw the State from some of its economic activities, in order to step up expenditures for, and increase State involvement in the social sector. On the other hand, there have also been apprehensions that expenditures on social services and poverty alleviation programme would be adversely affected. A study (S Mahendra Dev and Jos Mooij) showed that as a proportion of GDP, the share of social sector expenditure has not increased during the reform period, except in 1999-2000. The shares in 1990's were lower than those of the 1980's. The most significant change, visible both at the centre and the states, is a shift away from rural development, starting from 1996-97. Within the rural development outlay at the Centre, there is a shift away from rural employment schemes to rural housing, water and rural roads. There is a shift from the traditional ways of addressing rural poverty to human development or basic needs intervention.

Indeed, since the mid-1990s a high proportion of Government expenditure has been allocated to the social sector, yet as a proportion of GDP, Social sector spending has not increased.

(b) Declining public investment in agriculture

Although private investment in agriculture was stepped up in the post-reform period of the 1990's in response to economic liberalisation of the economy (and favourable terms of trade,) real public investment continued to decline on account of fiscal compression and reduction in input subsidies. As a result, the development of infrastructure like irrigation, rural electrification, roads and markets has been a major causality (Hanumantha Rao C.H.)

The combined expenditure by the Centre and the State governments on agricultural research and education, which is the most important determinant of TFP in agriculture, stagnated around 0.5% of agricultural GDP over this period (PAL, JHA and Singh)

As the mid-term appraisal of the ninth five year plan points out "There is a strong compatibility between public and private investment, and inadequate public investment could lead to a 25% lower private investment as desired (GOI—Mid-term Appraisal of Ninth Five Year Plan)

(c) Deficiency in the provision of extension services

The glaring deficiencies in the provision of extension services in the recent period are revealed by the mid-term appraisal of the Ninth plan. It points out that the credit extended to agriculture from the commercial banks constituted around 12% to 13 % of the total net bank credit in recent years as against the target of 18% (P65).

The short falls in public investment and in the provision of agricultural service account for the failure of agricultural supplies to respond to the favourable incentive frame work created by macro economic reforms including trade liberalisation in the 1990's (Hanumantha Rao 2001). The average annual growth of GDP in agriculture and allied sector slowed down in the post reform period of 90's when compared to preceding decade, while growth of crop output, especially food grain output decelerated (GOI 2001). The experience of the 1990's clearly demonstrates that far from trade liberalisation dampening the performance of agriculture, the failure of public investment and effort is responsible for the inability to benefit from trade liberalisation by stepping up and diversifying agricultural output in a cost effective way.

(d) Small cultivators and new technology

After the introduction of the new Economic Policy in 1991, the cost of cultivation has gone up due to increase in input prices. Small producers resort to marketing the - distress surplus and increasing costs of cultivation render them more dependent on large landowners for high interest loans. In a scenario of unequal distribution of land and resources, embrace of new technology by small cultivator far from leading to greater income diffusion, deepen their dependence on those with economic, social and political power (Kalpana Wilson,).

The major effort on domestic front for ensuring the viability of Indian agriculture has to be focussed on raising productivity by stepping up public investment and by accelerating the evolution and adoption of cost reducing technologies. Institutional reforms for augmenting and managing the infrastructure and other services through participatory processes such as Water Users Association, Water Shed Development Committees and Self Help Groups. Such reforms at the grass roots levels hold the key to improving the viability of Indian agriculture in the wake of trade liberalisation (Hanumantha Rao 2001).

Pragathi Bandhu Program i.e. SHGs of small and marginal farmers along with labour exchange program has emerged as the effective program for addressing the problem of rural poverty and agricultural backwardness.

Part-II

Micro credit and rural poverty

It is claimed that NGO led micro credit is an effective and financially viable alternative to the existing method of addressing rural poverty through the provision credit. Over emphasis on micro credit, as part of the program of NGO, even to the neglect of other developmental measures such as agricultural, technical, extension services, education, skill training, has been questioned. Micro credit is necessary for the poor to take up income generating activities but it is no panacea. NGO's should provide micro credit along with other services (Mukbul M. Ahmed).

The emergence of micro credit as an alternative in recent years has questioned the fundamentals of the rural credit system in the developing countries for channelling the credit to the poor. Following this transformation even the substitution of the existing rural credit system is being recommended. A study (Pallavi Chavan, R. Ramakumar) shows that micro credit programs have been able to bring about a marginal improvement in the beneficiaries income. However, the beneficiaries have not gained much by way of technological improvements, given the emphasis on 'survival skill'. It also indicated that NGO led micro credit programs and institutions such as Grameena Bank have been successful in reaching their target groups of poor more effectively than the state led programmes and institutions. Micro credit programs have generated positive change in the income of beneficiaries, but this change has only been marginal. There has not been any discernible contribution to the improvement on skills, and technology adopted by the beneficiaries.

Micro credit policy in India

Indian Banking policy attempted to involve the public banking network in the provision of micro credit to the poor through the SHGs. A paper by NABARD has referred to the Indian policy on micro credit as "relationship banking" against "Parallel banking" in other countries (Jayaraman).

Banks adopt the approach of group lending and peer monitoring for lending to the SHGs. Such a policy has three variants. In variant I, the public banks act as a SHG promoting institution. In variant II, public banks and borrowers (SHGs) are linked through facilitating agencies. In variant III, both the facilitating and intermediating functions are played by the NGO's. Nearly 70% of all the SHGs were of the kind of variant second, while 16% and 14% of the groups belong to variant III and I respectively (Annual report 2000-2001, NABARD).

Part-III

Self-Help Groups—Empowering the vulnerable towards the sustainable development

It has been accepted that one of the prominent problems of the rural poor is the inadequacy of the institutional credit. To expect the system to achieve the social objectives of providing the credit to the poor and the marginal farmers, which requires intensive work in the field in order to identify the potential borrowers and advice and follow-up, utilisation and recovery was unrealistic.

An analysis of the credit needs of the poor revealed that they require small but regular and timely loans for consumption, whereas their options were restricted to programs designed and approved by the government which did not cater to these needs. There was no mechanism to tune the size of projects and estimate to the micro situation. Banks schedule of recovery did not conform to actual trends in returns. Banks finance projects on the basis of viability. But the farmers prefer to invest on a package of options where the risk is spread rather than in one large income-generating project. Further, the wide gap between the numbers of loans a bank branch of a bank managed and the actual need also indicate that the system is inappropriate. For example, one branch has advanced a maximum of 50 loans under the anti-poverty scheme during a year, while the 102 credit groups within this branch service area advanced over 5000 loans every year to the poor (Fernandes. A.P.-The Myrada experience—Alternate Management systems to savings and credit of the rural poor—p. 8). It is in this background of obtaining institutional credit becoming a bitter proposition for the rural poor that alternative sources of credit become important. This led to the emergence of 'Credit Management Groups. initiated by NGO-MYRADA in Tamilnadu, A.P., and Karnataka, `Self Help Groups. by SKDRDP in Belthangady taluk in Karnataka State, SHGs by public Banks.

Self Help Groups

A Self Help Group (SHG) is a homogeneous group of rural poor voluntarily formed to save whatever amount they can conveniently save out of their earnings and mutually agree to contribute to a common fund of the Group to be lent to the members. The SHGs are generally promoted by voluntary organisations to ameliorate the problems of the economically weaker sections of the society especially in the villages.

Data on SHGs show that the number of SHGs formed through public banks has grown rapidly in the 1990's (Annual Report, 2000-01, NABARD). However, the evaluation paper by NABARD makes the case that variant III is likely to be found more convenient by Banks for credit linkage in the coming years, when very large number of SHGs would be required to be linked by small sized branches of banks" (Ibid. p. 17).

SHG programme is recognized as the highly effective experiment in rural development. Importance of SHG hails from ensuring progress by effective utilisation of the resources and creating awareness among the rural poor families about their capacity.

SKDRDP an NGO has organized SHGs in the Belthangady and Karkal taluks of DK and Udupi districts of Karnataka State in a novel way befitting to the local environment and conditions in the name of Pragathi Bandhu. The concept of "Pragathi Bandhu" has opened a new horizon in the all round development of the poor farm families in the rural area.

Genesis of Pragathi Bandhu Programme

With the assistance provided by the Sri Kshetra Dharmasthala Rural Development Project (SKDRDP) the small and marginal farmers were able to build sufficient infrastructure in their land. For further improvement they did not have the credit facilities. Recognising the fact that credit was the missing link in the development chain, the SKDRDP encouraged formation of homogenous SHGs known as Pragathi Bandhu Groups. These SHGs were organised with the following objectives.

- Sustainable development of rural resources
- Promotion of self dependence and mutual help
- Promotion of thrift
- Provide access to informal and dependable source of credit
- Enhancement of general standard of living

Mode of organisation: Each SHG consists of five to 10 members having equal land holdings and economic status

Labour exchange: Labour exchange is an unique feature of PBP. Human resources are effectively utilised in the development programmes through labour exchange. Each week on the specified meeting day, all the members of SHG meet at the farm of a member farmer and contribute labour for his farm development. The SHGs are able to carry out all their farming/developmental activities through labour exchange programme without much financial burden on the beneficiaries. This had firmed up bonds of peer support. It also ensures planned implementation of the development projects of each and every family due to exchange of skill and experience in agriculture and development.

Thrift: Every member saves Rs. 10/- per week.

Credit Management: The informal credit to the members is one of the most significant activities of the group. Based on the savings of the group, the group can borrow an amount equal to four times of their savings from any bank.

Repayment: The repayment is made on weekly basis

Utilisation: For proper utilisation of the loans and credit management, necessary training is imparted during the monthly meetings. The group sanctions loans to its members on the basis of need. However, priority is accorded to productive loans.

Federation of SHGs: The federation of PB groups plays a vital role in the growth and organisation of activities.

Progress of Pragathi Bandhu Groups—An Impact analysis: Pragathi Bandhu (Partners in Progress) programme is a new experiment in the area of SHGs by Shri Kshethra Dharmasthala Rural Development Project (SKDRDP). Pragathi Bandhu Programme (PBP) aims at achieving progress by ensuring effective utilisation of land resources, financial resources & human resources possessed by the rural poor families by involving them in three main activities like labour exchange, savings and credit management.

A field study was conducted to find out the impact of PBP in the last five years. A survey of 80 families of PBP revealed the following points.

- 61.25% of the P.B. members possess less than three acres of land and belong to the group of marginal farmers.

- Every family has completed on an average five developmental projects under labour exchange programme.
- Every family on an average has undertaken Rs. 25,525.00 worth of work under labour exchange and every family in the last five years worked 222 Mandays under LE programme.
- On an average every family has borrowed Rs. 12,642.00 and 94.06% of the loans are utilised for predetermined purpose.
- 100% punctuality in loan repayment and 52.75% borrowers repaid before the due date.
- Progressively shifted to commercial crops
- Land under irrigation increased by 40%
- Considerable increase in income—the number of families having less than Rs. 10,000 annual income has declined from 26 to 2.

Thus, PBP has facilitated the poor farmers to frame their own developmental plans and effectively exploit their resources. It has assisted in generating employment and ensuring effective utilisation of the available human resources. PBs have opened new horizons to the rural life by inculcating the habits of hard work, habit of thrift, free from bad habits and imbibing the qualities of leaders.

The new policy of the RBI and NABARD made it possible for the local banks to lend directly to the groups based on the group performance, as an institution is a welcome feature that will reduce the extent of dependency on the promoting voluntary agency.

Conclusion

Voluntary initiative in the form of SHGs with multiple functions like micro credit, thrift, labour exchange and assetisation are creating alternative for government led programmes and provide safety net under the conditions of WTO ravages. Post-reform scenario suggest that there is a need at domestic front to be united for alternative packages, which will complement the governments reduced role in the development activities.

REFERENCES

1. Chavan Pallavi, R. Ramakumar (2002): "Micro Credit and Rural poverty" EPW, March 2002
2. Dev. S. Mahendra and Jos Mooij (2002): `Social sector expenditure in the 1990's,' EPW, March 2, 2002
3. Fernandes A.P., "The Myrada Experience—Alternate management systems to savings and credit of the rural poor"
4. GOI (2000); Mid-Term Appraisal of Ninth Five year plan (1997-2002) Planning commission New Delhi
5. GOI (2001) Economic Survey 2000-2001, Ministry of Finance, New Delhi
6. Jayaram, "Micro Finance: Retrospect and Prospects", Occasional Paper—20, NABARD, Mumbai
7. Mukbul M. Ahmed (2000); 'Distant voices: Micro Credit Finance and views of the NGO Field Workers in Bangla Desh' Journal of Rural Development, Vol. 19(2) NIRD Hyderabad.
8. NABARD, Annual Report (2000-2001).
9. Pal, S.D. Jha and A. Singh (19771); `Agriculture Research and Education in India' NCAER, New Delhi.
10. Rao Hanumantha C.H. (2001): `WTO and Viability of Indian Agriculture', EPW, September 8, 2001.
11. SKDRDP (2001), Annual Report.
12. Wilson Kalpana (2002); 'Small Cultivators in Bihar and New technology' EPW, March 2002.

20

WTO—Strategic Implications For the Indian Business Unit

K. Balakrishnan

Introduction

The implications of international institutions and treaty obligations (IITOs) such as WTO, GATS, TRIPS and TRIMS for the Indian economy, Indian business and the working class have been commented upon by scholars in considerable depth. Similar attention has not been paid to the implications for the individual business unit (IBU)—what economists call micro-economic analysis. We consider in this paper the decision-making space that the IBU is confronted with in the changed scenario caused by WTO regime. For this purpose we consider only those IBUs where operational and strategic management controls vest with Indians, where the top management is physically located in India and where the bulk of operational revenues originate in India. Excluded therefore, are multinational businesses operating in India, NRI organisations with Indian operations, Indian multinationals and predominantly export oriented organisations. Being considered are small and medium enterprises (SMEs) and large business houses in the private sector. These account for the bulk of corporate contribution to GDP, exports, tax revenues and employment. The rationale for this choice system is the fact that the IITOs referred above operate essentially on the territorial principle co-terminus with national sovereignty. The decision space for the excluded categories is much larger with greater scope for constraint breaking. For the sectors being considered the exercise of strategic choice is now along a paradigm shift.

Organisation and Limitation

This paper is organised in three main sections. *Section 3* explores the universe of strategy options available to any IBU. *Sections 4 to 7* is a detailed analysis of each of these strategic options with respect to the various sub-sectors under manufacturing classified by type. The analysis considers the different impacts of IITOs on these sub-sectors and then arrives at a set of propositions which either forecasts the impact of IITOs or suggests action modifying its effects. *Section 8* is a broad set of policy prescriptions which is aimed at the Union Government and has as its objective the preservation and strengthening of the domestic Indian owned manufacturing sector.

The analysis does not consider the impact of IITOs on the service sector. The sub-sectors of the service industry are so varied—hospitality, health, retailing and distribution, logistics, education, entertainment etc.—that strategy implementation is quite varied across each of them. Each of these sectors, consequently, deserves to be addressed separately.

The Framework of Strategy Formulation

Strategy formulation begins with an analysis of the environment along four levels—the internal environment of the firm; the operating environment; the industry environment and the remote global/domestic environment. Environmental analysis leads to the choice of one among three generic and fourteen grand strategies. Let us first examine the impact of IITOs on environmental analysis.

The basic mandates of IITOs are essentially two. Firstly, the treatment of all businesses irrespective of origin-by-nationality on equal footing—this is the well-known free trade principle—and implies not only the dismantling of tariff barriers but also restraint on maximum tariffs. Secondly the realisation that free trade across national boundaries can be possible when not just the physical but also the intellectual properties of business enjoy judicial protection from arbitrary private or governmental infringement. Both these mandates are creating the paradigm shift in India—removal of tariff protection creates a new class of foreign based competition in the domestic market which is now to be faced. The hitherto extremely low level of intellectual property protection in India has resulted not only in rampant IPR violations and even entire business models based on such violation, but also widespread ignorance of what constitutes intellectual property. For the Indian IBU therefore neither geography nor internal process now contributes to boundary maintenance.

In the internal analysis of the firm the question that arises is whether any external IPR is being violated. The subsequent question is whether there is any internal IPR that needs protection. If the answer to the first question is in the affirmative, then transaction costs for the IBU are bound to rise. The bulk of Indian IBUs operate with knowledge available in the public domain and therefore the answer to the second is likely to be in the negative. In the minority of the cases where the answer to this question is positive then a careful examination is required of the kind of protection warranted by circumstances; legal protection is time-consuming and often prohibitively expensive. Access control methods quite often could be a temporary substitute.

Internal analysis usually employs financial ratio analyses for a snapshot picture accompanied by careful

SWOT analysis for a broader and dynamic view. The impact of IITOs on the SWOT analysis will be to reveal the possibility of considerably increased number of competitors with higher product quality, lower prices and better financial health. These represent the `threats'. At the same time the IBU's product-market scope is no longer constrained by geography and tariff barriers. These represent the `opportunities'. Both the strength and the opportunity are conditioned by the existence of strong non-tariff barriers.

Four types of generic strategies are possible—a firm can adopt a cost leadership based approach, a broad differentiation approach or a focussed low cost/ differentiation approach or some combination of the first two. The managerial theory of competitiveness is derived from the concept of positioning which basically mandates that for a firm to be effective, it must deliver value to the customer in a manner that is meaningfully (to the customer) different along some variable from that of its competitor. Given that the defining characteristic of the SME is resource constraint, it is natural that the most popular strategies tend to be the low cost approach and focussed differentiation.

The Cost Leadership Approach

The focus of low cost approaches in the Indian IBU has hitherto been on administrative control—elements of overhead costs, control of wage costs by trimming flab accumulated under protection and by substituting high cost experienced workforce with low cost new entrants. This focus will very soon exhaust itself and the low cost approach will need to address dynamic areas–cost/value relationships along the entire value chain and the extension of the basic value engineering concept from manufacturing to administration and management. Addressing these dynamic areas will impact outsourcing decisions and automation. Many IBUs will find that the make or buy decision continuum will shift towards the buy decision on cost reasons. The new supplier will be from a set consisting not only of other Indian units specialising in the outsourced product or service but also global ones. Moderating this choice will be two sets of cost elements.

One: transaction costs and inefficiencies involved in the import of goods into the domestic tariff area (DTA). Generally the cross-border competitor wishing to operate in the Indian DTA will face the same levels here and therefore this cost element will be competition-neutral.

Two: infrastructural costs such as high power tariffs (both direct costs and costs imposed by poor quality), inland transportation, internal tariff regime and real interest rates. This set of cost differentials impacts only the domestic player and its effect therefore to influence the outsourcing decision in favour of the foreign supplier.

The interplay of these two sets of cost elements will decide the extent of outsourcing. For many SMEs however search and establishment costs related to cross border outsourcing can be prohibitive. This is the economic and strategic justification for geographic clusters-whether called industrial estates, EPZs or SEZs. The ideal cluster is one comprising a number of units of a mother industry surrounded by ancillary units. From this we come to Proposition 1 that:

Proposition *1: The role of government in ensuring the survival of SMEs under the impact of IITOs is the creation of Special Economic Zones with the objective of reducing transaction and infrastructure costs for the members.*

The role of automation on the low cost approach will be not only in the shop-floor but in administration and management (A&M). The traditional focus of automation/ computerisation in A&M has had more to do with the replacement of law value added manual clerical activities by machine Wage costs have therefore been the driver. This will change along two dimensions: automation/ computerisation will be used to eliminate non-value added activities and more creatively, as a force multiplier.

It can be seen from the above analysis that while the low cost approach remains the strategy of choice for many Indian IBUs even with the evolution of IITOs, the variables involved in the making of strategic choice and the nature of implementation are strongly impacted.

The cost leadership strategy for the large Indian IBU with a pan-Indian market presence will be differently impacted. Such businesses tend to be in commodity markets-paper, chemicals, cement, petroleum products etc. where the number and strength of brands is not high. Except for the structural tendency to oligopoly in unregulated markets, this sector comes closest to the classical concept of perfect competition. While one of the foci of the low cost approach will be in the areas of A&M, the dynamic area of cost leadership is not so much the outsourcing decision along the value chain as that of scale and design dependant process efficiencies. Many of these units are in the continuous process sector where manufacturing labour costs are not the significant factor. The WTO mandate of low tariffs and open borders implies that the products of this sector of foreign origin will enter the domestic Indian market if there is a cost-backed price advantage. The only method to preempt this is for Indian IBUs to rapidly reach international scales of plant size. This is however only a necessary and not a sufficient condition given that other significant cost elements such as power tariffs and the real interest rate are significantly higher than in international markets. To counteract this the large Indian IBU pursuing the cost leader strategy needs to attempt two things—pursue even greater economies of scale than is the current international norm to offset the cost disadvantages and secondly engineer even greater efficiencies into the process.

Both of these call for access to large amounts of low-cost capital. If this is not available either due to governmental policy flip-flops or due to stock market inefficiencies, the large Indian IBU will tend to out-locate its manufacturing operations. Proposition 2 therefore is:

Proposition 2: *Capital market inefficiencies and government policy instability will compel the large Indian continuous process IBU to relocate abroad and result in the evolution of the Indian multinational.*

Let us now consider the case of the large Indian IBU with a pan Indian presence which is not a continuous process unit and which follows a cost—leadership strategy. Many industries fall within this classification—automobiles, consumer durables, FMCG, machine tools, electronics etc. This case is analogous to that of the SME as far as manufacturing is concerned with the significant difference that marketing strengths in the areas of distribution, promotion and branding are more substantial. Marketing costs are viewed more in the nature of investments necessary to secure survival and therefore cost control devolves back to manufacturing. The significant element here is wage costs. Much of the confusion and controversy over industry's attempt to control this element (popular debate is about retrenchment, sweat labour and the lack of job—really speaking this should be income—security) is because of the tendency to view wage costs as only labour-hour costs. In reality wage costs include not just the rupee amounts paid out to or on behalf of labour but also the costs arising out of low levels of productivity and reskilling and the infirmities and rigidities in the labour market that make it impossible to calibrate labour input with production requirements. Where the option exists therefore the IBU in this segment will increasingly outsource production activity. For technically complex products outsourcing from another medium scale unit is unlikely to provide any significant cost advantage. For simpler products it may be viable to source under controlled conditions from the SSI sector where labour costs are much lower. The advent of IITOs will simply mean that the large Indian IBU is no longer restricted to the DTA for outsourcing requirements and can simply shift abroad. Labour market reforms in line with international trends will arrest this process.

Proposition 3: *Unless addressed, labour market infirmities will cause the flight of large scale discrete manufacturing abroad.*

The Broad Differentiation Approach

A strategy dependant on differentiation is designed to appeal to customers with a special sensitivity to a particular attribute of the value-delivery system. Note that we are not limiting ourselves here to the value-embodying artifact (which is the physical product or service) alone but the entire spectrum from wants-identification to want-fulfillment. Broad differentiation simply means that the IBU is addressing itself simultaneously to a number of sets of customers each with their set-specific sensitivity to different attributes and fairly obviously followers of this strategy tend to be the large players. Such a strategy calls for the following skills and resources in the organisation.

- Strong marketing skills.
- Product engineering
- Creative flair
- Strong research capability
- Corporate image of quality/technology
- Strong cooperation from distribution channels

As can be seen, the broad differentiation strategy is almost entirely manufacturing independent. To a large extent therefore IBUs in this segment will be indifferent to the impact of IITOs with one significant exception, which we will see shortly. In many sectors such as white goods and automobiles where engineering input into product design is considerable, competitive differentiation leads to an explosion in industry-wide product development. The key element here is the availability of a critical mass of product development skills and facilities. Low cost in this situation, while definitely an advantage, is certainly not the paramount factor in deciding the physical location of design and development and R&D. The impact of IITOs on large Indian IBUs will be to free them now to locate their product development and R&D centres in the most advantageous location, *anywhere in the world.* It must be noted that what we are discussing here is the pure broad differentiation strategy where the IBU is not attempting to blend in elements of the cost leadership approach. Thus we come to Proposition 4:

Proposition 4: *Indian IBU following a pure broad differentiation strategy will tend to setup/relocate product development/R&D centres abroad with little impact on manufacturing.*

The Focussed Approach

A focus strategy anchored in a low cost base or a differentiation base, attempts to best meet the needs of a particular market segment. If anchored in a low cost base coupled with a proximate geographic approach, we are then back to the situation of Proposition 1. If while retaining the low cost base, the geographic approach is not limited but the product/application/value element is, then the scale of operations will be large. In this case the analysis now takes us back to Proposition 2. An interesting variant is the focussed differentiator where low cost is not so critical as the ability to uniquely meet a client's needs. Such an IBU is indifferent of the effects of the IITOs as long as minimal requirements of foreign market access are met. These IBUs can grow to the top end of the SME sector. Proposition 5 states:

Proposition 5: *Focussed differentiators with unique value propositions will grow their Indian manufacturing facilities being unaffected by IITOs.*

The success of this strategy depends on having a global approach as far as market is concerned. The role of the Government here is fairly limited, the basic requirement being that multinational marketing efforts are not hampered by transaction costs and inefficiencies in areas such as provisioning of foreign exchange for marketing expenses incurred abroad, for the purchase of cost-effective used plant and machinery, and for meeting warranty obligations.

The Combination Approach

A broad differentiator aiming to achieve cost leadership is essentially trying to take up an unassailable position. Such IBUs are obviously not in commodity markets. Many products in their life cycle move from being initially commodities (transparent products) to branded ones (opaque products) and then revert to commodity status under the impact of hypercompetition. With the Indian market being in a developing stage, with per-capita consumption of most products being well below developed country standards, it will be a long while before the scope for the broad diffentiator is exhausted. However the ever present fear that under IITO provisions a well heeled foreign competitor could enter the Indian market and significantly ramp up the scale of marketing expenditures will tend to make cost leadership as a strategy component attractive. The IBU will then retain a part of manufacturing in-house in order not to lose manufacturing skills but out-source as much as possible from either SMEs or foreign locations (owned or otherwise) unless labour market infirmities are removed.

Proposition 6: *Broad differentiators with unique value propositions who also seek cost leadership will base their manufacturing strategy on labour market conditions:*

Policy Prescriptions

Having considered the set of all strategy options for the sectors of interest, we will now work out the policy prescriptions for the Indian Government.

(a) For the survival of a large number of SMEs operating essentially in the domestic market either as ancillaries, as units focussed on a specific target industry, or serving the replacement market, the role of the government lies in promoting clusters where all types of transaction and infrastructural costs are minimised. The important point to be noted here is that *such clusters need not have an export orientation.*

(b) For the survival of the large scale discrete manufacturing sector labour reforms are mandatory. While there is no direct effect of profligate government spending, the indirect effects of the resultant policy (especially taxation policy) instability will stunt the growth of this sector.

(c) It is necessary to adopt and institutionalise best practices in the capital market both in the equity and wholesale debt sections to enable the large Indian continuous process units reach international levels of cost efficiencies both by scaling up plant sizes and by M&As.

(d) The strategy analyses and the set of propositions clearly indicate that corrective action taken by government to prevent the deindustrialisation of India under the impact of IITOs will as a corollary also promote exports. Both the cost leader and the focussed differentiator in the SME segment will find global competition in local markets. The best way to face this will be, to use military terminology, to shift the battle to the enemy's territory. We will thus find that the drivers of manufacturing exports, foreign exchange earnings and the domestic economy shifting from export led growth to growth led exports. All of the above is, of course, management of the supply situation. Demand side management will have to be through a judicious mix of fiscal and monetary policies, discussion of which is beyond the scope of this paper.

REFERENCES

1. Filiho, P.V. "Environmental Analysis for Strategic Planning" *Managerial Planning,* January—February 1985 pp. 23-30.
2. Hill, C.W.L. "Differentiation versus Low Cost of Differentiation and Low Cost A Contingency Framework". *Academy Management Review,* July 1998, pp. 401-12.
3. Murray A.I. "A Contingency View of Porter's Generic Strategies" *Academy Management Review,* July 1988, pp. 390-400.
4. Reimann, B.C. "Sustaining a Competitive Advantage" *Planning Review,* March—April 1989, pp. 30-39.
5. Scherer, F.M. *Industrial Market Structure and Economic Performance* 2nd ed. Skokie III: Rand McNally 1980.
6. Ansoff, H.I. Strategic Management of Technology "*Journal of Business Strategy,*" Winter 1987, pp. 40-48.
7. *La Bell, D. and O.J. Krasner* "Selecting Environmental Forecasting Techniques from Business Planning Requirements" *Academy Management Review,* July 1977, pp. 373-83
8. Fifer R.M. "Cost Bench Marketing Approach Functions in Value Chain" *Planning Review,* May 1989, pp. 18-27.
9. Hergert, M. and D. Morris "Accounting Data for Value Chain Analysis" *Strategic Management Journal,* March 1989, pp. 175-88.
10. Langley A "The Roles of Formal Strategic Planning" *Long Rane Planning,* June 1998, pp. 40-50.

11. Porter, Michel E. {From Competitive Advantage to Corporate Strategy" *Harvard Business Review,* May-June 1987, pp. 43.
12. Prahalad C.K. and G. Hamel "The Core Competence of the Corporation" *Harvard Business Review* 68, no 3(1990), pp. 79-91.
13. Miller D. "The Generic Strategy Trap" *The Journal of Business Strategy,* January-February 1992, pp. 37-41.
14. Pearce, J.A., II "Selecting among Alternative Grand Strategies" *California Management Review,* Spring 1982, pp. 23-31.
15. Allio, R.J. "Formulating Global Strategy" *Planning Review,* March-April 1989, pp. 22-29.
16. Marucheck, Ann; Ronald Pannesi; and Carl Anderson "An Exploratory Study of the Manufacturing Strategy Success in Practice" *Journal of Operations Management 9,* no. 1, pp. 101-23.
17. Roth Kendall; David M. Schweiger, and Allen J Morrison, "Global Strategy Implementation at the Business Unit Level: Operational Capabilities and Administrative Mechanisms" *Journal of International Business Studies* 22, no. 3 (1991), pp 369-402.

21

Technological Implications of Globalisation and WTO

N.P. Suryanarayana

Introduction

With information explosion on all branches of knowledge, world has become small and compact. Environment consciousness of advanced nations has made technologies and advancements in its large-scale utilisation, a hard task. Mineral wealth of the world on the one hand and agricultural capability on the other have raised several technological implications between nations for technology transfers. Political policies of developed, developing, and under developed nations under one umbrella like WTO has made this issue much more complicated. MNCs are faced with very high risk decision involving high investments and large groups of organised employees. In this context, Indian Industries are faced with acute marketing problems and consequent financial problem. As a satellite problem, a number of small and medium scale industries dependent on large industries are threatened for a total closure. In this context, a hard choice between petro-chemical based industries on the one hand and agro based industries on the other hand are faced with challenging technological implication for growth compromises.

India is an old country with rich traditions. Due to continuous exploitation of agricultural and mineral resources, over centuries, by external rulers and large population over years we have now become poor. This poverty while due to large population, is also due to poor management of our resources. Particularly, British rule brought in a new dimension of "National Inferiority Complex". This has become an internal enemy of our progress in post-independence period.

During the post-independence period, a series of Five year plans were taken up for fast development of our standard of living. Bullock cart economy changed to "Automotive economy in Transport Sector". 'Cotton wear' (Khadi) changed to synthetic fabric. Manual transport for internal movement of goods changed to elevators and conveyors. Above all, in the core sector of agriculture 'Plough' changed to 'Tractor' and chemical fertilizers were adopted in place of agrobased fertilisers. If these changes are viewed critically these plans pushed India to an oil based economy. Agriculture and transport industry started thriving making astronomical increase in our oil import bills. Although, a simultaneous attempt was made to produce oil indigenously it was largely due to heavy import of technology which benefitted other than a common Indian citizen. Much worse impact has been, export of our progressive people to advanced countries. Nationality become a sense of contempt and today. We live in a cloud of economic distress and self contempt of our own talents in all fields of human activity. Craze for imported goods, craze for settling abroad by highly educated people (on whom this poor country has invested huge amounts from its resources), accepting only imported models for all activities are creating unusual tensions. Seal of "in collaboration with ...."has become a market gimmick for sales.

WTO and globalisation of business activities would mean one quality, one price and centralised production of large volume at lowest cost of production. To persue this idea, Multi National companies under new arrangement would move towards places where raw materials are available at low costs and personnel can be hired at smaller prices. This has already started in the area of information technology. MNCs have started opening their software develop centres here and hiring people at small prices and exploiting the huge human resources of IT area.

However, the objective of this presentation is to look at these WTO implications in a sunrise area like Polymer Science and Technology. Polymers are becoming important in many areas of core economy like transport, textiles, housing, food, paper pharmaceuticals etc., Implications of globalisation and MNC participations within the regulations of WTO would pose serious problems in this area. Automotive Tyres and Tubes sector has already shown the results by a steep decline of over 17 percent in truck and bus tyres production. PET (Poly Ethylene Terpthalate), nylon, carbon black and a host of petrochemical based products have exceeded the production and are facing acute pile up of stocks.

Globally, however petroleum based products are gradually being replaced by agro-based products which are eco-friendly and bio-degradable. This change has given a fiat to fast development of agro-based technologies and concepts of value added agriculture. Even in areas like medicine and pharmaceuticals plant and animal products are fast replacing petro-based products.

Objective of this presentation is to compare petrobased technologies Vs. agro based technologies and its likely impact on world trade agencies.

Petroleum Based Technologies

Briefly, crude oil is subjected to distillation and fractionation. This would separate petrol, diesel, kerosene, gas and other fuels. There is a well developed type of technology called "off stream products". These can be broadly divided as

1. *Aromatic Stream.* Consisting of benzene, tolume Xylenes. These form basis of a number of drugs, pharmaceuticals, dyestuffs and solvents. When subjected sulphuric acid treatments yield mixed sulphates which are detergents and have almost totally replaced laundry soaps.

2. *Saturates* are hydrocarbons like methane/ethane/ butane etc. which are fuel (gas) and waxes (paraffin wax) and form raw materials to candles, matches pharmaceuticals and plastics and rubber additives.

3. *Olefines* are unsaturated hydrocarbons like ethylene, butylene etc. which can be polymerised as such or as their reaction products to a family of plastics called vinys like polythene, acrylcis styrenics polyvinylcloride (PVC's) and others.

4. *Dienes* are more unsaturated than vinyl and can polymerise to very long coiled chains containing residual unsaturation which is usable for vulcanisation like natural rubber and hence form a source of various synthetic rubber.

5. *Pitch or Petroleum Tar* also known as mineral rubber is used for surfacing road. Along with some other polymers mineral rubber is extensively used as durable road construction material.

Todays industrial world is dominated by petro-chemicals and are covered by hundreds of patents for which directly or indirectly WTO will be involved.

Agrobased Technologies: Cover a wide range of materials:

1. Forest wealth consisting of flora and founa of different parts of earth. A wide variety of woods,

herbs, animals, insects have been exploited over years. Changes in the world conditions and concern for eco-balance has largely limited this exploration. Sandal wood, teak, ivory, honey, bees wax, rosins and camphour, ivory and many other products and their related technologies.

2. Food products like paddy, wheat, potato, fruits, vegetables etc.
3. Cashcrops and plantations products like sugarcane, coffee, tea, tobacco, rubber, coconut, arecanut pineapple etc.,
4. Spices like pepper, asplodia etc.
5. Medicinal plants like cinchona, tulsi, bilwa, neem etc.,
6. Farm animals like sheep, goat and poultry.

There are a large number of patents covering yield, processing and preservation of these products. These again come in the purview of WTO trade agreement.

Basmati Rice episode is a typical example of patents laws coming under the WTO trading norms complicating the issues of such nature.

Large number of commercial products coming under petro-chemicals group area under ecology problem issues. Consequently, a large number of patents are now under issue for world rights for food processing methods and products. In the area of pharmaceuticals a large number of herbal compositions are under legal perview of WTO for commercial use. 'Turmeric' is a typical example. A number of steroid drugs now banned are being replaced by herbal preparations protected by patent.

Protection of Intellectual property rights is not a new concept to traditional Indian practices "Amrutanjan" Painbalm, Bedekar's Pickles, Lijjat papad or MTR Idlimix has been well known examples. Yet under WTO such traditions would not hold water.

A time has now arrived where we have to understand, interpret and act in a direction to protect ourselves from exploitation of our traditional talents under WTO. This calls for a rapid action technical force to translate these eco-friendly plants and agro-based technologies to well protected patented procedures. This would ensure an equitable share of world trade and rightful place for the Indian technologies.

Such a step only would ensure the interest of Indian farmers, Plantation personnel and small and medium sale industries. In rapid changes taking place in all sectors example Petrol to Alcohol, detergents to fatty oil soaps. Recycled thermoplastics to bio-degradable packing materials etc. India and Indian state of the art of technologies can play vital role in just distribution of wealth among nations for the larger interests of well being of humanity as a whole.

22

WTO and Indian Pharmaceutical Industry

R.L. Jagadhish, K. Sivachithappa, Mahadevaiah

Introduction

This paper analyses the present scenario of Indian pharmaceutical industry (IP) in the context of WTO trade regime. The P.I. of the country is a vibrant, high technology based growth oriented industry attracting attention of the world for its immense potential to produce high quality drugs and P-formulations. The PI is characterised by very intense competition with about 24000 companies.

Due to pressure from the developed countries, across the world uniformity in patent laws is being implemented under WTO. Presently, different countries have different patent types and life period. WTO has decided upon a product patent life of 20 years in all countries. However, to ensure a smooth transition and provide local players in the developing countries, ample time for gearing themselves, a moratorium up to the year 2005 has been provided. So, new products i.e. drugs introduced after this date will have to be accorded product patent protection. However, existing pharmaceuticals and new products that will be introduced in the interim period will all continue to be reverse engineered in nations which do not have product patent laws.

The inclusion of Trade-Related Intellectual Property Rights (TRIPS) into the mainstream of the WTO system establishes new disciplines for many countries in copyright, trademarks, industrial designs and patents. Two groups of issues dominate the debate on intellectual property in India—patents for pharmaceuticals and agricultural chemicals; and the implications of the WTO agreement on products based on local species.

It has been said that India was violating its obligations on pharmaceutical and agricultural chemicals patents. While the Government—along with foreign multinationals—is keen to implement the WTO agreement, it has faced resistance from local drug manufacturers and consumers.

The Indian Drug Manufacturers, Association (IDMA) protested stating that the prices of drugs shall go up by 5 to 20 times as a consequence of accepting the TRIPS proposals. However, the government claimed, "once the crutches of weak patent law are removed, we can successfully negotiate with research-based international companies...to boost export earnings, create more employment...and benefit from the transfer to technology". The government had some reservations about the TRIPS Agreement. But it signed the deal, taking the view that the package of agreements in all areas of trade—the result of the 1986-94 Uruguay round of negotiations—was on balance in India's interests.

The crux of the matter is that when the world is moving in one direction, it makes no sense for India to move in the opposite direction. India can emerge as a strong world partner. This is not happening overnight. As a developing country, India has a 3-year transitional period (until 2005) for giving full patent protection for pharmaceutical and agro-chemical products. This precious time can be carefully utilised by the P.I. of India for its economic advantage.

23

WTO and Textiles Industry

R. Meenakshi

International trade is a highly dynamic phenomenon. It involves a number of complex transactions which cross national borders. The nature of the transaction is such that more than one national law/rule/policy applies on the transaction. Uniform rules on trade transactions are a must in today's world where goods export are in the region of more than five trillion.

The WTO is the only international body dealing with the rules of trade between nations. Thus, WTO and the various WTO agreements have become an integral part of the international trading. WTO's success story centres round the effective involvement and active participation of its member countries. There is a general perception that WTO agreement on textile industry is difficult for Indian industry to practice. This is not an illusion. Of course it is not easy to say with full confidence about India's position as a net gainer or a loser from WTO Agreement on Textiles and Clothing as there are both plus and minus points on this issue. Hence, a nutshell review of WTO and Textiles in India is captured here.

Textiles and Clothing In India

The textiles and clothing industry is the largest

manufacturing sector of Indian economy accounting for 20% of national industrial output and providing means of living to 30 million people. Textiles (i.e. yarn, cloth, fabrics and other products not made into garments) constitute 37% of India's total exports, over half of which consist of cotton fabrics. India earns more than $ 11 billion per year. India has the largest cotton acreage in the world and cotton is the dominant fibre in the Indian industry. Indeed under the liberalised environment of both domestic and external sectors with abundant supplies of cotton, large skilled work force, low wages, improved technology and due to modernisation, India should be in a position to emerge as a major force in the global textile markets despite the stiff competition from countries like China, Malaysia, Taiwan, Hongkong and even Pakistan, Bangladesh and Indonesia. Market access is a key issue for India in multilateral trade negotiations. The Agreement on Textiles and Clothing (ATC) negotiated during the Uruguay Round was seen as a potential area of benefit for the developing countries, with estimates at that time even suggesting that over one-third of the total benefits from the Uruguay Round would result from the liberalisation of the world trade in textiles and clothing in the wake of the phased abolition of the quota regime and its integration into WTO/GATT discipline.

The anticipated benefits, however, have not materialised. This is largely because the integration process has not been commercially meaningful. In other words, market access for Indian textiles has not increased significantly. Compounding the problem are the various measures taken by importing countries (United States, European Communities, Canada, Norway, Austria and Finland) such as anti-dumping actions, transitional safeguards and discriminatory rules of origin which nullify whatever little market access resulting from implementation of the ATC.

ATC and The Uruguay Round

The key elements of the ATC, which was finalised during the Uruguay Round, are as follows. (i) Setting up of a time-frame for integration of textiles and clothing products into WTO (GATT-1994) disciplines—i.e. integration of textiles (or abolition of quotas) within a time frame of 10 years in four stages—abolition of quotas on specified products to be 16 per cent of the total volume of imports into the quota countries in 1990 on the date of commencement of the agreement on 1st January, 1995: 17 per cent on 1st January, 1998; 18 per cent on 1st January, 2002; and the remaining 49 per cent on the final day of the transition period i.e. 1st January, 2005. (ii) Progressive growth of quota limits during the period of transition preceding final integration of the textile sector into GATT. For products remaining under quota, at whatever stage, the Agreement lays down a formula for increasing existing growth rate. Thus, the annual growth rate should be 16%, 25% and 27% higher than the growth rate established for the previous MFA restrictions under MFA bilateral agreements in the three stages. (iii) Application of safeguard mechanism during the transition period. A specific transitional safeguard mechanism allows members to impose restrictions against individual exporting countries if the importing country can show that both the overall imports of a product and imports from the individual countries are entering the country in such large quantities as to cause (or to threaten) serious damage to the relevant domestic industry. Setting up of a time frame for elimination of quotas is the singular achievement of the ATC given the fact that textile trade has been under a discriminating regime since the early sixties. The growth in quotas envisaged in the interim also goes beyond the MFA maximum of 6 per cent in many categories under restraint especially to the US and some categories, especially garments, in the European Union (EU). The additional access gained on account of the growth on growth rates granted under the ATC, although no substitute for the elimination of actual restriction, is also a significant improvement. Apart from the above, the ATC also recognises the need to strengthen GATT rules and disciplines through tariff reductions and bindings, elimination of non-tariff barriers etc. as part of the integration process. The ATC also provides a mechanism for supervising the implementation of the agreement by establishing the Textiles Monitoring Body (TMB). A periodic overview of the agreement before the end of each stage of integration by the WTO Council of Trade in Goods has also been envisaged. Of the above, the two most significant features of the ATC are: (i) the phase-out of restraints on a pre-determined schedule and within a stipulated period of 10 years and (ii) an improved, multilateral policy of additional restraints and other measures during the phase-out period through the Textile Monitoring Body (TMB) envisaged in the ATC and on both these counts, the operation of ATC has fallen short of the expectations of developing countries, including India. Since 1995, the ATC has taken over from MFA. By 2005, the textiles and clothing sector is to be fully integrated into normal GATT rules. In particular, the quotas will come to an end and importing countries must follow the principles of GATT. The importing country can choose any product for integration so long as the stipulated percentages are met.

Integration Process—Tardy Implementation

The process of integration of items has been very reluctant and tardy, especially in the case of the US & EU. In effect, commercially meaningful integration has not been done. An analysis of the integration process in the first two stages initiated by the US & EU shows that it has not led to removal of restrictions on any item under specific restraint from India. Canada and Norway, on the other hand, who are also operating quotas under the ATC have significantly reduced the restraints under the phase-out programme during the first two stages.

While Canada has removed restrictions on several clothing products in 1998. Norway has removed all restraints on clothing by 1998 and on bed linen with effect from 1999. Norway currently operates restraints only on fishing nets in a few countries. The developed countries appear to have adhered to the strictly 'legal' requirements of the integration process, without taking into account commercial considerations. The Council for Trade in Goods of the WTO in its review report on the eve of the second stage of integration (July 1997) also concurred that a large number of quotas remained in force, with members fulfilling only the minimum legal requirement.

Textile Monitoring Body (TMB)

The TMB is the only legitimate body within the ATC which can interpret the different provisions of the ATC and ensure that these provisions are properly implemented by the members. But the track record it has created during its brief period of operation is not very encouraging. The functioning of the TMB has not given any indication of the commitment of the WTO itself to the implementation of the ATC. The structure of the TMB is such that in any issue, it tends to get divided into two distinct blocs of importing country members and exporting country members. The result is that on many disputes they end up issuing a finding rather than making a recommendation. And in some of the serious disputes, they are not even able to issue a finding and merely admit that they have no consensus to say anything about the dispute. The apparent division of the TMB into two blocs and its tendency to wash its hands off serious disputes would tend to erode its relevance, and also convert it into a sort of deal-making body. And in case where the parties refuse to make or accept a deal, the dispute goes to a WTO Panel. In fact, dispute settlement in the textile sector may become a lot more smoother if the disputes are handled directly by the Dispute Settlement Body (DSB), as in the case of the other sectors.

Safeguard and Other Anti-Import Actions

A tendency to replace QRs with other disguised anti-import measures has been evident in both the US and EU especially after the finalisation of the ATC in December 1993. The EU pre-empted the impact of the ATC by accelerating the anti-dumping drive in the textile sector during 1994. Repeated action was initiated by EU in the case of imports of PTFY from India. The United States proposed as many as 26 new restraints globally during the first year of the ATC. The ostensibly social new issues such as those relating to child labour, labour standards, wages and working conditions/workers' rights, environmental and ecological standards and even fire safety standards have been invoked both by the EU and the US, and linked to trade, as thinly veiled protectionist measures all too frequently in the textile sector. An important element of the ATC is the linkage of the integration process to the issue of market access. Article 7(i) of the ATC mandates members to achieve improved access to markets for textiles and clothing products through measures such as tariff reductions and bindings as part of the integration process and with reference to the specific commitments undertaken by the members as a result of the Uruguay Round. With the unequivocal commitment to phase-out MFA restriction within a definite time period of 10 years, it is not surprising that the developing countries facing quantitative restrictions on imports of textiles and developed countries imposing QRs on imports of textiles and clothing products should seek reciprocal market access in the textile sector by seeking reductions in tariffs and removal of non-tariff barriers in the developing countries. India has granted access for textile products under the MOUs signed with the US and the EU. The market access has been granted by calibrating the removal of QRs and tariff reductions over a 10 year period, coinciding with the 10-year integration period of textile products into GATT. The peak tariff levels of textile items have been progressively reduced to 25 per cent for yarns, 35 per cent for certain made-ups and 35 per cent for priority garments. QRs have also been removed for large number of textile products and most of the remaining products in 2002.

Most of the imports appear to have taken place from the countries in the South-East Asian region. In order to ensure that low cost and poor quality imports of textile products do not unduly distort the domestic market, a scheme of specific duties has been envisaged along with the ad valorem duties in the MOUs signed with the US & EU.

Apart from the above, the transition period has also seen: (i) Unilateral changes in the Rules of Origin (by the US) restricting market access. (ii) Delay in prompt approval of special flexibilities committed under the India-EU MOU. (iii) Growing preference for regional parts/Customs Union in order to circumvent meaningful liberalisation of textile trade. With the developed countries showing varying degrees of commitment to the process envisaged in the ATC, developing countries like India will come under increasing pressure to liberalise trade by removing restrictions. There is thus a need to remain vigilant during the remaining years of the operation of ATC and renew efforts to resist attempts to restrict trade by recourse to new methods of protectionism.

The Results

The integration programme implemented by the importing countries have been very meagre and have not been in line with the spirit of the ATC.

- The importing countries should be persuaded to apply growth-on-growth presently provided under Article 2, 14 for stage 3 with effect from 1st January 2000 instead of 1st January 2002.
- The period of 10 years provided for removal of all QRs on textiles and clothing products be adhered to and the integration programme be implemented in good faith by the deadline of December 31, 2004.
- TMB should be made more effective by directing it to make a recommendation in each case referred to it and provide a clear finding rather than observations, on each measure or action reviewed by it.
- The developed countries should avoid resorting to unreasonable anti-dumping/anti-subsidy and other anti-import actions as a means of protecting their textile industries;
- Sparing use of transitional safeguards based on standards established in the context of WTO dispute settlement mechanism. Thus, while reviewing of safeguard action if it is found that the market data provided by the importing country does not establish a situation of serious damage or actual threat thereof for the product, all requests for restraints issued by the same importing country to other exporting countries for the same products based on the same market statement should automatically be treated as invalid. Not more than one safeguard action should be permitted on a given product of a particular exporting country by any importing country during the currency of ATC.
- There should be no unilateral change in the rules of origin to the detriment of developing exporting

countries. Further, since the process of harmonisation of rules of origin of various countries is being undertaken in the committee of Rules of Origin, no member country should be allowed to make any further changes in the rules of origin till the harmonisation process is completed.

Dumping

India is facing the threat from the EU in the matter of dumping. To make its domestic industry competitive, the EU has imposed anti-dumping duties on Indian textile exports. The duties were imposed in several slabs ranging up to 24.7% since November 1997. India, therefore, dragged the EU to the DSB of the WTO for imposing unwarranted anti-dumping duties on its textiles exports. It also complained that the EU had failed to consider India's special status as a developing country before imposing the duties on June 12, 1997.

The complaint was lodged under Article III. 3 and IV. 3 to the DSB and under Section 2.4 of the Anti-dumping Practices (ADP)., According to this article, a product is considered to be dumped only if the export price of the producer is lower than the price charged for home consumption in the country of export.

EU's imposition of anti-dumping duties on imports of cotton bed-linen from India violated free trade rules. The ruling was a major victory for Indian textile exporters, most of whom were in the private sector. The EU, contended in front of the appellate panel that the European textile industry had suffered declining profitability and prices depression and therefore slapped anti dumping duties.

The WTO has also ticked off the EU for "failing to explore the possibilities of constructive remedies" before levying the anti-dumping duties. "EU had acted inconsistently with the provisions of ADP agreement and has nullified or impaired benefits accruing to India under the agreement" The EU would contest the WTO ruling against the anti-dumping duties on exports of cotton bed-linen from India Rs. 400 crore. India has to defend the ruling or the appellant panel and prove that the EU has gone against the provisions of the ADP agreement thus putting itself at a disadvantageous position. There is a requirement for India to approach the WTO to prevent frequent anti-dumping laws by importing nations trying to curb its exports, India has to ensure that anti-dumping does not become a tool in the hands of a few developed countries.

China's Entry into WTO and Its Implication for India

China's entry into the WTO is a double-edged sword for India. India's share of world exports stands at a meager 0.8% while China enjoys a 3.3% share of the total world exports. China is ahead of India both in terms of trade openness as well as its promised commitment to further trade liberalisation. As per the commitments made to the WTO, weighted average tariff rates in India in 2005 will be around 30%, while in the same time frame China will reduce average tariff rates to 9.44%. The Indian policy makers must be aware that China is fast emerging as a supplier of cheap labour intensive goods in the world market. It is one of India's main competitors in nearly every major export sector.

China's entry into WTO is generally is in India's interest in both trade and foreign policy primarily because China's absence undermines the legitimacy of the multilateral trading system in which India has a major stake. Secondly, bilateral sources of trade friction, notably with regard to accused Chinese dumping of chemicals in India, is easier to resolve because China is in the ambit of the WTO's DSB. Thirdly, China shares India's point of view on various WTO issues. It is having more diplomatic clout than India and for the benefit of third world countries might be able to break EU and US in the multilateral organisation.

India has welcomed the move to facilitate China's entry into the WTO in the hope that the entry of China into multilateral organisation increases the access of India's textiles into Chinese markets and China is also coming out of its non-transparent regime of export subsides. The key question is whether China will get quota free access in textiles by January 1, 2005 when the clause in Agreement on Textiles and Clothing comes into the force. If China gets that; India will face more competition in textiles.

In fact, the phasing-out of textile and apparel quotas by 2005 will enable China to worst market share from other low-cost Asian producers. The textile sector in India is already feeling tremendous competitive advantage of their bottom line and many textile units are on the verge of closure. The Chinese are exporting to India a wide range of low-cost consumer goods that have a mass market in India such as kitchen ware, textiles, electronic items, furniture, toys, cosmetics, footwear, and accessories. Armed with competitive advantage of low price the Chinese are moving in new markets at a feverish pace and Indian exports also come under serious threat with the entry into the WTO.

Competition from New Players

The challenges the Indian exporters face are not only from trade barriers in importing developed countries. The removal of quotas, which have been restricting, imports from specific sources means freer competition among exporters. The EU and US will buy from the lowest cost suppliers, and India will often, but not always, be among them.

In 1993, a study of seven countries found that the price of cotton yarn per kilo was cheapest in India at US $ 2.79

compared to others. This is the result of overall labour and raw material costs being cheaper in India.

Some argue that the ending of quotas will increase competition between developing countries trying to capture a bigger slice of these markets. Exporters fear that freer imports permitted under the GATT could lead to dumping of low-cost fabrics from China and other South East Asian countries into India. Under these conditions, India can invoke the WTO agreement on anti-dumping.

When these exporters enter a quota-free market in 2005, they may face stiff competition from more competitive countries. As of today, our garments are of an average standard, but to face competition, India will have to drastically improve its quality and productivity standards.

This will require not only state of the art machinery, but also attitudinal changes on the part of entrepreneurs and the government. Unless the industry emerges as a world leader exploiting all the competitive elements within the 10 year transition period, it will end up as back bench player.

There is evidence to suggest that these fears may come true. Countries such as Thailand and Indonesia have increased their share of world clothing exports from 0.7% and 0.4% in 1980, to 3.2% and 2.3% respectively by 1994. Over the same period a country such as Bangladesh, with zero exports in 1980 has today managed to capture 1% of the world market.

Recent studies indicate that India is beginning to lose some market shares to its rivals. In one survey of US textile and apparel imports, it is found that China and Hong Kong had higher market shares than India. In certain categories, they observed that other Asian low cost producers namely Pakistan, Bangladesh and Indonesia had higher market shares. They are emerging as close competitors to India.

However, India's strength is that it is a producer of cotton cloth, unlike some of its rivals, who are dependent on imports.

Liberalisation Reshapes the Industry

However, the industry has made considerable adjustments in order to maintain its international competitiveness. Over the past decade, India has acquired the productivity and modern technology to enable it to compete with Hong Kong, Korea and Taiwan, as well as the newer exporters such as Indonesia and China.

The Government has allowed garment exporters to import essential textile machinery and equipment at concessional duty rates. It has set up the National Institute of Fashion Technology to cater for the research and training needs of the fashion industry, thus enhancing the industry's international competitiveness. As the country is not very strong in the weaving and processing sectors, the government has initiated steps to establish a technology upgrad action fund for garment making units.

Since the Indian government embarked on a liberalisation programme in 1991 several large private enterprises have entered into joint ventures with foreign firms. These strategic alliances include considerable foreign direct investment, technology transfers and brands licensing. They provide useful insights into the ways in which the Indian textile and clothing industry is being reshaped by the country's liberal economic policies and increasing globalisation.

Privatisation has encouraged some well-known private firms to revive public sector enterprises that had been incurring losses. A study by Textile Outlook International (1996) profiles 10 textile companies in some detail. These include high profile firms such as Mafatlal industries, LNJ Bhilwara Group. Birla VXL and Coats Viyella, who are leading manufacturers of yarns, fabrics and ready-made garments.

The companies are endowed with a highly skilled labour force, often trained abroad, and state of the art of manufacturing technology. Mafatlal for instance, has emerged as one of the largest fabric exporters in the country, with foreign sales of Rs. 3.9 bn per year. Similarly, companies such as Silvia Apparel, an Indo-Italian alliance with a US $ 600m turnover, are now 100% export orientated. As a result of being located in export processing zones within India, these companies are exempted from government export quotas.

As a result of the structural changes associated with investment in physical and human capital, the government's liberalisation policy and the removal of all quotas by 2005, textile output is forecast to expand by 138% by the year 2005.

Winners in the End

Recent studies suggest that India has a lot to gain from the ATC. A study on the impact of the Uruguay round on India's cotton textile industry by Tata Economic Consultancy Services (TECS, 1994), indicates that exports are set to rise dramatically.

According to projections by TECS (1994), EU imports of ready-made fabrics will double by 2004, as a result of the elimination of quotas. US imports are expected to treble over the same period. Already there is some evidence to substantiate these predictions.

It is expected that the removal of quotas will lead to a fall in consumer prices for textiles, thereby increasing demand in importing countries. The demand is expected to be fuelled further by rising incomes as a result of the Uruguay round agreements as a whole. According to another prediction, apparel output could more than double (i.e. expand by 24%) between 1995 and 2005, compared to an increase of only 114% without the agreement on textiles and clothing.

But in reality, the gains are not there for India to go for claim. India feels that commercially meaningful integration has not been done. India argues that the intended benefits of the ATC involving phasing out of quotas have not been realised by developing countries. The restraints under the ATC were used almost exclusively to protect the markets of US and EU against imports of Textiles and clothing from developing countries. An analysis of the integration process in the first two stages initiated by the US and EU shows that it has not led to removal of restrictions on any item under specific restraint from India. These major countries have most integrated such products on which there were no quotas restriction in any case during the first two stages. Therefore effective phase-out of quotas had been minimal in the two stages till 1-1-98. In the third stage till 1-1-2002 also the trend was likely to be the same. This will mean that most of the quotas may continue upto 31-12-2004. It is sad to note that in the case of India 90% of its exports will be liberalised only in the last phase. The functioning of the TMB has not given any indication of the commitment of the WTO itself to the implementation of ATC. The developed countries resorted to unreasonably anti-dumping/anti-subsidy and other anti-import actions as a means of protecting their textile industries. Hence, India could not achieve improved access to markets for textiles and clothing products through measures such as tariff reductions and removal of non-tariff barriers.

Conclusion

India is facing the threat from US and the EU. India claimed that the transitional safeguard measures on her wool coats by the US were inconsistent with ATC. At last, the US announced that the measures were withdrawn due to India's complaint in the panel report of DSB. India dragged the EU to DSB for imposing unwarranted anti-dumping duties on its textile exports. Added to this, China's entry into the WTO is a double edged sword for

India. Ultimately, the extent that India will gain from ATC depends on its cost competitiveness, size of the market, high productivity, good quality, modern technology, better infrastructure, skilled manpower, research and training needs of the textile industry.

Part—IV
WTO and Environmental Policy Issues

24

World Trade Policy for Environmental Sustainability

Odeyar D. Heggade

One of the new paradigms that deserves serious discussion is the issue of how to use trade policy for environmental sustainability (or sustainable development or sustainable human development). The recent trends of globalisation in trade and global environmental concerns and health concerns have necessitated such a discussion. This paper focusses on this theme.

I. Trade Policy and Environmental Protection

The World Development Report 1992 has tried to raise the following three vital questions and answer them:

(a) What are the environmental effects of trade liberalisation?

(b) Should trade policies be used to influence environmental standards in other countries?

(c) Should trade policies be used to enforce or implement international environmental agreements?

Regarding the first issue there is growing unfound fear that trade liberalisation shall further accentuate the pollution around the world. Recently controversies arose about the negative impact of the North American Free Trade Agreement on air, and water resource quality in Mexico and the southwest of USA, the liberalised export trade of cassava to European Union lead to soil erosion in Thailand; and the Ghana's exchange rate depreciation causing deforestation. These environmental degradations were there even before trade liberalisation in the concerned countries. But "using trade restrictions to address environmental problems is inefficient and usually ineffective. Liberalised trade fosters greater efficiency and higher productivity and may actually reduce pollution by encouraging the growth of less-polluting industries and the adoption and diffusion of cleaner technologies". (WDR, 1992: pp. 67).

The pollution is not caused by trade liberalisation but arises on account of failure of markets and governments to appropriately price environmental resources. Thus, trade policies, it is pointed out that, "are a blunt and uncertain tool for environmental management because they influence the use of environmental resources only indirectly. Indeed, modifying trade policies to deal with environmental problems may worsen degradation. Thus, restricting the export of logs, as in Indonesia, raises returns to the domestic wood processing industry and may contribute to inefficient and high cost production that could worsen deforestation. Usually, more direct instruments than trade policies are available for combating deforestation, soil erosion or industrial pollution. Trade liberalisation should be accompanied by better use of these targeted policies". (Ibid).

Thus, the argument is trade controls worsen environment whereas trade liberalisation creates incentives for environmental protection. This claim is partly correct and partly dubious. The claim that trade controls increase pollution is correct, in the sense that the foreign exchange hungry LDCs may continue to produce with older technologies causing more pollution although there are trade barriers over certain goods in the importing industrial countries. This is because of the smallness of export market which may not induce the LDC's to adopt a high-cost clean technologies. The other part of assertion—trade liberalisation encourages the adoption of clean technologies is dubious—since there are no evidences. In fact, the MNCs are bringing old technologies as they were doing earlier even now in the fields of power, petro-chemicals and metallurgical industries. The MNCs are trying to adopt clean technologies in their subsidiaries located in LDCs which produce goods for consumption in the MDCs. This is a 'dual' standard.

The second question is more normative. It is based on the presumption that the MDC's have the responsibility to protect global environment by initiating punitive actions by way of imposing countervailing duties on the exports of the LDCs with high pollution emission levels. This idea was put forward in the 1989 Uruguay Round of trade negotiations but there was of consensus about it. The imposition of countervailing duties for environmental concern is a trade control which cannot be uniformly applied and can not be universally justified. Because there are some "variation in environmental standards across regions and countries is justified by differences in priorities and in capacities to assimilate pollutants or cope with resource degradation. When countries (typically the bigger and richer ones) use trade policy to impose their environmental standards, the effect is to protect domestic producers from foreign competition. Applying the same standards to domestic production and imports may be justified when, as with cars or pesticides, consumption leads to environmental damage. But even there, environmental concerns do not warrant uniformity across countries". (Ibid.).

A study by Dean (1992) for GATT reveals that the LDCs in general do not invite foreign investment in "dirty" industries by lowering and diluting environmental standards. Because the environment costs are just a fraction of the total output value—nearly 0.5 per cent, an average for all US industries in 1988 and only 3 per cent for the highly polluting industry. That means private foreign investments generally do not flow into countries with low environmental standards popularly called "pollution heavens". The experience of Chile, however, indicate the opposite: it is cheaper for MNCs to use clean technologies as they do in their home countries the MNCs if they like can contribute to environmental protection and improvement.

The third question is again normative: it explores the potency of trade policies for implementing international environmental agreements. This is undoubtedly, a right perspective. The World Bank has already started linking its lending operations to implement the 'Montreal Protocol' on environment. In case of trade the implementation of international environment agreements may ultimately take the form of "trade sanctions" against countries which violate their accepted commitments about preservation of biodiversity or green house gas emissions.

In this regard the WDR (1992: p. 67) on "Development and the Environment" observes that:

> "Trade measures to implement environmental agreements include the Montreal Protocol, which phases out ozone—depleting chemicals; the Basel convention (which entered into force in May 1992) for controlling the transboundary movement and the disposal of hazardous wastes; the convention on International Trade in Endangered Species (CITES), which supports the embargo on ivory trade. The use of trade instruments could be justified in some of these cases. For instance, restricting trade in hazardous and toxic wastes, as under the Basel convention, is appropriate if the capacities of many countries to monitor and dispose of these wastes are in doubt. But in most countries the scale of such trade is small in comparison with the volume of hazardous

wastes being generated domestically. Therefore, the concern should minimise the production of these wastes and to devise ways of ensuring their safe disposal. A total ban on all trade in hazardous and toxic wastes would be counterproductive because it would prevent the development of collective arrangements for treatment and disposal even where individual countries, as in Western Europe, can specialize in safe and low-cost disposal".

Therefore, there is scope for using trade policy for environmental sustainability only on selective basis. In fact, the careful scrutiny of foreign investment proposals from environmental sustainability perspective and persuading MNCs to use 'clean technologies' in host countries and increased emphasis on environment friendly approach to domestic industrial and agricultural production and its exports could be more potent instruments for environmental improvement rather than trade controls and trade sanctions imposed by the industrial countries.

The USA has imposed some health standards on the level of pesticides use in the case of traditional and non-traditional food imports from developing countries. This is followed by other industrial countries. The excessive use of pesticides is found to be the main environmental cause for cancer. So the high health standards in importing industrial countries shall slow down agricultural diversification and its exports from LDCs. Thus, the farmers, particularly the small farmers should be trained in integrated pest management and bio-engineering of crop varieties which are effective alternatives to chemicals.

II

Alternatives for Global Environment Protection

Further, it is not desirable to advocate trade policy (i.e., trade controls and trade sanctions) against exports of LDCs where threats to environmental sustainability are real and complex in the sense that without addressing seriously the problem of existing poverty and its likely increase in the context of globalisation towards which the MDCs also owe responsibility, trade policy used for environmental sustainability lead to deprival of right to livelihood and fair opportunities for sustenance of the life claims of the people of LDCs. Under such a situation trade policy not only discriminates between the people of MDCs and LDCs at present, but it will prove to be a futile tool for environmental improvement in LDCs.

It is unfortunate that the recent global attempts at strengthening the links between environment and development have not addressed adequately the problem of poverty. The Human Development Report of 1997 has been very critical of the neglect of poverty reduction from the perspective of environmental sustainability. The 1997 Human Development Report (pp. 114) observes that:

"The commitments made at the United Nations Conference on Environment and Development (UNCED) in 1992, encapsulated in Agenda 21, give equal weight to poverty and environment, recognizing the intrinsic relationship between the two in the context of sustainable development. But the political appeal of environmental issues in the North has allowed environmentalists to steal the show during the follow-up to the conference. Agenda 21 recognizes that a specific anti-poverty strategy is one of the basic conditions for ensuring sustainable development. But this kind of focus on poverty has been missing from the global mechanisms established to support and monitor implementation of Agenda 21.

The UN Commission on Sustainable Development, charged with monitoring follow-up to UNCED and Agenda 21, has not made poverty a theme of its discussions. And the Global Environment Facility the financing mechanism for meeting the global environment goals of Agenda 21, is not geared to take account of the poverty-environment relationship. Meanwhile, the UN Commission on Social Development, charged with monitoring follow-up to the World Summit for Social Development, where poverty was the central concern, does not view poverty reduction in the context of its relationship to environmental protection and sustainable use of resources".

The missing of poverty reduction concern in the recent global attempts is termed as a "fault line" by 1997 HDR. Thus, it lays emphasis on formulating and implementing an environment sustainable development strategy to help the poor. Therefore, the 1997 HDR (pp. 114) has suggested the following policy initiatives:

- Improving environmental health.
- Sustaining natural resources and eco-systems to ensure food, shelter, living space and livelihoods for poor people.
- Maximising the potential of environmental protection activities to create sustainable employment and income.
- Supporting local communities in their role custodians of their environment and natural resources.
- Ensuring rights of tenure, land use and access to local resources and credit for poor people.
- Accelerating technological innovations needed to increase productivity and sustain livelihoods in marginal environments.
- Another method suggested for controlling global pollution is the use of "tradable permits". This could be a next best alternative for dealing with global pollution rather than trade policy. For this purpose the setting up of an international

authority is suggested. Such an authority may be empowered to issue "tradable permits" which enable the polluters to emit pollutants upto a specified quantity. This agency may also be authorised to lease the tradable permits for definite time period and use the revenue so derived to finance international environment projects or such tradable permits may be issued without a price.

The allocation of "tradable permits" may be highly flexible allowing the countries which do not use their permits in full to sell or lease such surplus permits. This method is based on pay for 'ecological space' principle applicable equally to all countries. It would make high polluters to pay more and help to avoid a few countries abusing world's environment without a price.

The scheme of tradable permits according to 1994 HDR suffers from two major problems:

> "First, it demands an international consensus on total permissible emissions of greenhouse gases—a consensus that might be difficult to reach. Second, if the distribution of permits were based on income, the largest share would go to industrial countries. If it were based on population, most would go to developing countries though this would be the most equitable system since each person has an equal right to use the earth's atmosphere. An intermediate solution would be to allocate half the permits on the basis of population and the other half on the basis of GNP." (HDR, 1994: pp. 68).

As it is well known that the industrial countries are the largest polluters. If they want to continue with current levels of emissions and if the allocation of tradable permits is adjusted for population and GNP then the MDCs will have to buy tradable permits from LDCs. This entails a significant transfer of resources from industrial countries to the LDCs. Such transfers would be around $500 billions to

$1 trillion per year. These resource transfers are neither aid nor charity. They will be the consequence of a market mechanism that would impose a price on large polluters who over consume the global common property resources.

The system of tradable permits has the advantage of generating funds for financing environmental improvement programmes in LDCs and further creates strong incentive to reduce pollution at global level. These two advantages are not found in a trade policy that imposes trade controls or sanctions to protect the global environment.

Therefore, the trade policy has its own limitations to contribute to effective environmental sustainability. The trade policy linked to high health standards might seriously and considerably impoverish the LDCs by reducing their exports. In view of this danger it may not be possible to obtain a general consensus regarding using trade policy for sustainable development. Thus, as it is shown already, instead of a trade policy, the collective efforts at reducing global poverty, encouraging MNCs as well as domestic enterprises to adopt clean technologies, and devising a system of tradable permits adjusted to population and GNP could be better alternatives for achieving the goal of environmental sustainability or sustainable development in the future.

REFERENCES

1. Brahmananda, P.R. (1997), The Emerging International Economic Paradigm. A. B. Shetty, Memorial Lecture delivered at Mangalore University, November, Mangalore.
2. Nayyar, Deepak (1995). Globalisation: The past in our Present (Presidential Address, 78th Annual Conference IEA), Chandigarh.
3. World Bank (1992), World Development Report: Development and the Environment, Oxford University Press, Oxford.

4. UNDP, (1994), Human Development Report, Oxford University Press, Newyork/Oxford.
5. World Bank (1994). Making Development Sustainable, Washington D.C.
6. UNDP (1997), Human Development Report, Oxford University Press, Oxford.
7. GATT (1992). "Trade and the Environment" (A Background Paper by Dean), In International Trade 1990-91. GATT Secretariat, Geneva.

25

WTO and Its Environmental Policy

S.N. Yogish

International trade is an "engine of growth" has been the belief of many countries and also international organisations. This belief originated in Adam Smith's writings and has continued to influence the policies of a large number of countries in the mid-twentieth century. In recent years, many new issues have come to the forefront to influence the trade patterns. The concern of environment is one which has been exerting dominant influences in the world trade.

Environmental Implications on International Trade

Today, serious issues have arisen over the relationship between environmental damage and international trade. The relationship between trade and environmental policies has emerged as a major topic of debate. In some areas international trading rules are seen as a limit on the ability of countries to protect national and global environment resources. Trade policy analysts view trade restrictions for environmental purposes as a new form of protection. They argue that free trade as being environmentally destructive and in favour of placing restrictions on trade in the name of environmental protection. In such cases, there is a problem.

GATT/WTO and Environmental Standards/Rules

GATT has been set up with the purpose of framing rules and procedures to be followed by nations in their international trade relationship. It is especially aimed at reducing the barriers to trade to get nations to refrain from putting tariffs and quotas on imports and in general to move toward conditions of free trade among nations. One section of the GATT agreements are related to non-tariff barriers such as excessive inspection requirements, excessive product specialisation and so on.

GATT was never seriously concerned with the interface between trade and environment. But in course of time environmental protection became a major concern, and state framed appropriate laws. Sometime these came to be challenged before GATT Dispute Settlement System.

The issue of trade and environment was not on the agenda of the GATT Uruguay Round of Multilateral Trade Negotiation (1986-94) which led to the adoption of the Final Act under WTO.

The Final Act contains a number of agreements with implications for trade environment issues. These include:

- The Agreement of Agriculture.
- The Agreement on Trade Related Aspects of Intellectual property Rights (TRIPS).
- The Agreement on Subsidies and Countervailing Measures.
- The Agreement on Technical Barriers to Trade (TBT).
- The Agreement on Sanitary and Phyto-sanitry Measures (SPS).

The WTO Agreement establishes a Dispute Settlement Body (DSB) which is to discharge the responsibilities laid down in the understanding on Rules and Procedures governing the Settlement of Disputes, an integral part of the Final Act.

The Committee on Trade and Environment (CTE) has a twofold mandate, to identify the relationship between trade measures and environmental measures in order to promote sustainable development and to make appropriate recommendations on whether any modifications of the provisions of the multilateral trading system are required compatiable with the open, equitable and non-discriminatory nature of the system.

Use of Trade Measure for Environmental purposes

The United Nations Conference on Environment and Development (UNCED) has recognised that trade in conjunction with sound macro economic and environmental policies can make an important contribution towards sustainable development. Trade is an instrument of economic growth which increases the resources available for environmental protection. At the same time, environmental protection is aimed at preserving and developing natural and ecological resources which are needed to sustain a continuing expansion of trade. Environmental and trade policies need not conflict with each other. Then why environmental policies may lead to trade friction?

Environmental Policies and Trade

In recent years, many new issues have come to influence the trade patterns. The concern for environment is one which has been extracting dominant influences in the world trade. Environmental policies can affect trade in many ways. They are:

- Environmental measures aimed at *Production Processes* may indirectly affect trade through their impact on industrial competitiveness and industrial location decision.
- Environmental policies aimed at *Products* may have direct impact on trade (that is costs of compliance with product regulation and consumer preferences for green products).

- In some cases, environmental protection measures may act as a non-tariff barriers to trade.

Some aspects of environmental policies have an important impact on trade between nations. It pays special attention to the issue of standards, in particular the potential impact of standards on market access and international competitiveness. Environmental policies are based on certain measures such as direct and indirect controls including pollution charges, subsidies and tradeable permits, voluntary industry agreements, creation of markets through the extension and definition of property rights and liability arrangements. It is also necessary to classify environmental policy measures based on standards in terms of:

(i) Ambient standards

(ii) Emission standards

(iii) Technology standards

(iv) Performance standards

(v) Product standards

The emission, technology and performance standards can be classified together as *Processes and Production Methods (PPMS)*. Ambient standards can rarely be implemented. Thus, distinction between process and product standards is important.

Two conditions must be satisfied to make international economic changes beneficial to all the countries in the World.

(i) The sustainability of eco-system on which the global economy depends must be guaranteed.

(ii) The economic partners must be satisfied that the basis of exchange is equitable.

The introduction of policy measures to protect the environment has potential implication not only for the domestic economy but also for international trade. For example, the processing of certain raw materials pulp and paper, oil can have substantial environmental side effects. DCs have generally been more successful that LDCs in seeing to it that export product prices reflect the costs of environmental damage and controlling that damage. Thus in the case of exports from DCs, these costs are paid by consumers in importing nations including LDCs. But in the case of exports from LDCs, such costs continue to be borne entirely domestically, largely in the form of damage costs to human health, property and eco-systems.

The adoption of costly pollution control measures in certain countries will in principle alter the international structure of relative costs with potential effects on pattern of specialisation and world trade. In particular, there has been a concern that the LDCs with their emphasis on economic development rather that environmental protection will tend to develop a comparative advantage in pollution-intensive industries over time. In consequences, LDCs will become the "heavens" for the world's dirty industries.

Is WTO an Anti-environment Organisation?

The inter-face between trade and environment encompasses a range of issues that have been identified by the WTO committee on CTE. WTO is far from being the anti-environment organisation. Prof. B. S. Chimni has cited out two cases:

(i) United states—Import Prohibition of certain shrimp and shrimp Products. (Shrimp—turtle case 1998).

(ii) European Union Measures concerning Meat and Meat products (Harmones) 1998.

There is an urgent need to contest the anti-environment image of WTO. Northern NGOs and academics are playing a dual strategy on the trade-environment front: On one hand pressurising WTO rules to accommodate their environment concerns and on the other hand, seek to put the trade-environment issue on the agenda of the next round of trade negotiations. Third World countries have been supported the second strategy and not the first strategy. Thus the Third World countries must challenge the anti-environment image of WTO.

The two cases brought before the Appellate Body of the WTO show that the WTO has gone a long way in integrating environmental concerns with the objective of free trade. On April 10, 1996 the U.S. Court of International Trade in its decision in Earth Island Institute Versus Christopher case ordered that shrimp imported from all countries which had not adopted adequate policies to protect sea turtles be barred. It is based on U.S. Public Law of Section 609. India, Pakistan, Thailand and Malaysia challenged this before WTO panel. The panel on the basis of reasoning analysed it and concluded that the import ban on shrimp products as applied by the U.S. was not consistent with the article XI: I of GATT 1994. Some of the interpretations developed by the panel were subsequently rejected by the Appellate Body in a bid to arrive at a balanced view on the relationship between trade and environment.

In EC-Harmons case (1998) two panels dealt with separate complaints by the U.S. and Canada against the European Union concerning the prohibition of imports of meat and meat products derived from cattle to which either the natural harmones or the synthetic harmons had been administered for growth promotion purposes.

The Agreement on SPS (Sanitary and Phytosanitary Measures) addresses government regulation and import bans regarding food safety and disease-spreading products to protect human, animal or plant life or health. SPS measures are however to be applied only to the extent necessary and within the territory of the member. They are to be based on scientific principles and not maintained without sufficient scientific evidence.

Thus, WTO has been projected as an anti-environment organisation because it tends to evaluate measures designed to protect the global environment from the standpoint of the principles and goals of free trade. Environmentalists pointed to the record of WTO as evidence of its anti-environment position. But the WTO Appellate Body has, through a series of interpretative steps in shrimp-turtle and EC-Harmons cases sought to balance and integrate trade and environment objectives. It is to be noted that WTO has tried to use the absence of clean and detailed rules regarding the environment protection.

Environmental Concerns in Trade and its Implications on Developing Countries

Changes in environmental concerns in trade may have serious implications and consequences for LDCs. The purpose of strict emission standard is to protect human health. But in some cases, it is not a matter of a human health but one of environmental protection. In recent years, Denmark placed a ban on the use of non-refillable drink containers from neighbouring European countries. These countries objected saying that the ban was really just a way of protecting Danish drink producers from competition.

The inter-relationship between environmental issues and trade problems has recently raised the possibility that environmental standards will be co-opted by those whose interest is primarily to protect themselves against international competition. Environmental factors now give them added ammunition. In a recent case, the U.S. barred imports of tuna from Mexico that had been caught using methods that cause excessive mortality among dolphins. The question here is whether Americans really do have a substantial willingness to pay for protecting dolphins or whether this was just being used as an excuse by U.S. tuna companies to shield themselves from foreign competition. Environmental policies are mainly framed out of the need to change the unsustainable pattern of development in developing countries. But the impact of these policies of developing countries which had accepted GATT Principles hinders them to move away from attaining sustainable development. The environmental policies being evolved are misused by developed countries at various levels. developed countries are talking constantly about saving the environment. But they have failed to take steps to limit their over-consumption of environmental and natural resources. Environmental issues are today being misused by developed countries as non-tariff barriers and it would be further deteriorating the international terms of trade of many developing countries.

The Third World countries must reject the possibility of the use of unilateral trade measures to promote environment protection and campaign for a co-operative solution which emphasises a dialogic and rewards-based approach. It was viewed that "co-operative" solution are more stable than coercion.

WTO-CTE Report emphasises the importance of market access opportunities in assisting developing countries to obtain the resources to implement adequate developmental and environmental policies, determined at the national level and provide income-generating activities for the poor. The co-operative solution stresses an incentive or rewards-based approach. The Third World countries must evolve an effective strategy not only to keep these forces at bay but to ensure that it can pursue an independent and self-reliant of sustainable development.

In recent years, there is decline in multilateral co-operation in general and a negative attitude to dialogue on development in particular. It is argued that introduction of an environmental dimension further complicates the search for such co-operation and dialogue. But it has also been realised by all that the failure to bring the interaction between resource depletion and rising poverty will accelerate global ecological deterioration. Reforms at an international level are now needed to deal simultaneously with economic and ecological aspects in ways that allow the world economy to stimulate the growth of developing countries while giving greater weight to environmental concerns. How to reconcile environmental quality with trade? New dimensions of multilateralism are essential to enhance human progress.

Part—V
Regional Trading Arrangements and India

26

Economic Integration of Developing Countries With Special Reference to SAPTA and ISFTA

Francis Cherunilam

There has, indeed, been such a proliferation of regional economic integration schemes that most countries in the world are members of—or discussing participation in—one or more trade blocs known as regional integration agreements/arrangements (RIAs). Such agreements have been concluded among high-income countries, among low-income countries, and, more recently, starting with the North American Free Trade Area (NAFTA) between high-income and developing countries. In fact, many countries belong to more than one RIAs. According to WTO, over 200 RTAs have been notified to the GATT or WTO over time. Currently over 150 agreements are in force, most of which have been concluded recently. Since 1995, over 100 agreements covering trade in goods or services or both have been notified to the WTO. A major part of the world trade now occurs within actual or prospective trading blocs. Japan and Korea are two notable exceptions to membership in any RIA.

A World Bank Policy Research Report on Trade Blocs observes that during the last decades of the last century, the move to regionalism has become a headlong rush.

According to this Report, the recent period has witnessed qualitative, as well as quantitative, changes in regional integration schemes due to the following three major developments.[1]

The first is the recognition that effective integration requires more than reducing tariffs and quotas. Many other barriers have the effect of segmenting markets and impeding the free flow of goods, services, investments, and ideas, and wide ranging policy measures—going well beyond traditional trade policies—are needed to remove these barriers. This so-called deep integration was first actively pursed in the Single Market Program of the European Union (EU), and elements of this program are now finding their way into the debate in other regional agreements.

The second is the move from 'closed regionalism' to a more open model. Many of the trading blocs that were formed between developing countries in the 1960s and 1970s were based on a model of import substituting development and regional agreements—with high external trade barriers—were used as a way of implementing this mode. The new wave of regional agreements—including resurrection of some old agreements—have generally been more outward-looking, and more committed to boosting, rather than controlling international commerce.

The third development is the advent of trade blocs in which both high-income industrial countries and developing countries are equal partners in agreements designed to bolster the economies of all the member countries. Perhaps the most important example of this is the North American Free Trade Area (NAFTA), formed in 1994 when the Canada-U. S. Free Trade Agreement was extended to Mexico. EU has linked with the transition economies of Eastern Europe through the Europe Agreements, and has developed the EU-Turkey customs union and a

Mediterranean policy potentially incorporating agreements with nearly every Mediterranean country. There has been discussion of replacing the EUs trade preferences of the Lome agreements with reciprocal trade agreements with these developing countries.

As the Report observes, these developments have occurred against the backdrop of globalisation. New technologies and more liberal trading regimes have led to increased trade volumes, larger investment flows, and increasingly footloose production.[2]

Rationale of RIAs of Developing Countries

Economic integration of developing countries has been advocated by many experts as a means to accelerate economic development and strengthen their trading and bargaining power vis-a-vis the developed economies. The South Commission also emphasised this. The United Nations Conference on Trade and Development (UNCTAD) has felt that "Regional economic groupings, integration or other forms of economic cooperation should be promoted among developing countries as a means of expanding their intra-regional and extra-regional trade and encouraging their economic growth."[27] The countries participating in the Second Session of the UNCTAD reaffirmed "...that trade expansion, economic cooperation and integration among developing countries is an important element of an international development strategy and would make an essential contribution towards their economic development".[3]

Berry et. al observe that, LDCs enter into integration schemes for somewhat different purposes from those of advanced nations. Integration offers LDCs a means for simultaneously solving two trade problems: (1) It provides an opportunity for free trade with other countries that are at similar levels of development and are thus able to compete on equal terms, and (2) it presents a way to trade with advanced countries without being harmed by their superior economic power. Yet the promotion of trade is not necessarily the main reason why LDCs form integrated groups, as it is for advanced countries. A more urgent goal is to generate economic growth and development. The gains from integration are fundamentally similar for developing countries and advanced ones, but with some important differences. The less-developed nations have possibilities for proportionately greater benefits because they have so much further to so. In addition to the opportunities that integration offers for acquiring individual industrial specialities and trading the products of these with other members, union can improve the allocation of resources.[4]

The domestic market of many less developed countries is limited by the low per captia income and the small size of the population. This naturally comes in the way of achieving economies of scale and industrial development. It is hoped that the increase in the size of the market due to integration will, therefore, remove this obstacle. It "....may be fair to say that if the less developed countries are determined to industrialise irrespective of the social cost, industrialisation through regional integration should be preferred where feasible. The reason is simple; Regional integration can support larger and more efficient production units." It is observed that there "...is much less interest in trade creation through destroying inefficient producing units existing in the member countries than in trade diversion—shifting purchases from the rest of the world to member countries, and more constructively the achievement of economies of scale."[6] After all, the labour that goes into the trade diverting activities is seldom withdrawn from other useful activities. More often than not, such labour is drawn from the ranks of the unemployed or underemployed, and its opportunity cost is very low, near zero.

Economic integration of developing countries is beset with problems—it has even been argued that integration can do pretty little to improve the economic performance of these nations. The following paragraphs give a very brief account of some very important factors that come in the way of economic integration of developing countries.

Integration Schemes of Developing Countries

A number of integration schemes have been initiated by less developed countries "...and have experienced varying fortunes, raising questions of both of the efficiency of existing schemes and soundness of the theoretical and policy arguments upon which they are based."[7] Thus, the integration so far, achieved has meant continuing interference with unfettered multilateral trade. While these arrangements may be argued to be a movement towards freer international trade it is fair to note that they have frequently been seen (at least in Latin America) as a *medium-term* alternative to non-discriminatory dismantling of tariffs.[8]

For many developing countries in Latin America and Sub-Saharan Africa, regional trade agreements have been a key element in their policy agendas over the past three decades.

Regional integration has long been a priority in Sub-Saharan Africa, where, in the past thirty years, all the countries have joined regional integration schemes. However, none of these schemes has been successful, for a variety of reasons, including the fact that the Sub-Saharan countries did not trade with each other a lot and are not what one would call natural trading partners.

Similarly, Latin American countries have been involved in regional integration schemes since the late 1950s.

Regional trade agreements among developing countries include the Latin American Free Trade Association (LAFTA), the Central American Common Market (CACM), the Andean Pact, and the Caribbean Common Market (CARICOM) in Latin America; the Economic Community of

West African States (ECOWAS), the Preferential Trade Area (PTA), the Economic Community of Central African State (CEEAC), and the Southern African Development Coordination Conference (SADCC) in Sub-Saharan Africa; and the Gulf Cooperation Council (GCC) in the Middle East.

There has been a move to establish a Latin American Common Market consisting of Brazil, Argentina, Chile, Uruguay and Paraguay.

In the post-World War II period, the erstwhile Soviet Union and East European countries sought to foster economic development via the integration scheme of Council for Mutual Economic Assistance (CMEA or COMECON). With the dissolution of the CMEA in 1991 following the political changes, the regional trade of the Eastern bloc also collapsed.

The *Association of South East Asian Nations* (ASEAN) was formed by the Bangkok Declaration, 1967, by five countries, viz. Indonesia, Malaysia, The Philippines, Singapore and Thailand, with a view to accelerate economic progress. Brunei joined the Association in 1984. While the ASEAN does not function as a regional trade arrangement, it has become an effective interlocutor for cooperation in economic matters and foreign affairs with OECD.

The ASEAN now constitutes a larger-market for Japan than does the United States. For two of the members—Indonesia and Malaysia—Japan is now the leading trade partner for exports as well as imports.

The economic growth rate of the ASEAN which is richly endowed with natural resources has been very high. This region accounts for the lion's share of the world's natural rubber, palm oil and tin. It is also an important producer of sugar, coffee, timber, petroleum, nickel, bauxite, tungsten and coal.

The ASEAN Free Trade Area (AFTA) is a notable RTA. Other important RIAs include the Southern Common Market (MERCOSUR) and the Common Market of Eastern and Southern Africa (COMESA).

Objectives

A look at the objectives of RIAs and the determinants of their success will be helpful to evaluate the integration schemes of developing countries. RIAs have several objectives. The motivation to form trading blocs may vary from region to region and from country to country. Nevertheless, as Shiells suggests, the following motivations seem to play a key role in the formation of trading blocs.

1. To obtain economic benefits from achieving a more efficient production structure by exploiting economies of scale through spreading fixed costs over larger regional markets, increased economic growth from foreign direct investment, learning from experiences etc.
2. To pursue non-economic objectives such as strengthening political ties and managing migration flows.
3. To ensure increased security of market access for smaller countries by forming regional trading blocs with larger countries.
4. To improve members' bargaining strength in multilateral trade negotiations or to protest against the slow pace of trade negotiations.
5. To promote regional infant industries which cannot be viable without a protected regional market.
6. Finally, to prevent further damage to their trading strength due to further trade diversion from third countries.

Regional agreements frequently have political objectives and non-economic dimensions, including national security, enhancement of bargaining power, and bolstering the credibility of reforms (economic and political). The attainment of such political objectives depends primarily on agreement design, as this determines the size and distribution of net economic impacts.[9]

Determinants of Success and Roadblocks to Integration Schemes of Developing Countries

There are certain conditions to be satisfied for the success of an economic integration. However, the economic structure and conditions of the developing countries, by and large, do not satisfy some of these conditions. The important factors include the following.

1. A customs union would lead to a net economic welfare if the economies of the partner countries are actually very competitive, or similar but potentially very competitive, or dissimilar because under such situation the trade creation will outweigh trade diversion. But "...if we apply the criterion of trade creation and trade diversion to the developing countries, it would not be possible to justify integration among them. The developing countries are in fact are producing similar products and also they are competitive. But the similar goods—mostly the primary products—that they produce are not for selling among themselves, but they are for the market in the developed countries. Unless they industrialise and diversify their production, they cannot develop complementarity. Since the conditions of complementarity and competitiveness cannot be fulfilled by the developing countries, integration among them will not lead to greater trade creation."[10]

2. A customs union would increase economic welfare if the trade among the member countries could be substantial, i.e., the partners should constitute the major market for the principal exports of each of the members. Further, the success of an integration scheme also depends on the proportion of the world's production, consumption and trade which is covered by the members of the union. The developing countries do not, however, satisfy these two conditions, namely, scope for substantial intra-regional trade and substantial share of world's production, consumption and trade.

Apart from these unfavourable economic factors, there are certain practical problems with respect to economic integration of the developing countries.

First, there are political difficulties, Governments of this region would not favour sacrifice of their freedom, sovereignty and autonomy by integration. Further, political differences and narrow nationalistic views are "...formidable obstacles to the integration of developing countries. This is more true of the developing countries of Asia and Africa which have national rivalries and boundary disptues."[11]

Secondly, the relatively poor and weak countries may have the apprehension that the relatively advanced and strong countries of the group would eventually dominate the entire customs union. The "...lagging country becomes frightened, that by giving its partners free access to its market, it will never be able to start any industry. Thus Bolivia refuses to join Latin American Free Trade Association (LAFTA) on the ground that it would impede its development rather than assist it. It regards LAFTA as a device to speed up the development of Mexico, Argentina, and Brazil—now leading in the area—at the expense of the slower countries."[12]

Thirdly, in spite of their geographic proximity the less developed countries are not economically unified; they lack adequate transportation and other communication and infrastructural and institutional facilities for successful unification. "Forming a single land mass, as they do, the EEC members for the most part have an economic advantage over the outside world in the markets of the community."[13] In contrast, "...in the developing countries, many of them with only exterior lines of communication (as noted for Argentina and Chile), there is no natural unity, and the artificial unity of political resolve is difficult to sustain. The fact that benefits for one member are costs for the others is divisive."[14]

Fourthly, the unequal distribution of the gains from integration due to the unequal economic status of the developing countries themselves makes them less enthusiastic about integration. "As evidenced from the experience of the EU countries, the gains will not get distributed equally even in the case of member countries whose economic status is not very much different initially. If integrated production units are established guided by considerations of economies of scale, it is possible that industries might get concentrated in a few partner countries.[15]

Fifthly the loss of revenue from customs duties, which is an important source of revenue for the governments of the less developed countries, tends to reduce the attractiveness of economic integration to these governments.

Thus, a number of obstacles come in the way of economic integration of the less developed countries. However, measures like those mentioned below.[16] have been expected to promote regional economic cooperation and trade liberalisation among developing countries.

1. Development of regional trade infrastructure i.e., provision for economic intra-regional transport facilities, etc.

2. Establishment of regional institutions to facilitate intra-regional trade i.e., expansion of clearing or payment union, Regional Reserve Bank, regional import-export credit facilities, regional trade information centre, etc.
3. Effective implementation, improvement and widening the scope of regional 'commodity communities' i.e., coconut, tin, etc.
4. Plan harmonisation and regional investment projects i.e., exchange of experiences in national planning and economic aspirations, development of regional investment plans, standardisation of policies regarding investments from outside the region, etc.
5. A planned effort in the direction of reduction of tariffs and trade barriers between the member countries and possible agreements on common policies vis-a-vis non-regional countries i.e., a product by product or systematic reduction of intra-regional tariffs, etc.

RIAs help achieve greater economic integration at a regional level, without adversely affecting global liberalisation initiatives. However, "making regional integration an effective element of national development strategies is a great challenge. Regional agreements can reduce the frictional costs of trade by harmonising regulations and standards. By making national policies a part of international agreements, regional agreements can increase the credibility of reform initiatives and strengthen security arrangements between partners. They can be vehicles for governments to test the waters of freer trade. By reducing trade barriers on a subset of partners, however, countries generally increase the real cost of their imports, reduce the flow of technology from nonmember countries, and increase dependence on particular export markets. Great care is required to ensure that such costs are compensated by other gains. If not, membership may hinder, rather than promote, development."[17]

A major problem of RIAs is that they promote regionalism at the expense of multilateralism. The negative production and consumption effects are the results of this problem. It is very important that as regionalism grows the greater benefits of the *first-best* policy and the ultimate goal-multilateral free trade, are not neglected. Regional arrangements should be conceived and implemented in a manner that harnesses them securely to the long-run goal of multilateral liberalisation, so that the arrangements develop as building blocks and not stumbling blocks, to such liberalisation.

A Performance Appraisal of RIAs of Developing Countries

The RIAs, in general, present a diverse picture of the extent of success.

Experience shows that regional agreements among the developing countries would be less successful than those among the developed countries.

According to an IMF study,[18] regional arrangements in industrial countries initially contributed to an increase in intra-regional trade, although recent evidence is less conclusive. In the EC and EFTA, for example, intra-regional trade increased markedly in the first ten to fifteen years but levelled off or decreased in later years. The study cites several reasons why the industrialised country arrangements tend to increase intra-regional trade and face implementation problem than their developing country counterparts.

First, trade liberalisation is principally carried out in differentiated manufactured goods. This can be achieved without major shifts in factor proportions and entails relatively lower traditional adjustment costs, particularly in terms of labour dislocations.

Second, industrial countries are in a better position to absorb structural adjustment costs within the context of steady growth.

Third, the industrial countries have postponed structural adjustment in sensitive sectors.

The following paragraphs also indicate several differences between the RIAs of developed and developing countries.

Many RIAs have failed, in part because of low complementarity in member countries' trade (i.e., countries' production structures are largely similar and their exports match the imports of their trading partners only poorly). In such a setting, countries have little to gain from regional arrangements and should focus mainly on unilateral or multilateral trade liberalisation.

A trade complementarity index can be used to provide some indication of the likelihood of successful integration in possible new RTAs. The index is zero when no good exported by one country is imported by the other, and one when the shares of one country's imports correspond exactly to those of the other's exports. Michaely suggests that the higher the index the more likely is a proposed regional trade arrangement to success in stimulating trade between its members.[19]

There is a wide range between the index values for previous successful and unsuccessful arrangements at the time they were formed. Index values for the EU Six averaged 0.53, while an even higher degree of complementarity existed between the trade of the United States and Canada. In contrast, the index for the unsuccessful LAFTA was less than 40 per cent of the EU/ U.S.-Canada average. The Andean Pact index (0.07) shows that the export structures of Bolivia, Colombia, Ecuador, Peru, and Venezuela were almost completely dissimilar from those of their imports at the time this arrangement was initiated. Among recent arrangements, complementarity among NAFTA members is an high as among the early EU members. In Mercosur (Argentina, Brazil, Paraguay, Uruguay) the average complementarity index of 0.29 is about half that of the most successful precedents, though the index is closer to 0.35 between the two central partners-Argentina and Brazil. This suggests that while the arrangement has a reasonable chance of promoting trade among members, countries must avoid an inward-looking "regional bloc" approach that deemphasises continued multilateral or unilateral trade liberalisation as has sometimes happened in regional arrangements with high trade complementarity. Much the same could be said for two prospective RTAs, the expansion of NAFTA to the rest of Latin America and APEC in the Asia-Pacific; their complementarity indices are around 50 to 60 per cent of the EU/U.S.-Canada average.[20]

Sub-Saharan African countries have low trade complementarity. The index for twenty countries averages only 0.09. This strongly suggests that the structure of African countries' exports and imports differ so widely that RTAs efforts hold little promise for accelerating industrialisation and growth (regional cooperation can, of course, be beneficial in other areas, such as joint border projects and consolidation of peace). Liberalisation of trade barriers in the region either unilaterally or within a multilateral framework appears to be a far more promising option.[21]

It has been observed that developing countries have been more successful in other areas of cooperation, including agricultural research and development, and coordination of investment incentives, than in producing large or sustained increases in intra-regional trade.[22]

There have been many reasons for the poor results of RIAs of developing countries. A World Bank Report reveals the following reasons.[23]

1. In a number of cases (CARICOM and the Central American Common Market in Central America; UDEAC in Africa) inter-regional conflicts have made it difficult to liberate trade.
2. In many blocs, such as the Andean Pact, participants sought to rationalise production by allocating specific markets to designated producers instead of allowing the competitive process to determine the allocation of production. These designed producers were not necessarily the most efficient; nor were tariffs low enough in relation to the rest of the world to provide external competition. Consequently, the expected benefits from rationalisation of production or increased competition have been limited.
3. Trading opportunities and pro-competitive effects have been limited by the small size of regional markets in comparison with the rest of the world.
4. Regional trading blocs have frequently produced similar products, limiting the opportunity to exploit differences in skill or endowments.
5. Political interest in these arrangements has not always been translated into effective implementation of economic goals. The overall impact of these arrangements, has, therefore been limited.
6. Few developing country regional groups removed barriers across the board.
7. Strong vested interests in import competing industries and weakened external environment also thwarted efforts to liberalise intra-regional trade.
8. Inappropriate macroeconomic policies and political and institutional factors have also impeded implementation.

The South Commission observes that a basic handicap for regional organisations has been inadequate support from their member countries. It is clearly essential that this attitude should be reversed if the schemes are to gain the necessary strength.[24] The problems indicate the courses of action needed for making the integration schemes successful. The fact that the developed countries are 'extensifying' and intensifying integration schemes reveals certain important facts. Integration schemes have considerable benefits, if properly carried out. Secondly, this trend in the North will create more problems for exports from the South to North. Therefore, it is essential that the South also actively pursues such schemes, to mitigate the adverse effects of the integration of the North as well as to make better utilisation of the resources and development potentials of the South through cooperative endeavours.

According to a World Bank Policy Research Report, one reasonably firm conclusion is that for most developing countries, and especially for the poorer ones, a North-South RIA with a large industrial country is likely to be superior to a South-South RIA with a developing country. The reasons are the following:[25]

1. South-South RIAs are more likely to generate divergence with the less developed member losing relative to the more developed one.
2. South-South RIAs are more likely to generate trade diversion.
3. North-South RIAs are more likely to generate useful transfers of technology.
4. North-South RIAs are more likely to provide lock-in mechanisms in the area of politics (such as democracy) and economics (in terms of policy credibility).
5. Given the industrial partner's superior institutions, a North-South RIA may provide more benefits from "deep integration" than a South-South RIA.

6. Given a larger endowment difference between member countries in a North-South RIA than in a South-South one, a developing country may be able to better exploit its comparative advantage in a North-South RIA.
7. The developing country partner is unlikely to capture most of the above-mentioned benefits of North-South integration unless it undertakes economic reforms.

Other conclusions include

1. For any RIA, lowering external trade barriers (up to the optimum level) is beneficial: it will increase the RIAs gains or reduce its losses.
2. Though there are substantial benefits from a Customs Union, compared with an FTA in terms of simplicity or intra bloc trade regulations there are also costs in terms of loss of sovereignty, difficulty in setting the common external tariff and sharing the tariff revenues. Thus, most recent RIAs have been FTAs, and mostly North-South ones where these costs of forming a CU are likely to be high.
3. For middle-income countries—such as the members of MERCOSUR or ASEAN—there may be sufficient gains from scale and competition effects to justify a RIA between them, but fully capturing these effects will require "deep integration" measures, and expansion and contraction of sectors and firms decided by the market.
4. However, if a middle-income country is located close to a large industrial RIA—such as Mexico, and Eastern European and Mediterranean countries—then it is likely to best capture the benefits of enhanced scale and competition by joining that RIA.

Role of WTO

The WTO has an important role to play to improve the environment to enable the developing countries to benefit more from RIAs. The World Bank Policy Research Report points out that this requires:[26]

1. Changes in WTO rules to benefit developing countries.
2. Improvement and enforcement of the rules.

With reference to the first it is recommended that:

1. Industrial countries should fully open their markets to developing country exports, particularly those from least-developing countries.
2. The WTO should modify its rules concerning trade blocs to create a presumptive right of association.
3. In return, developing countries should accept the disciplines of Articles XXIV and V for their RIAs.

The recommendations in respect of the second are that:

1. The WTO enforces the disciplines of Articles XXIV and vigorously in the CRTA, especially those on coverage and depth of liberalisation.
2. The WTO define, the rules more rigorously: On "substantially all trade," we advocate 9$ percent of trade after 10 years and 98 per cent after 15; on "other restrictive regulations of commerce," we advocate inclusion of the abolition of internal barriers, such as safeguard actions and anti dumping duties.
3. The WTO uses the dispute settlement procedure to enforce the rights of third countries not to face increases in protection either directly or indirectly through the use of tools such as rules of origin.

SAPTA

The Sixth SAARC Summit held in Colombo in 1991 strongly mooted the idea of a SAARC Preferential Trading Arrangement (SAPTA) and the Foreign Ministers of all the member states (India, Pakistan, Bangladesh, Nepal, Sri Lanka, Bhutan and Maldives) signed the Agreement on II April 1993 during the Seventh SAARC Summit in Dhaka. SAPTA became effective from 7 December 1995.

The basic principles of SAPTA are as follows:

1. Overall reciprocity and mutuality of advantages.
2. Step-by-step negotiations and extension of preferential trade arrangement in stages.
3. Inclusion of all types of products-raw, semi-processed and processed.
4. Special and favourable treatment to LDCs.

The special treatment of LDCs include allowance of favourable percentage points, application of relaxed rules of origin, favourable terms for technical assistance, duty-free access, deeper tariff preferences, removal of non-tariff and para-tariff barriers, negotiation of long-term contracts to support sustainable exports and provision of special facilities with regard to shipping and documentation, preparation and establishment of industrial and agricultural projects, training facilities and support to export marketing etc. possibly linked to co-operative financing and buyback arrangements.[27]

The share of intra regional trade in the total trade of SAARC countries is very insignificant. This has not increased even after the formation of the SAARC. There was, in fact, some fall in the intra-regional trade after the coming into effect of the Association. During the decade commencing in 1985, it declined from 4.5 per cent to 3.5 per cent. The share of individual countries' trade within the region varies.

While the share of the region in the total exports of Maldives, Nepal (17-18 per cent in 1994) and Bangladesh (12.8 per cent) is fairly high, that of India (0.5 per cent) and Pakistan (1.6 per cent) is very low.

The share of the region in the members' imports also shows a skewed pattern. While only about 0.5 per cent of India's imports originate from SAARC countries, it is fairly high in respect of Nepal (18.3 per cent in 1994). While India and Pakistan have been enjoying trade surplus in the intra-regional trade, all others have been confronting deficit. High levels of tariff and non-tariff barriers have been affecting the trading between SAARC countries.

All the SAARC countries have implemented substantial reduction in tariffs and also modified their tariff structures as part of the on-going economic policy reforms. These changes have been carried out with a view to improving the efficiency of domestic industries. This process in itself should help the expansion of intra-regional trade. But the presence of non-tariff barriers in different forms are acting as constraints to realise the potential for trade expansion.

The SAPTA is expected to play an import role in boosting the intra-regional trade. According to the country perspective exports on SAPTA, this preferential arrangement would benefit SAARC countries due to the following reasons.

1. The countries can substantially reduce the transport and transit cost because of geographical continuity among the members.
2. Capital goods produced within the region may be more compatible to the factor endowment of member states than those imported from developed countries.
3. The increasing competition among the member states would result in technical efficiency in existing industry as marginal firms might be

forced to reduce their cost. Resources will be reallocated away from less efficient firms and monopolies protected by the tariff wall will no longer be in a sheltered position.

4. As economic ties get stronger and countries become committed to common economic goals, political problems will gradually recede. When economic benefits gain significance, amicable environment may evolve for dissolving political problems.

5. Regional cooperation may also pave the way for regional banks or corporation which might be influential in promoting regional investment in larger projects.

It is intended to develop SAPTA into a South Asian Free Trade Area. (SAFTA), The SAARC Council of Ministers which met in December 1995 reached an agreement to realise the objectives of SAFTA preferably by the year 2000 but not later than 2005.

Today, SAARC countries' share in total world trade is not even one per cent, and their trade among themselves lingers below 3 per cent of their total foreign trade. This compares poorly with more than 60 per cent for intra-EU trade of their global trade and nearly 40 per cent for North America, and East Asia.

According to a study by the international Food Policy Research Institute (IFPRI), the intra regional trade would expand by more than $800 million following SAPTA, which was more than double the then existing trade. India exports to the region was expected to double, increasing by almost $270 million. According to the IFPRI study, the target gains accrue when liberalisation is across the board for all trade partners. Economic welfare in that case is expected to improve by nearly $ 5600 million per year. Much of the improvement will occur from the intra-SAARC trade in food products and primary commodities. The chief gainers of this would be Bangladesh and Pakistan who would lead the increase in inter-regional food imports.

Although some liberalisation measures have been taken following the establishment of SAPTA, some of them are regarded as flawed or inadequate. It is even suspected that the concession exercise is just so much playing to the gallery. Consider, for example the fact that the majority of the products offered concessions by members are not being imported by them at all. It is, therefore, not surprising that preferential imports cover only a very small percentage of the total intra-regional trade.

It is also argued that the approach of SAFTA to introduce trade concessions, initially, on a product-by-product basis is a drag on trade liberalisation. There are, however, provisions in the agreement for across-the-board tariff reduction as well as for adopting a sectoral approach to reduction in tariffs. The product-by-product approach may be justified on the ground that the developing countries need to exercise more caution in the matter of trade liberalisation. Further, members will not benefit from tariff concession on many products as they already have equal, or better, levels of tariff preferences and market access under other arrangements.

It is also pointed out that many items with large intra-trade potential are not extended the trade preferences.

There is a view that what is needed is a customs union and not a free trade area because a free trade area has an important problem that goods from a non-member country may enter a member country and from there freely flow throughout the free trade area causing damage to the domestic industry/agriculture of some of the members. The 'rule of origin' designed to check this does not work. In practice, effectively.

Indo-Sri Lanka Free Trade Agreement

According to the Bilateral Free Trade Area Agreement signed by India and Sri Lanka on 28 December 1998, a large number of items will be eligible for duty free trade. India has offered to permit as much as 1000 items on zero duty from Sri Lanka and Sri Lanka will allow duty free imports of 900 items from India.

The main objectives of this Free Trade Agreement, according to its preamble, are the following.

1. To promote through the expansion of trade the harmonious development of the economic relations between India and Sri Lanka.
2. To provide fair conditions of competition for trade between India and Sri Lanka.
3. In the implementation of this agreement both the countries would pay due regard to the principle of reciprocity.
4. To contribute, in this way, by the removal of barriers to trade to the harmonious development and expansion of world trade.

The agreement also provide for safeguard measures under which if any product, which is the subject of preferential treatment, is imported into the territory of a contracting party in such a manner or in such quantities as to cause or threaten to cause serious injury in the importing country to the agreement, the importing country with prior consultations except in critical circumstances suspend provisionally without discrimination the preferential treatment accorded under the agreement.

The contracting parties are also free to apply their domestic legislation to restrict imports in cases where prices are influenced by unfair trade practices like subsidies or dumping. This agreement would have long-term consequences as other members might try to "multilateralise" it within the SAARC region by demanding similar preferential treatment within the trading arrangement bloc.

It is feared that the India-Sri Lanka Free Trade Agreement would very adversely affect the farmers of India as several cash crops would enter India duty free from Sri Lanka depressing their domestic prices.

As India is a very large market, the Free Trade Agreement is likely to benefit Sri Lanka a lot and the benefits to India may not be much as Sri Lanka is a small market.

REFERENCES

1. World Bank. *A World Bank Policy Research Report on Trade Blocs,* Oxford, Oxford University Press, 2000, p. 13.
2. *Ibid.,* pp. 3-4.
3. Cited by B.S. Sreekantaradhya, 'Economic Integration among Developing Countries with Special Reference to South-East Asia', *Economic Affairs,* September and October 1973.
4. Brian J. L. Berry et. al., *The Global Economy in Transition,:* Prentice Hall International, New Jersey, 1997, p. 419.
5. Miltiades Chacoliades, *Principles of International Economics,* McGraw-Hill Publishing Co., New York, 1981, p. 275.
6. Charles P. Kindleberger, *International Economics,* D. B. Taraporevala Sons and Co. Pvt. Ltd., Bombay, p. 1976, p. 186.
7. A.I. MacBean and P.N. Snowden, *International Institutions in Trade and Finance,* George Allen and Unwin, London, 1981, p. 173.
8. South Commission, *The Challenge to the South,* Oxford University Press, New Delhi, 1992, p. 197.
9. Josel Ritzen in the *Foreword to A World Bank Policy Research Report on Trade Blocs, op. cit.*

10. Sreekantaradhya, *op. cit.*
11. *Ibid.*
12. Kindleberger, *op. cit.* p. 18.
13. *Ibid.* p. 187.
14. *Ibid.* p. 187.
15. Sreekantaradhya, *op. cit.*
16. Trilok N. Sindhwani, *Economic Feasibility of an Asian Common Market,* Sterling Publishers Pvt. Ltd., New Delhi, p. 1975, p. 178.
17. Ritzen, *op. cit.*
18. IMF, *Regional Trade agreements,* Occasional Paper No. 93 (the main points were reported in the *IMF Survey,* April 3, 1992).
19. Michaely, cited by World Bank, *Global Economic Prospects and Developing Economics,* New York: The World Bank, 1996, pp. 20-1.
20. *Ibid.,* pp. 20-1.
21. *Ibid.,* pp. 20-1.
22. *IMF Survey,* April 13, 1992.
23. World Bank, *World Development Report 1992,* pp. 107-108.
24. South Commission, *op. cit.,* p. 197.
25. World Bank, *A World Bank Policy Research Report on Trade Blocs, op. cit.,* pp. 90-1.
26. *Ibid.,* pp. 117-8.
27. Information for this section has been drawn considerably from B. Bhattacharya and Vijaya Kath, *Regional Trade Agreement: SAPTA and Beyond,* Occasional Paper 3, IIFT, New Delhi, 1996.

27

SAARC and India

H.R. Krishnaiah Gowda

Introduction

South Asian Association for Regional Co-operation, shortly called SAARC, is born as a result of the efforts to increase co-operation in international affairs among the less developed countries. The idea that if mutual co-operation among South Asian countries is developed, it will be conducive to creation of an environment for development of these countries, was the basis for establishment of SAARC. It was rightly realised in the early years of the 1980's that an association was necessary for co-operation among South Asian Countries. After a series of discussions, seven countries namely, India, Bangladesh, Pakistan, Nepal, Bhutan, Sri Lanka and Maldives established a regional association in December 1985. These seven countries joined together with mutual trust in order to create an environment conducive to their development.

Basic Principles

Article II of the Chapter of SAARC lay down the following principles:

1. Co-operation within the framework of the Association shall be based on the respect for the principles of sovereign equality, territorial

integrity, political independence, non-interference in the internal affair of other states and mutual benefit.

2. Such co-operation shall not be substitute for bilateral and multilateral co-operation but shall complement them.
3. Such co-operation shall not be inconsistent with bilateral and multilateral obligations.

Significance of SAARC

It was firmly believed that the establishment of SAARC was a logical response to find a solution to the common problems affecting the South Asian countries. The then Prime Minister of India, Shri Rajiv Gandhi, who participated in the inaugural meeting of SAARC, gave a call to the concerned countries to get the idea of their development materialised by remaining out of the conflicts and tensions which are acting as serious hurdles to progress and prosperity of the region.

As its name itself suggests, SAARC is a plan for development. The basic objective of the SAARC is to arrange for mutual co-operation and association with a view to improve economic and social development by making an optimum utilisation of physical and human resources.

Establishment of SAARC is undoubtedly a milestone in regional co-operation. The share of member countries of SAARC in the total world population is 23 per cent. The population of these countries is about 1350 million. These countries account for only 3.3 per cent of the total land area of the world. Hence population density in the member countries of SAARC is about two times of that of low income countries.

Most part of the people in the world live in SAARC countries. All these countries are low income countries with less than 500 dollars of per capita income.

The Role of India in SAARC

India accounts for about two-thirds of the total population of SAARC countries. As against this, population of Maldives is only 1.85 lakhs. Its land area is just 298 square kms. Bhutan is a very small country with only 1.5 million population. Sri Lanka is an island. Maldives is an archipelago. Nepal and Bhutan being land-locked countries, their access to sea routes is only through ports of India and Bangladesh.

India has a dominant role to play in SAARC. Though India suffers from a number of economic problems, it is definitely in a position to help other member countries, particularly the tiny and the least developed ones.

There exists ample scope for development of co-operation between India and other member countries in the fields of education, training, research, indigenous medicine and system of treatment. India can help the fellow member countries in the fields of agriculture and industry. Considerable scope also exists for co-operative ventures in energy development, communications and transport and tourism.

India has a significant role to play in the growth of SAARC. It can play a leading role in bringing about co-operation in the field of tourism and trade among the member countries.

India's dominant position, geographically and economically, should have been an asset for SAARC. But this has not been so. There is mutual distrust among members. This is more so towards India. These member countries are competitors in the international market. For example, this is true of India and Bangladesh with respect to Jute and India and Sri Lanka with respect to tea.

Geographically, India's dominant position in the region can very well be understood with the help of the following table.

Table 27.1: SAARC Members-Geographical Area

Country	*Area (Thousand Sq. Kms)*
India	2973
Pakistan	771
Bangladesh	130
Nepal	143
Sri Lanka	65
Bhutan	47
Maldives	0.3

Source: World Development Report 1998

India Possesses a geographical area of 2973 thousand square kilometres. In contrast, Malidves geograhical area is just 0.3 thousand square kilometres. When compared with India, some countries are small and the remaining are tiny. This amply goes to prove the role that India can play in the region.

Table 27.2: Population and GNP Percapita

Country	*Population (Million)(1997)*	*GNP Percapita (Dollars)(1997)*
India	961	390
Pakistan	137	490
Bangladesh	124	270
Nepal	23	210
Srilanka	18	800
Bhutan	0.7	400
Maldives	0.3	848

Source: World Development Report 1998

The above table indicates that India is the biggest country in terms of population in the SAARC region. In terms of GNP Percapita, only Bangladesh and Nepal are poorer than India.

Exports of India are diversified when compared with those of other member countries of SAARC. This has given an edge to India over other countries in the field of international trade. Again India's share in the total exports and imports in the region is phenomenal.

India accounts for over 40 per cent of the exports and over 20 per cent of the imports of the intra-regional trade in SAARC.

Conclusion

Some studies have shown that regional trading arrangements have utterly failed. It is argued that these arrangements cause trade diversion than trade creation. The basic argument behind this thinking is that when a small group of countries come together to form a trading arrangement, it is accomplished at the cost of a wider trade bloc and a natural scope for trade expansion among a very large number of countries. A small group of neighbouring countries will be sharing many a similarly including production and occupation structure and basic economic problems. In such a situation, a regional trading arrangement will never help in any way expansion of trade among member countries. Instead, it may throttle the initiatives and efforts to develop trading relationship with developed countries.

A World Bank study has also come to the conclusion that trading arrangements between developed countries and developing countries are necessary in the interest of both these groups and also from the point of view of improvement in world trade.

The view that RTAs will cause trade diversion is not scientifically proved. Instead, this type of an arrangement can be a morale booster to poor and small countries to come together and to develop cordial trade relationships with the developed ones.

SAARC can very well become a forum for member countries to articulate their views before the developed countries.

In its seventeen years of existence SAARC has been able to show proper direction in the development of many small countries of South Asia. But basically an argument has been found in some quarters that bilateralism is against the principles of multilateral co-operation. The argument runs on the line that if a small group of countries unite among themselves and develop co-operation in trade, commerce and other economic affairs, it may thwart the efforts in the direction of expansion of economic relations among the nations of the world. But the achievements of SAARC have amply shown that it has complemented multilateral co-operation and has not stood in the way of trade and commerce among the countries of the world.

REFERENCES

1. Dominic Salvatore, International Economics, 1995, Himalaya Publishing, House, Delhi.
2. Francis Cherunilam, International Economics 1999, Tata McGraw-Hill publishing Company Limited, New Delhi.
3. World Bank Atlas, 1999.
4. World Development Reports, 1998, 2000-01.

28

SAARC—'A Distant Dream of Perfect Cooperation'–An Abstract

B. P. Veerabhadrappa
H. G. Devaraj

The SAARC involving seven countries India, Bangladesh, Pakistan, Nepal, Bhutan, Sri Lanka and Maldives was formally launched in December 1985. The birth of SAARC was a logical response to the problems facing the region. The fundamental goal of SAARC is to accelerate economic and social development through optimum utilisation of their human and material resources to promote the welfare of the people of South Asia and to improve their quality of life. The principle of SAARC believed in the cooperation within the framework of the Association based on the principles of sovereign equality, territorial integrity, political independence, non-interference in the internal affairs of other states and mutual benefit. With about 1200 million inhabitants, the SAARC accounts for over one-fifth of the world population. The density of population in the SAARC countries, which have only about 3.3 per cent of the world's land area, is very high, nearly double when compared to the average density of the low income economies as a whole. A major share of the world's poor lives in these countries. All these are low income economies, which have common features and problems which are characteristic of the developing countries. There are a number of areas which offer scope for development through mutual help and cooperation. Some such areas have already been identified and some follow up has been made by making organisational arrangements to forge greater cooperation and interdependence among the people of the region in meteorology, health, civil aviation, shipping, agriculture, communication and renewable sources of energy.

There are however, a number of important problems which affect the relationship among these countries. Border disputes, ethnic issues and differences in political outlooks and affiliations, cause mutual mistrust among the members and there are no signs of substantial improvement of the situation in the near future. The members are well aware of the implications of these problems. The share of intra-regional trade in the total trade of SAARC countries is very insignificant. This has not increased even after the formation of the SAARC. There was, in fact, some fall in the intra-regional trade after the coming into effect of the Association. The share of individual countries trade within the region varies. The share of the region in the members imports also shows a skewed pattern. High levels of tariff and non-tariff barriers have been affecting the trading between SAARC countries. But the presence of non-tariff barriers in different forms are acting as constraints to realise the potential for trade expansion. The SAARC Preferential Trading Arrangement (SAPTA) is expected to play an important role in boosting the intra-regional trade. It is intended to develop SAPTA into a South Asian Free Trade Area (SAFTA). Today SAARC countries' share in total world trade is not even one per cent, and their trade among themselves lingers below three per cent of their total foreign trade. Although some liberalisation measures have been taken following the establishment of SAPTA, some of them are regarded as flawed or inadequate. It is also argued that the approach of SAFTA to introduce trade concessions, initially, on a product-by-product basis is a drag on trade liberalisation. There is a view that what is needed is a customs union and not a free trade area because a free trade area has an important problem that goods from a non member country may enter a member country and from there freely flow throughout the free trade area causing damage to the domestic industry/agriculture of some of the members.

29

SAARC: Where Does It Stand?

Lija Ramachandran. K

Abstract

This paper examines the regional co-operation in South Asian countries and the role of SAARC using the trade growth a decade before and after the formation of SAARC. The study, shows that SAARC, as a regional arrangement is necessary as an economic co-operation rather than as a trading bloc. This is mainly because of the low intra-regional trade among them and further formation of preferential and free trade area results in a trade diverting union bloc and not as a trade creating one in South Asia.

Introduction

A major development, characterising global trade in recent years, has been the growth and proliferation of regional co-operation arrangements. Regional economic co-operation has been adopted as a means of expediting the process of economic development by many countries across the world. South Asia is not an exception to it. South Asian Association for Regional Co-operation came into being in 1985 with seven countries of the region. This paper aims to discuss the nature of regional co-operation operating in South Asia. Though the 'second wave' regionalism stimulated the region to participate in the move much later compared to other regions, the move towards regional co-operation started in the 50s and 60s. However, it became a reality only in the 80s. The region is characterized by common history and almost same sort of traditions. There is ethnic, social and cultural link between the people living in the region. South Asia, as a region has some unique features. With only 3.5 per cent of landmass, it has 20 per cent of the world's population to sustain; its GNP is only 2 per cent of the world's GNP and its per captia income is among the lowest in the world.

Regional Co-operation

The term regional economic co-operation basically implies collaboration among a group of nations comprising the region on economic matters so that each member nation is able to derive greater benefits than what would be possible in the case of normal economic relationship without co-operation. It has been adopted as a means of expanding the process of economic development by many countries across the world. It plays an important role in overcoming the disadvantages in the international trade and attaining better allocation of resources within the region. The spillover effects produced by regional economic co-operation leads to co-operation among various activities within the region. In the pace of globalization, regional economic co-operation and integration, especially among developing countries, can greatly help expanding world trade (Raghavan, 1995).

In this context, it is important to examine why countries are going for regional co-operation in order to accelerate the trade performance when they have the option of unilateral and multilateral liberalisation either through domestic policies or through the institutions viz. WTO.

There are essentially two different ways of opening up of the economy i.e., firstly, each country open up unilaterally and secondly, through trade agreements. The latter may be regional (including bilateral) or multilateral agreements. Economic theory points out that unilateral openness as the best policy for small countries, since it helps to ensure better resource allocation and hence maximise the well being of the community as a whole (Saez and Gabriel, 1999). However, the possibilities of taking full advantage of trade benefits do not depend only on the domestic policies adopted by the country, but also, and fundamentally its trading partners. Moreover, unilateral openness of a country is not necessarily reflected in openness of the markets of its trading partners. For example, it does not necessarily have any effect on their customs practices or the way they adopt and administer technical barriers, nor does it eliminate the restrictive practices applied by countries through the adoption of anti-dumping measure. Through agreements, it is possible to achieve preferential, assured and predictable openness, which facilitates the development of export projects. One of the main objectives of these agreements is to correct market failures that unilateral openness cannot correct itself. They are designed to reduce the transaction costs faced by private agents when taking investment decisions. Asymmetrical information, market flaws, and uncertainty, lack of transparency and the existence of permanent incentives to depart from certain pattern of behaviour increases the cost of operating in international markets. In this context, agreements have two essential functions to play. Firstly, the elimination and regulation of trade barriers through the provision of a framework for co-operation, and secondly, the reduction of transaction costs. As far as multilateralism is concerned, the speed and depth of trade openness that can be achieved at a multilateral level are limited, whereas preferential or regional agreements make it possible to take advantage of the economies of scale offered by a broad market and to incorporate more employment, technology and innovation, which are central elements in economic development, provided that the rules of origin are simple and are aimed at the creation and not the diversion of trade. The rationale for the inclusion of Article XXIV of GATT supports this argument. This article is an exception to the multilateral institution, which is based on the principle of most-favoured-nation (MFN) and national treatment. However, according to Bhagwati (1999), this exception is permitted in cases where it is difficult to reduce the trade barriers. Moreover, it may act as a supplemental practical route to universal free trade.

Theoretically, it is proved that when small countries form a trade bloc with a large country, the former can enhance its trade performance and thus welfare as it will provide an enlarged market for its products. But when small countries form their own trade bloc, it may result in trade diverting one and the region as a whole will suffer due to its increased costs of trade within the region. Panagariya (1999), support this argument. As the region at the aggregate level produces less than one per cent of the world output and that highly efficient producers are spread around the world, a regional bloc among within South Asia is unlikely to yield the any effect on trade flows within the region. Before going to the details of trade performance, we can examine the developments in region before and after the formation of SAARC.

SAARC: A Decade Before and After

As far as economic co-operation among South Asian nations is concerned, some specific factors are identified as favourable to the development of trade within the region. Geographical continuity and proximity of these countries gives a substantial freight advantage and closer ties in co-operation of different sectors. However, most of the economies in the region were highly protected. During the period of 1958-74, the ratio of exports and imports to national income has declined sharply (Aggrawal, 1979).

Moreover, intra-regional trade among the SAARC countries was very low. We can examine the growth of trade a decade before and after the formation of SAARC and see whether regional co-operation has increased the trade flow within the region.

Table 29.1A: Intra-regional exports: 1976-1985 (annual average growth as %)*

To *From*	*Bangladesh*	*India*	*Pakistan*	*Sri Lanka*
Bangladesh	0	133.3	27.3	47.5
India	12.4	0	45	18.5
Pakistan	38	16	0	18
Sri Lanka	40.9	52.2	–1.6	0

Table 29.1B: Intra-regional exports: 1986-1995 (annual average growth as%)*

To *From*	*Bangladesh*	*India*	*Pakistan*	*Sri Lanka*
Bangladesh	0	112.7	–5.1	125.1
India	11	0	24	25.5
Pakistan	16.2	21.1	0	5.4
Sri Lanka	7.3	31.6	3.2	0

It can be seen that Bangladesh's export growth within the region is higher than compared to other major countries even before the establishment of SAARC and after it. As far as India is concerned, its export growth has declined both before and after SAARC except in the case of Sri Lanka during 1986-95 period. In the case of Pakistan, its export growth to India has increased, whereas its exports to other SAARC nations show a declining trend. Sri Lanka's exports show a declining growth over the period of two decades. However, the above tables show that the export has showed a declining trend after the formation of SAARC.

Table 29.2A: Intra-regional imports: 1976-85 (annual average growth as%)*

To / *From*	*Bangladesh*	*India*	*Pakistan*	*Sri Lanka*
Bangladesh	0	13.7	13.7	118.7
India	39.9	0	19.3	32
Pakistan	71.4	133	0	–2.9
Sri Lanka	45.9	23.6	18.4	0

Table 29.2B: Intra-regional imports: 1986-95 (annual average growth as %)*

To / *From*	*Bangladesh*	*India*	*Pakistan*	*Sri Lanka*
Bangladesh	0	28.2	13.7	118.7
India	60.1	0	24.6	39.2
Pakistan	0.8	24.1	0	7.8
Sri Lanka	91.9	19.6	4	0

**Source:* Calculated from various issues of International Trade

Statistics between 1975 to 1998

As far as import is concerned, the period 1976-85 showed not much progress among the countries except in the case of Pakistan where its imports growth to India has showed an annual average growth of 133 per cent. However, its import growth to India has sharply declined to 24.1 per cent during 1986-95. Apart from this, intra regional imports showed an increasing growth during the period of 1986-95.

Thus an over all picture given in the above tables is a mixed one. On the one hand, export growth has declined after the formation of SAARC and on the other hand, the import growth has shown an increasing trend. Examining the trade of a major country in the region viz. India we can see how far the dominant partner's trade affects the intra-regional trade and its growth.

Table 29.3: India's Trade with SAARC and The World Average Annual Growth (as%)

	Exports		*Imports*	
	SAARC	*World*	*SAARC*	*World*
1976-85	8.0	7.8	11.3	12.6
1986-95	19.7	14.2	9.0	15.5

Source: Calculated from Direction of Trade Statistics Year Book (IMF), various issues.

India's trade share with SAARC countries can be compared with its trade with the world. On export side, India's trade with SAARC has increased much faster than its exports to world between 1976-85 to 1986-95, whereas import has declined over the same period from SAARC countries while its import from the world has increased during the same period.

During 1975 to 1995, Indian export to SAARC and world is shown in the above figure. It can be clearly seen that even

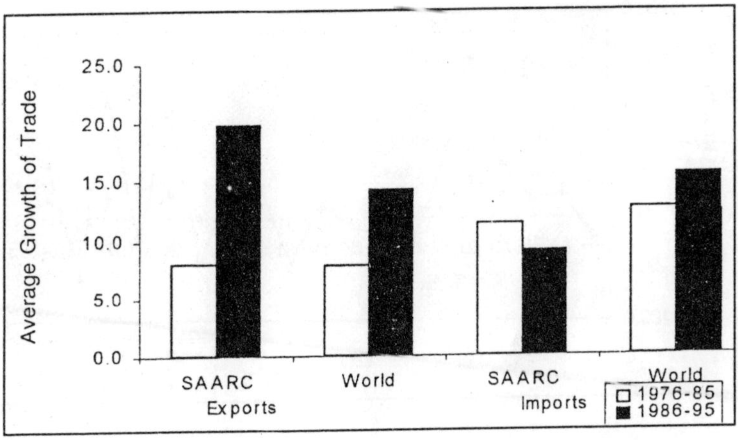

Fig. 29.1: India's Average growth of Trade with SAARC and World.

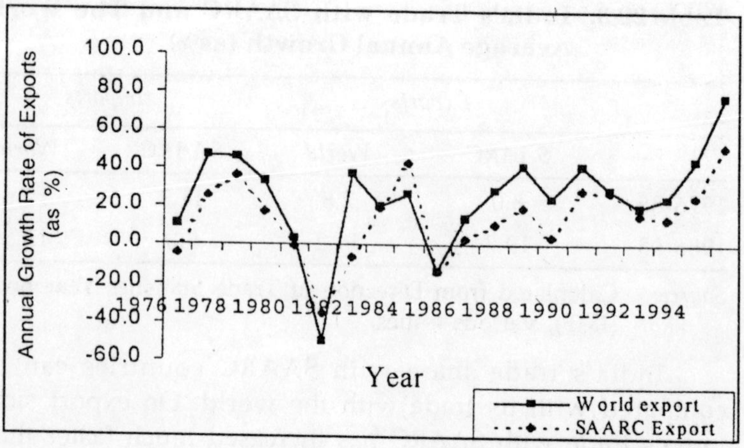

Fig. 29.2: India's Export Growth to SAARC and World: 1976-1995.

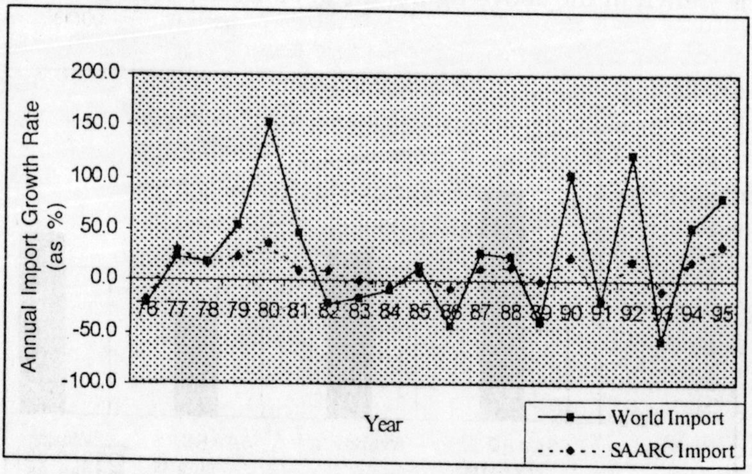

Fig. 29.3: India's Import from SAARC and the World: 1975-1995.

when India's exports growth rate has declined to negative, its exports to SAARC was not declined to the same rate. This is especially the case of 1980 to 1983. However, the growth rate of exports has been always less than its growth of its exports to world except during 1984-86 period. Moreover, the annual growth rate shows an interesting trend, that is, after the formation of SAARC, the export growth rate has not declined to zero or negative level. This may be mainly due to the liberalisation process, which started in mid 1980s and accelerated, in the early 1990s.

More or less similar is the case with import also except with high growth rate during late 70s and early 90s, when India's import from the world showed fluctuations.

Recent Trends

During the early 90s, most of the South Asian Nations started liberalisation process. These countries started opening their economy in order to cope up with the globalisation process, which got catalysed with the multilateral institutions like WTO. Though the process is slow, but moving towards opening up of the economy by reducing and eliminating tariffs and other non-trade barriers. Sri Lanka started its liberalisation process even early in the 1970s, whereas others started in 80s and 90s an indicator of openness is the trade integration ratio which is the ratio of sum of exports and imports to GDP. (Table 29.3).

Table 29.4 clearly shows that South Asian nations started opening up of the economy. However, among these countries India lags behind other nations in this regard. Sri Lanka's trade integration ratio is much higher compared to other countries. In 1989, it was 93.9 per cent, and it has increased to 123.6 per cent in 1999. Though a higher integration ratio is a sign towards moving the economies to integrate with the world economy, however, when we compared these countries with the other nations especially with the South East Asian

Nations, we can see that South Asian countries lag behind the rest of the world. Thus there is need to move further rather than following protectionist policies.

Table 29.4: Merchandise Trade (as % of GDP)

	1989	*1999*
South Asia		
Bangladesh	30	53.0
India	19.8	31.1
Nepal	30.5	-
Pakistan	52.3	62.6
Sri Lanka	93.9	123.6
Other countries		
Malaysia	211.4	333.7
Singapore	854.6	739.5
Indonesia	63.4	81.3
Thailand	123.6	171.2

Source: World Development Indicators, 2001

As mentioned earlier, regionalism may help in opening up of the economies and this is one of the rationales for the inclusion of Article XXIV of GATT. How far it is true in the case of SAARC is an important question. The intra-regional exports as a share of SAARC's total exports shows that regional economic co-operation may not be an alternative way for the improving trade share of these developing countries.

Table 29.5: Intra-regional Exports of SAARC (as % of total exports)

1970	*1980*	*1985*	*1990*	*1995*	*1996*	*1997*	*1998*	*1999*
3.2	4.8	4.5	3.2	4.4	4.3	4.0	5.3	4.7

Source: World Development Indicators, 2001

Intra-regional exports are abysmally small which is not sufficient to give impetus for further expansion of trade with in the country. In this context, it is better to think of SAARC only as a co-operation arrangement rather than a trade bloc and the move towards forming preferential and free trade areas may not be a successful experiment as far as South Asia is concerned. More over, even if these forces becomes a reality, then, the aftermath of it is that the region as a whole may suffer.

Conclusion

From the above discussion, we can see that the South Asian region has potential to improve its trade. But the establishment of SAARC may act only as co-operation arrangement and the formation of trade blocs may result in less favourable to the region as a whole. Concentrating on co-operation arrangement in specific sectors may yield better outcome and thus a sectoral approach within SAARC is the best alternative for the SAARC.

REFERENCES

Aggarwal, M.R. (1979), *Regional Economic Co-operation in South Asia,* S. Chand and Company Ltd., New Delhi.

Bhagwati, Jagdish (1999), Regionalism and Multilatoralism: An Overview In Bhagwati, Jagdish *et.al.* (eds.). *Trading Blocs Alternative Approaches to Analyzing Preferential Trade Agreements,* London: The MIT Press.

Panagariya, Arvind (1999), 'Trade Policy in South Asia: Recent Liberalisation and Future Agenda,' *World Economy,* 22, 3, 353-78.

Raghavan, S.N. (1995), Regional Economic Co-operation Among SAARC Countries, Allied Publishers Limited, New Delhi.

Saez, Sebastain and Juan Gabriel Valdes S. (1999), 'Chile and its Lateral trade policy', Cepal Review, Vol. 67. 85-99.

30

European Union, the Euro and India-An Economic and Business Analysis

Gajavelli V.Swamy

Introduction

The European Union (EU) is the association of countries formerly called the European community (EC) and prior to that known as the European Economic Community (EEC). The EEC became the EC when the issues handled in common moved from mainly economic and trade matters to include social and political aspects. EC became the EU when common tariff levels were applied by all members to outside countries and tariffs among the member countries were removed—EC transformed into a Customs Union.

The EU, which came into existence on 1st January 1993, is a major event in international political and economic relations and has caught the attention of the world. The collapse of the erstwhile USSR and the dramatic turn of events in Eastern Europe have significant bearings on North-South Relations as the countries of South undergo fundamental changes. Against this backdrop, the construction of the EU and its impact on developing economies in the context of changing North-South relations provide an interesting agenda for research, which is beyond the scope of this particular paper.

"The process of construction of the Union involved radical changes in the economic, commercial, trade and external policies of the EU. These changes, although mostly internal, would have significant implications for all other countries in relation to the Community, the issues in contemporary North-South relations and trade prospects of emerging economies at large".

Recently, the EU facilitated the transition of European currency (€) from a notional accounting measure to its acceptance as legal tender in twelve member states from January, 2002—with this EU transformed into a Currency Union. How big a deal is a currency union really? It is tremendous, say economists and analysts. A Currency union goes much beyond a free trade zone or customs union like the North Atlantic Free Trade Zone and does away with the very notion of fluctuations across currencies and exchange risk involved. The main objective of such arrangement being: **To create a unique European common market and bring-in the benefits of enhanced market competition and integration.**

Such European Integration will have far-reaching implications to India's foreign trade, capital inflows and growth prospects. Since the fifteen member EU is India's major trading partner and source of investment and aid, ahead of Japan and the U.S. It is in this context, this paper is an attempt to address some of these issues from the point of view of emerging challenges and opportunities for India's foreign sector and its growth prospects.

The paper is divided into three sections. The first section gives an account of European integration and its impact on India's business and industry. An attempt is made here to assess the implications to exporters and importers, exchange rate movements, currency risk and hedging prospects and the relevant strategic considerations for Indian corporates. The second section is an attempt to analyse the possible implications to India's foreign trade, investment flows and growth prospects. Also, it gives an appraisal of India's preparedness in terms of legal, banking and IT related changes. The third section examines the mega implications of the European integration and macroeconomic policies pursued by EU (for example, European Central Bank's monetary policy) to global economy, equity and bond markets in Europe and the rest of the world; and trade and investment flows into India. Also, it focusses on the issues of growing regionalisation of trade (such as EU, NAFTA, ASEAN and Mercosur in South America) and their implications to major currencies; and prospects for emerging economies like India in such an evolving scenario. The fourth section gives an appraisal of the expected benefits and risks arising out of Euro for the EU itself. Also, it critically examines the progress made by the EU towards a true integration, apart from providing summary and concluding remarks.

1. European Union, the Euro and Indian Business

The implementation of European Monetary Union (EMU) and the introduction of the Euro would significantly transform the way business is done by companies, at both strategic and operational level. Though the Euro represents new business prospects, the companies must develop new skills and capabilities to tackle and effectively manage the changes in the areas of accounting information technology, tax, treasury, legal and most importantly the financial and other information systems. Further, inadequate preparation to deal with the Euro may adversely affect the companies' very existence.

Some Issues Related to Business and Industry

Some of the challenges that the Euro will pose to the Indian corporates are mainly with regard to the following including an assessment of corporate strategies. Most corporates are already trying their best to adapt to the changing scenario.

(i) **Invoicing and Pricing:** Problem in pricing and invoicing occur when a company has to quote its products/services both in Euro and the legacy currencies (or in-currencies). While one-fifth of India's foreign trade is with Euroland, less than 10 per cent is invoiced in the EMU currencies. The immediate effect of the EMU will, therefore, be moderate, though there may be pressures from counter parties and banks to switch over to the Euro. Besides, it will be necessary to assess pricing and marketing policies followed by corporates. As currency barriers completely vanish by July 2002, transparency and efficiency gains for the markets will be enormous. Euroland contributes nearly 17.5 pre cent of world trade (compared to 15.9 per cent of the U.S) and synergies will only improve their share in the world trade.

(ii) **Risk-monitoring and Hedging:** A common currency does effect transaction costs at the margins and influence trade and capital flows between India and Eurozone economies. It means, Indian and European exporters and importers as well as European investors now need to hedge risk in one currency only-the Euro, instead of a multiple currencies like the DM and FFr. This clearly reduces the cost of foreign exchange risk monitoring and hedging. However, given the share of India's trade with Euroland and invoicing practices as mentioned above, the magnitude of this effect has been and is likely to remain moderate.

(iii) **Effect on Rupee**: There is not likely to be any significant impact on the rupee. We expect the U.S. dollar to retain the "intervention currency' status for the foreseeable period. However, as invoicing shifts to the Euro and its importance increases, the Euro-Rupee rate will be monitored more closely. For instance, during 1st Jan 2001 to 15th January 2002, the rupee has gained by Rs. 0.72 and the U.S dollar by about $ 0.05 against Euro. The result is that the weakening of the Euro against the dollar has reduced the export competitiveness of Indian firms from the rupee's depreciation against the dollar.

(iv) **Dollar-Rupee Risk Diversification:** The majority of Indian firms have atleast 80% of their foreign exchange transactions in US $s. This goes very much against the basic tenets of prudent risk management and diversification. For example, during mid-June to 11th August 2002, US$-Rupee rose 2.35%. An importer with 100% exposure to US $ saw its liabilities rise from a base of 100 to 102.35. Over the same period, when Euro-Rupee fell 4.63%, an importer with 25% exposure to the Euro saw its liabilities rise from a base of 100 to only 100.60. By diversifying into a more liquid market such as Euro-Dollar, the risk arising from the structure of the Indian rupee market (which is small, thin and illiquid with wide spreads) can be hedged. Trends in one strong currency, say US $, can be hedged by offsetting trends in another currency, say Euro.

(v) **Macro-environment, Forecasting and Budgeting.** It is very essential to understand the economic impact of the Euro to enable intelligent forecasting and to have an understanding of the overall economic performance of Euro-12 rather than individual economies. Euro involves following a single monetary policy and a largely similar fiscal policy across the member-economies; and also merging of capital markets.

The Euro's performance on the foreign exchange markets mainly depends on the underlying strength of the euro-zone economy. Over the past three years, 1999-2001, the US has been a better place to invest because its economy has performed well. Capital over flowed into the U.S from Europe in 2001 because most investors thought the U.S economy would recover from recession more strongly than the Euro-zone's. Consequently, the dollar continued to strengthen against Euro, even though the Euro-zone did not show it as quickly as the U.S. This essentially reflects the role played by 'perceptions' of the market players about the macro economic fundamentals of respective economies within the region.

(vi) **Re-conventioning and re-denominating.** Outstanding debt in the 'in-currencies' (pre-1st January, 2002 individual currencies and to be phased out by July 2002) need to be re-denominated into Euro only after 2002, but it will have to be reconventional in terms of floating rate indices, day count conventions, etc. The understanding is that the LIBOR (London Inter-Bank Offer Rate) for incurrencies will be replaced by the Euro LIBOR and that PIBOR, FIBOR (Paris/ Frankfurt) etc will be replaced by the Euribor. The day count for bonds is expected to be Act/ Act. These details should be agreed with one's counter parties. This holds good for derivatives as well. For option players, historical volatility

measures for risk analysis are available, obtained by creation of a 'synthetic euro'. tracked over a period of time.

(vii) **Corporates—Size and Business Strategy.** A currency union like the EU overcomes the trade barriers and the so-called 'home-country bias' created by exchange rate risk and facilitate a truly integrated market. Trade and investment flow within the region pick-up with corporates and countries competing purely on the basis of competitive strength.

Firstly, the Euro will greatly enhance sales and procurement opportunities as currency related barriers to the movement of merchandise, services and factors of production within EMU region will cease.

Second, The Euro region will also be an attractive investment destination as it may serve as access points to all the member countries and also the newly emerging markets of Central and Eastern Europe.

Third, Selecting a right business location in Europe will be easier for Indian corporates as exchange rate related concerns no longer matter for the choice of a right business location. Corporates could concentrate on other critical parameters directly related to the main concerns of the company such as production cost, technology, proximity to market centres and infrastructure.

Fourth, for banks the process of integration brings bit of bad news with good. The most significant impact for the Indian banks operating abroad is the elimination of exchange rate risk across the EMU region, which will encourage banks to buy/sell securities across the borders on a massive scale.

With the introduction of Euro, the notion of domestic currency become redundant taking away with the captive markets for foreign banks *on par* with domestic banks. The activity of M&As and restructuring that one can see in the European banking sector and their ramifications for their Indian subsidiaries (and also for Indian banks operating there) reflects this adjustment to a level-playing field.

Fifth, Indian firms with already established sales and production networks in Euro-zone will face more strategic challenges—in terms of the pricing of product and services. While on the one hand it will lead to larger local markets, on the other the companies will come under pressure from newly emerging competition, as in the case of European banking sector, within the region. The increased price transparency in this market will have an impact on price discrimination and the prices charged by a business for its goods and services in different markets in the region. This in turn might impact on existing packaging and labelling of products and on new product development. Thus, cost-cutting and innovation will be prerequisites for competitiveness and the future market position in an evolving scenario.

2. Euro-zone, the Euro and Indian Economy

The implication of Euro on India can be analysed in terms of its effect on trade, foreign aid, external commercial borrowings, FDI and portfolio flows, banking related issues and technology.

Prospects for Foreign Trade

The EU is India's biggest trading partner and source of investment and aid exceeding the contribution of both Japan and the U.S. Nearly 25% of our exports go to the region and imports from there make-up for about 30% of the total. Apart from the direct favourable impact on exchange risk monitoring and related costs (as mentioned in the above section), there is no immediate impact of Euro on India's exports and imports to, and from the Euro-zone. However, going by the trends in European corporate sector, it is quite possible that European firms will become more and more competitive as they would rationalise, streamline and become cost-efficient competitors. Further, the evolving markets of a gigantic size as Euroland would enhance market access and open up new opportunities for commercial ventures. This would imply that Indian firms have larger opportunities to be proactive and competitive. Sectorally, there could be more scope for software exports to the Eurozone. As recent experience shows Indian software companies are already able to access and diversify exports to Euro-zone countries.

Trade Invoicing

Indian exporters and importers are currently invoicing nearly 80% of its total trade in US $s. Switching over to invoicing in Euro by Indian firms depend on a number of circumstances. For example, POL products and fertilisers, which account for a major chunk of our imports, are denominated in US $s which is an international practice. Similarly, exporters and importers in other countries may still continue with US $ denomination. However, the European companies which were earlier invoicing in US $s prefer to shift to Euro. Indian firms would keep watch on international practices, preferences of their trading partners, possible natural hedge opportunities and their own considerations in such a shift in invoicing from US $ to Euro.

Foreign Currency Account/Deposits

These are basically nostro accounts of banks, foreign currency accounts maintained in India by banks such as EEFC/RFC accounts and foreign currency deposit accounts (FCNR-B) in DM. During the period of transition (i.e. introduction of Euro on 1st January, 2002 followed by complete withdrawal of national currencies by July 2002), banks can maintain nostro accounts in "in-currencies" or/ and Euro. Banks in India are already maintaining nostro accounts in Euro. With respect to foreign currency accounts, banks have been allowed to open accounts in Euro also. Similarly, in the case of FCNR (B) deposits, banks were permitted to offer 'Euro accounts' in addition to DM during the transition phase. In the case of existing fixed rate FCNR (B) deposits, the interest rates will continue till maturity. For existing floating rate deposits, as they are linked to Libor, banks have been instructed to use Euro Libor, the successor index. And for new deposits, banks have been allowed to link their interest rates either to Eurobor or Euro Libor.

Foreign Direct Investment (FDI) Flows

The Eurozone accounts for nearly 12% of the total FDI in India. Newly introduced Euro is unlikely to have an impact on existing investments, which are denominated in rupees. The investor can remit the funds in any convertible currency of his choice including Euro. However, in the case of GDRs if they are denominated in any of the 12 national currencies, the issuer can re-denominate them into Euro during the transition phase. As the physical arrival of the Euro will encourage Euro-zone governments to push-through much needed structural reforms and a broader and deeper Euro market would make the Euro more attractive to investors.

External commercial Borrowings

The introduction of Euro would go a long way in enhancing the financing opportunities for Indian firms who have been so far largely tapping the markets abroad in U.S $s in the form of bonds and syndicated loans. With Euro becoming attractive, competition between Us $ and Euro would become more intense and result in possible marginal reduction in spreads for Indian corporates. Moreover, Indian borrowers will now have greater access to Euro-zone markets in view of the larger investor base and a common financial market. For long-term financing, those firms which have natural hedge in Euro now find it attractive to borrow in Euro and take advantage of lower costs. Also, there is scope for raising dollar denominated and Euro loans in Euroland now.

Legal and Information Technology Issues.

There are no difficulties as such in Indian legal system regarding continuity of contracts *per se.* Under the existing foreign exchange regulations, Reserve Bank of India (RBI) has notified Euro as a permissible currency and hence settling payments in Euro is legal. However, a clause of continuity has been recommended for existing contracts which goes beyond 2002.

With regard to information technology, existing computer systems are already modified to recognise Euro, carry out and record relevant business transactions in the Euro. The modified systems must be able to provide a link between the in-currencies and the Euro as all the in-currencies are connected through Euro (atleast till July 2002, when all in-currencies will be phased out.) Thus, the systems will need to be made to handle orders in both the currencies which will require a thorough understanding of user interfaces with other linked subsystems and ledgers to ensure consistency throughout the financial information system. The businesses may also require a system functionality to match in-currencies/euro receipts with national currency unit invoices.

The significance attained more prominence as the IT impact of the change over coincided over broadly the same period as the Y2K problem.

Overall, the influence of the Euro and the underlying monetary union on the global economy, asset markets and the structure of international banking are anything but moderate. However, there are effects which Indian business, government and the banking sector need to monitor to explore the opportunities, given the size of the Euro-zone market.

3. European Union, the Euro and World Economy: The Underlying Macroeconomics and Policy Implications

Going by the experience of the last two years, it would be too early to be able to assess accurately how important the Euro will become in the international economy and financial system. It would take some more time for analysts, policy-markers, borrowers, investors and other financial market players to understand the Euro and its relative importance. However, one can assess the possible advantages and implications of the Euro and the underlying Macroeconomics and policy.

First, the impression among market analysts is that the Euro would become a more attractive currency for bond issuers. In fact, in the first month of its introduction in 1999, the Euro was the most popular currency for bonds issued in the international markets. It accounted for nearly 55% of the volume of new bond issues compared with 40% for the US $. This was mainly due to initial euphoria about Euro-denominated instruments.

Second, with Euro, the notion of domestic currency become redundant and the dominant strategy for European banking heavy weights would be to increase market share in the Par-European market. Thus, the persisting trend of M & As and consolidation is likely to continue in future. Size does matter, especially when domestic banks are loosing captive markets in the wake of Euro's introduction.

Third, indications show that the Euro is likely to become more attractive for the investment of Central Bank's official reserves. Currently, the US $ is by far the most important reserve currency world over. It is reported that well over half of official reserves are held in US $ denominated assets while about one-fifth are currently held in EMU currencies. According to Ashrof Laidi, Chief currency analyst at New York based MG Financial Group, some major Central Banks may decide to keep a larger part of their reserves in Euro. The People's Bank of China, the Bank of Japan, The Central Bank of Taiwan, and the Bank of England have all indicated that they may now divest part of their reserve holdings by acquiring the single currency. The shift to Euro assets by Central Banks around the world would be motivated by its strength, its increasing use as a transaction currency and the more liquid and deeper bond markets, among other factors. And there are indications of supporting factors that should help boost the Euro currency's value over both the medium term and long-term. The Euro zone's 'basic balance' - i.e. the sum of its current account balance plus long-term capital flows-is growing and this indicates that during the course of 2002, the Euro might at last appreciate. Other factors are also supportive of Euro like weaker oil prices, tumbling inflation rates, and an expected increase in the acquisition of Euro-zone companies by foreign institutions.

Fourth, the emergence of Euro, and the underlying EU will have far-reaching implications to major currencies (and the much-touted benefits of globalisation) more particularly to the US $. Indeed, considering regional trading arrangements such as NAFTA, EU, Mercosur in South America and ASEAN, more and more of international trade is occurring within regions. Statistics show that between 1982 to 1998, the proportion of U.S trade with countries in North, Central and South America increased from 29.31% to 37.1%, while Japan's trade with other Asian nations increased from 19.7% to 34.6%, and Germany's trade with other European countries which was already at a record high of 64% has increased to 77.6%.

This trend toward regionalisation of trade has important currency implications, making it of paramount significance to international financial management. The Euro currency (earlier it was DM which played a dominant role in Europe) is likely to become more dominant as the settlement currency in Europe, with the same being true for Japanese Yen in Asia. It is quite possible that the Euro could also emerge as an important anchor currency for other countries, particularly among countries in Central and Eastern Europe by virtue of their geographical proximity and possible economic linkages. Some of these countries may find it useful to peg their currencies formally or informally to the Euro or a basket of currencies with Euro carrying large weightage. *As a result, the role of US $, which has been the dominant global currency for price quotations and settlement of international payments, likely to be diminished outside the Americas in future.*

Fifth, the Euro is likely to become an alternate currency for invoicing next only to the US $. Approximately, 50% of the world exports is invoiced in US $s, almost four times the share of US in world trade. While nearly 20% of world exports are invoiced in EU currencies and 5% in Japanese Yen. In the long-run, it is possible that Euro would become an important alternate currency for the invoicing of international trade.

Sixth, it is quite possible that corporates would find Euro as a preferred currency for financial transactions. Trade finance could be more easily accessible to corporates in India and abroad as the European banks compete purely on their competitive strength and able to extend loans at attractive rates. Further, in the case of long-term financing those firms that have natural hedge in Euro may find it advantageous to borrow in Euro and take advantage of lower costs.

Also, with the elimination of exchange risk and the emergence of a single currency market, the scope for sector-specific funds expected to be more attractive. Therefore, raising funds for sectoral projects like financing of infrastructure projects become easier with the single currency.

Last, but not least, issue is with respect to the underlying macroeconomics and policy implications of the Euro on world trade, output and investments flows. With the advent of Euro, national central banks of the member countries have ceded monetary control to the European Central Bank (ECB)- based at Frankfurt. The German Bundesbank heavily influences the ECB's 'monetary stance' with inflation control as the prime target. However, this is often at the cost of the real economy and its growth prospects. Inspite of clear signs of global and European slow-down since the middle of 2000, the ECB foiled an interest rate cut till May 2001—its second cut since inception, while the Bank of England resorted to interest rate cuts thrice during the same period. For the Global economy in the long-term this kind of 'tight' monetary stance would imply that there would be an upward pressure on interest rates and consequent tightness in liquidity. This would dampen both the equity and bond markets in Europe and the rest of the world. For the world economy as a whole, it could mean that expansion/revival in output would be more moderate. This bound to affect trade and investment flows into India, and hence its growth momentum.

Thus, the implication to the global economy though difficult to assess accurately, the general perception is encouraging. How important is the role Euro would play and how fast it would impact on the global macroeconomy hinges on a variety of factors. More importantly, it would depend on how the expected benefits and risks evolve for all the players, and more particularly for the Euro zone economy itself (as examined below).

4. Benefits and Risks for European Monetary Union

There has been a lot of discussion about the possible benefits and risks arising out of Euro for the EMU itself. There is even greater interest in the implications for the rest of the world. It may be useful to highlight the differing view points in this regard.

Benefits

First, by eliminating different currencies, the Euro eliminates foreign exchange risk, including to counties that are members of the EMU.

Second, an immediate implication of the introduction of the single currency is the reduction in transaction costs. The costs associated with converting one currency into another, crossborder transfers by companies and hedging of risks are reduced.

Third, the current nationally based bond markets are transformed into a single market with common norms. The integration of financial markets is expected to boost the supply of new issues and instruments.

Fourth, the new funding and investment possibilities in the Euro-region are expected to become more efficient and competitive. As a result of increased price transparency and competition, financing costs of firms will probably scale down.

Fifth, the higher yield corporate debt market will in all likelihood become much large in the Euro with the elimination of foreign exchange risk. This will enable corporate credit risks to be priced more accurately.

Sixth, elimination of exchange rate fluctuations between legacy currencies or in-currencies is expected to lead to a significant increase in trade and investment within the Euro area.

Seventh, it is argued that giving other countries the ability to peg their currencies to a basket of hard currencies (say a mix of US dollar and Euro) might stabilise fixed exchange rate regimes.

Risks for EMU

First, it is held that different economies in the EMU are at different levels of business cycle, and hence there may be occasions when a single monetary policy appears inadequate to tackle the problem of growth and employment (-which is country specific-) in a desired manner.

Second the 'stability and growth pact' provides an excellent in-built mechanism to ensure fiscal discipline among the EMU countries. However, it is felt among some that the in-built mechanism may come under some stress during the initial periods.

Third, some concern has been expressed by some regarding absence of clear rules on 'seignorage' sharing and open market operations.

Fourth, since introduction of the Euro, there has been some degree of volatility and depreciation of Euro, against the US dollar. However, it is too early to formulate any medium to long-term view based on €-US$ exchange rate movements in the short-term.

Fifth, it is conceded that there would be significant reduction in transaction costs, but there are doubts about the extent to which this will get translated into cost reduction and efficiencies-given the fact that product and factor markets are still regulated in the Euro-zone economies to a significant level.

The Euro-zone and Prospects: Summary and Concluding Remarks

The primary objective of introducing a single currency is essentially to create a unique European common market and bring-in the benefits of enhanced market competition and integration for the Euro-zone economies. But the new currency has not really achieved the targeted objectives. Inspite of its initiation and experimentation over the years not really contributed to transform Europe into a vibrant economic entity. The governments resist to introduce structural/microeconomic reforms and industries are still protected from competition. Moreover, Europe's product and labour markets are highly regulated, which renders the very process of European Integration incomplete.

Coming to the macroeconomic management issues of integration, the reality is that different economies within the Euro zone are at different phases of business cycle and therefore ECB's uniform monetary policy proves, sometimes, inadequate to tackle the basic issues of low growth and unemployment (which are country-specific) in a desired manner. Especially, since membership of the Union also comes with tight 'fiscal discipline' enshrined in the Maastricht criteria which sets upper bounds on government budget deficits and hence the ability to revive their flagging economies by pump-priming will be muted. The ECB refuses to lower interest rates and the member nations cannot raise public spending either since it might violate the Maastricht norms. In 2001, Ireland faced a similar situation. Its attempts to raise budget deficit attracted a severe reprimand form ECB. The Irish opposition did not loose the chance to criticise the government against the perceived 'loss of sovereignty'. The IMF advised the ECB to go a bit easy on fiscal targets.

Another problem lies at the heart of Europe-Germany which is struggling to keep its budget deficit below 3% of GDP, inspite of impending recession. This is to adhere to 'the stability and growth pact' norms. The Pact, adopted at Germany's behest , provides that any country breaching the 3% ceiling could be subject to fines as big as 0.5% of GDP. Though there are let-out clauses for deep recessions, but Germany looks unlikely to qualify for such relaxations.

Is there a way out of this crisis-driven model of integration? Many eminent European leaders and policy-makers could come out with several solutions including a whole new round of political integration. One popular idea, promoted by both Lionel Jospin, the French Prime Minister and Romani Prode, the head of European Commission (EC), is the appointment of Mr. Euro who could represent the entire euro-zone in various international economic forums. Other suggestions include the harmonisation of corporate and other taxes and the creation of a bail-out fund to help counties in economic trouble. Because options open to countries with a national currency, notably devaluations and an independent monetary policy, are no longer open to members of the euro-zone. Hence Mr. Prodi suggests that the Union should greatly increase its central budget (implying that members pay taxes into a central pool), so that if a country hit by a shock specific to itself, then some of it could be transferred to help it tide-over the crisis. This federal fiscal structure is considered as the key to the success of the U.S, often touted as the oldest and the most stable currency union.

Though many eminent European leaders think that the logical end to the integration process is that of a closer 'political union', but that is not to say that Europe must now proceed to closer political union. On the contrary, the union has a new currency to reckon with and a daunting task of adhering to the stability pact norms. In case if the breach of the limit norms went unpunished, the down-side risk is that the new currency could suffer a credibility loss. And the problem is that the stability pact, far from creating more of flexibility, actually creates less and out of the reach of a member country, as in the case of the recent German experience.

The true flexibility and endurance that Euro-zone economy badly needs at this juncture can only come from removing remaining barriers to competition and further deregulating product and labour markets. More importantly the governments including Germany's must go ahead with the structural reforms to make their economies more vibrant and contribute to the very process of heightened market competition and integration.

Appendix: 1-What is the Euro? The Construction

With the arrival of the European Monetary Union on January 1, 1999 the European countries have begun replacing their national currencies with the euro, transforming the European Union (EU) into the world's largest single currency trade group. The union poses both challenges and opportunities to businesses which will now be operating in an open and transparent market.

Out of 15 nations which comprise the European Union (EU), only 11 (and later 12) adopted the Euro in January 1, 1999. The EMU is the largest single currency zone in the world with a GDP of eight trillion dollars. The new bloc will be an economic might account for 19.4% of the world GDP and 18.6% of the world trade as compared to the US which accounts for 19.6% of world GDP and 16.6% of the world trade and Japan which contributes only 7.7% of world GDP and 8.8% of world trade. Also, the unification is

Table 30.1: Key Statistics

1998	*Area (000 km2)*	*People (mn nos)*	*GDP (mkt pr)*
EU-15	3191	376	7495
Euro-11	2364	292	5774
USA	9373	270	7592
Japan	378	127	3327

expected to bring an additional growth in GDP (for the 11 member countries) of about 0.5-1% thus overtaking the US.

Apart from this, the formation of EMU will rake in many other benefits such as:

- Lower business costs with a single currency
- Rise in competition may reduce prices benefiting the consumers and making countries more competitive in the international markets
- Centralised fiscal and monetary policy will provide interest and inflation rates which are stable and under control
- Which will in turn encourage corporate investment

Starting Jan 1 '99, the currencies of member countries (11 countries which joined the EMU include Austria, Belgium, Finland, France, Germany, Ireland, Italy, Luxembourg, The Netherlands, Portugal and Spain) has been linked to the Euro with a fixed conversion rate. The local currency and the Euro will co-exist until July 2002 at the latest, after which the local currency will be replaced by the Euro.

Entrance criteria. The European Commission (EC), the EU's administrative body, has set up entrance criteria to ensure the countries that joined EMU had reasonable chance of succeeding in a single currency zone. These "convergence criteria" focused on stabilised inflation, exchange rate stability, sustainability of public finances and the ratio of public debt to GDP.

Qualification test for EMU members

Inflation rate should not exceed 1.5% above the average of best three Countries.

- Long term interest rate not more than 2% higher than the average rate of three member Countries with the lowest inflation rate.

- Budget deficit to be maintained within 3% of the GDP
- Public debt not exceeding 60% of the GDP.

Appendix 2: Legal framework

The main parts of the legal framework for the introduction and the use of the Euro are laid down in two European Council regulations:

No Compulsion-no Prohibition

The fundamental principle applicable during the transitional period (1 January 1999 to 31 December 2001) is that no enterprise or individual will be required to use the euro. The corollary will also apply; no enterprise or individual will be prohibited from using the euro in transactions where they deem it appropriate. Thus, obligations in legal instruments stipulating the use of one of the units possible, the national currency or the Euro shall be performed in the stipulated unit unless otherwise agreed by the parties. This rule ensures that economic agents will only have to use the unit to which they have agreed. To further clarify, if an enterprise or individual chooses to use the Euro and the counterparty of the transaction does not; the financial institution or bank is required, under European legislation, to convert to the chosen currency.

The principles of 'no compulsion' and ' 'no prohibition' concerning the use of the Euro were established during the 1996 Madrid summit. There is an inevitable trade-off between the freedom of the economic agents and that of the Member States. As a result of these trade-offs, enterprises may be faced with the following situations:

> It may not be possible in all countries to file tax returns for income taxes, value-added taxes, and customs and duties, in Euro from the start of the transitional period.

- It may not be possible in all countries to keep books and records and to file accounts in Euro from the starts of the transitional period.
- Other transactions with government bodies and agencies, such as payments of registration fees or sales and purchases, may only be possible in the national currency unit during the transitional period. However, as explained above, it is the obligation of your financial institution to convert the Euro to the national currency to effect the payment.

Payments in Euro During the Transitional Period

As from 1 January 1999 any amount denominated either in the Euro unit or in the participating member state national currency unit, can be paid by the debtor either in the euro unit or in the national currency unit.

The legal regulations enable debtors to settle their debts in book money (electronic form) by making a payment in either the Euro or in the national currency. Banks are under an obligation to convert such payments into the unit of accounts of the creditor.

When a business only maintains a bank account in the national currency, receipts in Euro must be converted into the national currency. The Euro regulations do not expressly address the issue of charging for the conversion of amounts between the national currency unit and the Euro unit. This will be subject to competitive forces.

Rounding

"Monetary amounts to be paid or accounted for when a rounding takes place after a conversion into the Euro unit shall be rounded up or down to the nearest cent. Monetary amounts to be paid or accounted for which are converted into a national currency unit shall be rounded up or down to the nearest sub-unit or in the absence of a sub-unit to the nearest unit, or according to national law or practice to a multiple or fraction of the sub-unit or unit of the national currency unit. If the application of the conversion rate gives a result which is exactly half-way, the sum shall be rounded up." The resulting among must be rounded to the nearest number in the smallest subdivision of the currency (i.e. 2 units to the right of the decimal). If the conversion results in an amount that is exactly the middle of the smallest subdivision of the currency, the amount is rounded up.

REFERENCES

1. Levi D. Maurice (1996): *International Finance The Markets and Financial Management of Multinational Business,* McGrawhill International, New York
2. Giri D.K (2001): *'European Union and India-A study in North-South Relations',* Concept Publications, New Delhi
3. Many Currency strategist now believe that the coming 12 months could see more strengthening for the euro, as it recovers ground lost since its launch as an electronic, accounting currency on Jan 1, 1999. Measured on a trade weighted basis, the Euro has declined every year of its existence—by 12% during 1999, 1% during 2002, and 2% in 2001.

   David Fairlamb (2000): 'A Real Currency with Real Impact', *Business Week,* Jan 4, 2002.
4. Rohit (1999): 'Where do we go? *Business India,* July 11, 1999

   Economists at Credit Suisse First Boston in London now predict that the single currency will rise by 10% during 2002.
5. It is a synthetic (cross) rate, say between € and US $, calculated from the rates of these two currencies against, a third currency, say Pound Sterling □. It gives lower and upper limits on the direct quotes/between, say € and US $.
6. Jon Bowen (1999): 'What the Euro means for Indian Business', *The Hindustan Times,* Jan. 17, 1999, New Delhi.

7. It is the tendency on the part of coporates and households to invest more in domestic assets and buy more from domestic producers in the face of foreign exchange rate risk and related costs.
8. In the case of European Currency Union (ECU), the impact of this has been quite significant. In the second quarter of 1999, just three months after the introduction of Euro, cross-border mergers and acquisitions (M & As) in euroland increased by 43%, a trend that persisted since then. The rise of the Euro has also deepened the pan-European debt-market and increased the available risk instruments significantly.
9. Of these, the UK is the most significant but does not belong to the currency union (the Pound sterling, continues to exist). Excluding U.K. the Union's rank drops by a couple of points, but remains significant.
10. Development Research Group (2000): 'EMU, Euro and India', *Reserve Bank of India* (RBI), Mumbai.
11. David Fairlamb (2002): A 'Real Currency' with 'Real Impact', *Business Week,* January 4, 2002.
12. Op cit.
13. Op cit.
14. Op cit.
15. Include North America, Central America and South America.
16. Development Research Group (2000): 'EMU, Euro and India', *Reserve bank of India* (RBI), Mumbai.

    Abheek Barua (2002): 'The Euro-Making it Work' *Economic Times,* 16, January, 2002.
17. Op cit.
18. The problem with this model is that crisis by their nature are unpredictable.
19. Economist (2002). 'Europe's Big Idea—The Euro', *The Economist, 5th* January, 2002, London.
20. Op cit.
21. Bairne, P.O. (1998): "Managing Risk in Euro Currency Conversions' *IT Journal,* volume XI, No. 6. June 1998.

22. Meier G(1994): *Leading Issues in Economic Development,* Oxford Press, New York.

23. Ugur, M (20002): *An Open Economy Macroeconomics Reader,* Edt. Routledge Publishers, London and New York.

24. Rajvade A.V. (2002): "Issues in Asset Liability Management' *Economic and Political Weekly.* Vol. xxxvii N.9 March 2, 2002.

25. Euroframe Forecast (2001): 'Short-term Prospects for the European Economy—Evaluating the current slow-down and aftermath of the September 11th attacks on the USA, 9th November, 2001.

31

Euro Denomination Bloc and India

M.G. Basavaraja

The regional trading arrangements (RTAs) are pursued for a variety of reasons. After Second World War, there was an increasing interest in integrating national economies at regional levels in the form of RTAs, though efforts in many cases have been floundered due to different levels of political, economic impediments. Since World War II, especially industrialised economies have significantly reduced their trade restrictions via The GATT/WTO, and the RTAs. Under the RTAs, member states agreed to impose lower barriers to trade within the RTA than to trade with non-member states. In the 1950s, West European countries began to dismantle trade barriers in response to successful tariff negotiations under the auspices of GATT. Trade liberalisation efforts in those countries were also aided by the establishment of OECD and the European payments union. Convertibility for most European currencies had been developed by 1958, and most quantitative restrictions on trade within this region had been eliminated. It was against this background of trade liberalisation that the European Union was established. Since its establishment the greatest ambition of EU was to have a single currency for all its member states.

The recurring dollar crisis during 1960s, and 1970s led to heavy pressures on the European exchange markets. This brought about wide fluctuations of exchange rates. The dollar devaluation (1971 and 1973), and the adoption of flexible exchange rate made the global currency crisis more precarious and the European monetary system (EMS) was conceived to pave the way for European monetary integration. The EMS commenced functioning from March 1979, and it created European currency union as the unit of account for mutual monetary assistance. The ECU occupied the same position as occupied by special drawing rights (SDRs) in IMF. Then also England did not join the ECU. From January 1, 1999, the ECU ceased to exist in its present form.

Table 31.1: Time Table of the European Monetary Union Key Dates

Year	*Event*
1958	The dream of single currency.
1998	European Summit selected Euro Members.
	European Central Bank was established, conversion rates into the Euro were fixed.
1999	European Monetary Union began.
2001	Greece joined the Euro denomination bloc.
2002	Euro Bank notes/coins became legal tender in Euro denomination bloc.

Source: 1. Economist (April 11, 1998). EMU: An Awfully Big Adventure, p. 4
2. Financial Express and Economic Times (Different issues).

It was disclosed in 1992 when Fortress Europe came into existence—borders that demarcate the member states would disappear, trading procedures would be simplified, uniform commercial laws would come into existence and there would be more choice for the people of EU.

The new year day of 2002 was a milestone in the history of currency notes/coins, as this day, Euro Bank notes/coins became legal tender in 11 EU member states namely France, Germany, Italy, Spain, Austria, The Netherlands, Belgium, Luxembourg, Portugal, Finland, and Ireland. A few other countries are also expressing their desire to join Euro Zone and those countries are to fulfil following conditions to get the entry into the Euro Denomination Bloc (EDB).

1. The rate of inflation in such aspirant countries should not exceed 1.5% points above the best three performing countries.
2. The rate of interest should not be more than two per cent points above the best three performing countries.
3. The debt, of the aspirant country, should not exceed 60% of GDP.
4. The fiscal criterion is that the budget deficit in a prospective member should be at most three percent of GDP.

Gains and Benefits of Euro

The EDB is the second largest economic area after the US accounting for nearly 2/3 of US GDP and around 16% of world GDP. A macro economic balance in such a large trading zone has major implications for price stability, financial and capital markets, business activities as also in travel and tourism. Some of the major implications of a single currency backed up by a sound monetary policy can be outlined as follows;

1. Now, for travellers in EDB, only one currency i.e., Euro is enough and one has to change money only once really, its is a wonderful benefit.
2. For compulsive shoppers, one can compare prices in the same denomination to enable a better decision making and choice.
3. Cost of transportation has reduced, especially with regard to cross border transfers by corporates. Formerly, transportation cost was too exorbitant.

4. Considerable lowering of foreign exchange risks especially for multi-country contracts within the EDB.
5. Transformation of nationally based bond markets into a single market with common conventions.
6. More efficient and competitive funding and investment possibilities.

Even though 50% of world exports are still denominated in Dollars, no doubt that the Euro has the potential to be the first full-fledged rival to the dollar. It also has the appeal to financial markets outside Europe since European capital markets will become more integrated. Liquid and user-friendly thereby pushing down transaction costs considerably. Increasingly corporate treasurers active in the EDB and naturally EDB countries benefit from this European Currency.

Now the largest companies of EDB countries are using the Euro immediately simplifying their accounting procedures and eliminating transaction costs within the EDB. Now Europeans have the means of directly comparing prices and costs across the continent which leads to increased corss-border trade in goods and financial services. In return for stability and low inflation the EDB countries have surrendered their monetary policy. The Finance Ministers of EDB have agreed on conversion rates of which their currencies are irrevocably fixed against the Euro. European Central Bank has established the exchange rate for the Euro against the dollar and other external currencies.

The Euro and The Dollar

About 292 million people live in EDB while it is 265 million in US. The total GDP of EDB is almost as large as that of the world's main economic power. The dollar of US roughly makes up 56% of international reserves eventhough US's share of the world economy is only 20%.

There has been a vibrant Euro bond market which challenges the US market in size. Equity markets are also set to grow in a borderless environment across EDB countries. The burgeoning pool of investible resources means that the cost of raising capital has been reduced. Over time, also because of the adoption of uniform standards, the transaction costs come down remarkably.

The introduction of Euro has brought about economic reform and an enlightened corporate governance structure in EU. The economic criteria laid down for admitting member countries into the EDB have resulted in lower inflation and lower interest rates.

But as things look now, the Euro has not been able to challenge US dollar's pre-eminence in the exchange rate. Despite high expectations, the Euro which started its trading debut in the currency markets in 1999 at an impressive $ 1.17, has remained weak in relation to the dollar. For most of the past three years, it has remained weak vis-a-vis dollar. More of investment capital flows from Europe to the U.S. than the otherway round. There are five important reasons for this- (1) Traditionally, US economy is strong. It has optimum size of population and more economic resources. It has lots of advantages in earning more and more interest rates for its Dollar loans. Over the past decade the technology boom came and went but the US, despite its highs and lows, and notch some impressive productivity gains.

2. The EU's nature of transition into a complete Euro involves some uncertainty. Perhaps a dent in the aggregate GDPs of the EU member countries is possible. Even more likely many central banks/ financial institutions who would welcome a second reserve global currency are adopting a wait and see attitude.

3. Another explanation is regarding Argentine crisis. Banks in Germany, Italy and Spain are over exposed on Argentine.
4. Further, Euro has to earn enough credibility to enter the league occupied only by the dollar. That takes sometime especially because the Euro experiment is unprecedented. The new institutions presiding over it, such as the European Central Bank, do not have the aura which the Federal Reserve System has had.
5. Despite the monetary union among EDB member states, the full integration is still some distance away. During the period of Euro's existence beginning January 1999, the Euro did not perform to its potential especially against the dollar. Apart from the strongness of Dollar, the growth of US economy has spectacular and the buoyancy was far beyond expectations. Market sentiments and spectacular activity went against the Euro and it fell to touch \$ 0.8320 on October 26, 2000. Subsequently, as the US economy moved southwards, the Euro reversed the sentiment and recovered in January 2001. However, this trend could not be sustained and it again fell sharply by July 2001.

But in the years to come, the Euro is expected to emerge as a second powerful currency at the global level bringing about a major diversification of official and private portfolios, bank deposits and bonds. Many countries, which denominate their trade in dollars may even consider shifting to the Euro making it a leading global currency. Such a change in international financial scenario will have far-reaching consequences for Europe, U.S. and for other countries as well.

Challenges of Euro for Indian Companies

The emergence of Euro as a currency of EDB, has posed some challenges for Indian companies. With the Indian currency composition heavily in favour of the US Dollars, with a share of nearly 75%, it might take some more time for Indian corporates to shift to Euro. But due to larger trade with EU, Indian companies have to incorporate changes soon. Many large US brokers are switching over to trade in terms of currency blocs.

The launch of Euro presents a serious challenge for the Indian exporting units as the development would not only make, the EDB market more integrated but competitive too. The exporting units, therefore, have to sell their goods at competitive prices by reducing their cost of production and by increasing the quality of their products. According to RBI study, the price elasticities of the major exports to the EU are large implying that an improvement in quality and cost reduction help to augment exports. However, income elasticities for most of the commodities are quite low. Hence, the key to augment exports from India to EDB and other EU member states crucially depends on the movement of income elasticities of major exports. From the EU's side, there are some impediments which Indian exporters have to reckon with—some tariff and non-tariff barriers. Many of India's market access problems, if closely examined revolved around differential rates of tariff or tariff quotes being applicable on different partners and India not being at the favourable end of it.

Implications of Euro for India

The EU, as glorified by its spokespersons, is India's largest partner in trade, investment and development cooperation. The economic relationship between India and the EU is becoming stronger in the multilateral trading system under the aegis of the WTO. The EU accounts for more than a quarter of India's exports and imports of goods. The EU is also India's biggest partner in development co-operation and the second largest source of foreign direct investment. The Indo-EU bilateral trade has surged in the 25 years. Indian exports to Europe were a paltry 1.8 billion ECUs in 1980, reached 4.8 billion in 1990 and in 1998 grew to 9.8 billion Euro. Indian exports in general grew at a rate of 11% but exports to the EU were even more dynamic-15% per annum.

The growth concerned not only traditional products such as textiles and agriculture but also includes machinery, cars, and chemicals. A parallel trend is noticeable for EU exports to India that from 2.4 billion ECUs grew to 6.4 billion in 1990 and reached 9.5 billion Euro in 1998. So the EU is continuing as one of the leading trading partners with Euro 25,661,00 two-way trade during the year 2000-01. It accounted for nearly 30% of Indian exports, many East European and African countries with whom India is having good economic relations are willing to join EU. Hence, India can avail of the opportunity of expanding trade with EU. Indian exports to the EU are mainly textiles, leather and leather products, pearls, chemicals, machinery, animal and vegetable products and miscellaneous manufactured goods.

Given the potential that exists between India and the EU in the fields of trade, investment and services, the emergence of Euro has major implications in facilitating the growth process in these areas, The Euro currency is already in use during trading, though the percentage of the trade in Euro varies widely and it is estimated that it is within a cluster of 10-30% of India's trade with EU. The Euro has provided a unique opportunity for Indian companies to increase their external competitiveness. This would require changes in their legal instruments for newer contracts to be drawn in Euro and also organisational changes in their electronic data inter change systems. In the EDB single monetary policy is coming into operation, so that factor prices may move in similar direction. Even if there is no

Table 31.2: India's Trade with Three Powerfuls of WTO and other Countries

(Rs. crores)

Country	*Exports* 1990-91	1997-98	1998-99	1999-2000	*Imports* 1990-91	1997-98	1998-99	1999-2000
1. EU	8951	32840	36361	40663	12680	37719	43274	44736
	(27.5)	(25.2)	(26.0)	(25.1)	(29.4)	(24.5)	(24.3)	(21.9)
2. USA	4797	25282	30289	36980	5245	13814	15314	15728
	(14.7)	(19.4)	(21.7)	(22.7)	(12.1)	(9.0)	(8.6)	(7.7)
3. Japan	3089	7056	6950	7379	3245	7972	10379	10206
	(05.6)	(5.4)	(5.0)	(4.5)	(7.5)	(5.2)	(5.8)	(5.0)
4. Others	15766	54923	56153	77903	22021	94671	108365	133913
	(52.2)	(50.0)	(47.3)	(47.7)	(51.0)	(61.3)	(61.3)	(54.4)
Total	32553	130101	139753	162925	43191	154176	178332	204583
	(100.0)	(100.0)	(100.0)	(100.0)	(100.0)	(100.0)	(100.0)	(100.0)

Source: Economic Division, Ministry of Finance, GOI.
Economic Survey Reports 1990-91 to 2000-2001.

equalisation, this could help in dispersing the trade concentration between EU and India from a few of the member states to the other countries within the EDB. Manufacturing, engineering, other related industrial sectors, information technology and related areas, food processing, banking and financial institutions are some of crucial business sectors in India which could reap immense benefits from the emergence of Euro as a real currency.

For those potential benefits to become a reality, a number of other pre-requisites will also have to materialise. This involves the greater administrative reforms in India, stability of the Euro itself, especially against the Dollar as also the levelling of the different economic cycles of the EDB. As already stated from the EU side, there are some impediments which Indian exporters have to reckon with-some tariff and non-tariff barriers. Many of India's market access problems if closely examined revolved around differential rates of tariff or tariff quotas being applicable on different partners and India not being at the favourable end of it. India is a big democratic country having the second largest population in the world. The relations between India and the EU are historic. India has given specific proposals to enhance the export potential of Indian goods, which include the GSP regime of EU which needs to recognise the meagre share of India in the basket of EU imports, improving bilateral trade in the textile sector, frequent countervailing actions India face etc. Imbalances in multilateral trading system which could not be perceived back in 1994-95 have now become apparent. Needless to say, that this trend must be reversed to grant development dimension to the WTO system. Trade is not an end in itself. The development deficit needs to be made good by the multilateral trading system.

With the present liberalised economic scenario, there is wide scope for broader economic, technical cooperation between India and the EU. There are wide opportunities in natural resources-rich India for capital resources-rich

European investors of all kinds-portfolio and direct. Many of our companies have listed their stocks on the European money markets. India has been a major beneficiary of official loans from EU countries. Now EDB countries are lightening their budgets and following fiscal discipline as a consequence of the monetary union. About 13 percent of India's external debt is denominated in Euro.

Concluding Remarks

The Euro has been a major achievement for the EU. It is expected to bring about greater relief to business people and tourists alike who have had their misfortune in losing value while covering from one currency to another during their visits to Europe. This apart, the Euro is also likely to lower transaction cost and bring about a stable price regime across the different countries of the EU. The Euro, in due course of time, is expected to acquire the advantage of emerging as high valued currency on par with the Dollar. As a result of this, developing countries like India will not face the international liquidity problem in their international trade. Indian exporters can look forward to new markets other than US and increased trade in EU countries following the introduction of Euro Currency. However, the emergence of Euro has made the EDB market more integrated and competitive. The exporters of India, therefore have to prepare themselves to sell their goods at competitive prices by reducing their cost of production and by increasing the quality of their products.

REFERENCES

1. Krugman, Paul R and Obstfeld (2000) International Economics—Theory and Policy (New York: Addision—Wesley) p. 618.
2. Sarma, Atul, Faber Gerrit and Mehta, Pradeep (1997) Meeting the challenges of the European Union (New Delhi: Sage Publications) p. 80.
3. Carbaugh, Robert (1999) International Economics (New York: South Western College Publishing) pp. 556-558.

4. Giri, D.K. (2001) European Union and India—A Study in North-South Relations. (New Delhi: Concept Publishing Company), p. 214.

5. Deutsch, Klans Gunter and Speyer, Bernhard (2001) The World Trade Organisation Millennium Round—Freer Trade in the Twenty-first century, (New York: Routledge) pp. 34-46.

6. Mathur, Vibha, (1999) India-European Trade Prospects and Impact of Euro (New Delhi: Indina Tax Institute).

7. The Hindu, Bangalore Edition, January 2, 1999.

8. The German News Vol. XL June-July 1999 and Vol. XLII, June-July 2001.

9. Andrews Edmund L. "The Euro Takes a Visible Form". The Hindu, January 3, 2002, p. BS-1.

10. ASSOCHAM Press Note. The Hindu, March 6, 2002. p. 17.

Index